Unders... and Teaching

Understanding Learning and Teaching

The Experience in Higher Education

Michael Prosser and Keith Trigwell

The Society for Research into Higher Education
& Open University Press

Published by SRHE and
Open University Press
Celtic Court
22 Ballmoor
Buckingham
MK18 1XW

email:enquiries@openup.co.uk
world wide web: www.openup.co.uk

and
325 Chestnut Street
Philadelphia, PA 19106, USA

First published 1999
Reprinted 1999, 2000, 2001

A catalogue record of this book is available from the British Library

ISBN 0 335 19831 7 (pb)   0 335 19832 5 (hb)

Library of Congress Cataloging-in-Publication Data

Prosser, Michael, 1949–
    Understanding learning and teaching : the experience in higher
education / Michael Prosser and Keith Trigwell.
        p.   cm.
    Includes bibliographical references (p.) and index.
    ISBN 0–335–19832–5 (hc.). — ISBN 0–335–19831–7 (pbk.)
    1. College teaching—Australia—Case studies. 2. Learning.
Psychology of—Case studies. 3. Education, Higher—Australia—Case
studies. I. Trigwell, Keith, 1949–   . II. Title.
LB2331.P766   1998
378.1'25—dc21   98–23978
                                                                CIP

Typeset by Graphicraft Limited, Hong Kong
Printed in Great Britain by St Edmundsbury Press Ltd, Bury St Edmunds, Suffolk

Contents

Preface   vi
Acknowledgments   viii

1 Learning and Teaching in Higher Education   1
2 A Model for Understanding Learning and Teaching in
   Higher Education   10
3 Students' Prior Experiences of Learning   26
4 Students' Perceptions of Their Learning Situation   58
5 Students' Approaches to Learning   83
6 Students' Learning Outcomes   108
7 Experiences of Teaching in Higher Education   137
8 Understanding Learning and Teaching   164

Appendix – Approaches to Teaching Inventory   176
References   180
Index   188
The Society for Research into Higher Education   195

Preface

This book has several dimensions. It is above all a book for those who are interested in the scholarship of teaching and learning in higher education. It focuses on the students' experience of learning and links ideas from that research to the teachers' experience of teaching in higher education. In this respect, the book complements and bridges the messages in two of the more popular, current higher education texts. It contains an extension of the student learning research used to underpin the message in *Learning to Teach in Higher Education* (Ramsden, 1992) and it links the learning focus adopted in *The Experience of Learning* (Marton *et al.*, 1997) with the experience of teaching. For university teachers it provides an approach to the scholarship of teaching and guidance on the application of scholarly ideas in university teaching.

While it is written from the same perspective as both the books mentioned above, its message differs from both in suggesting that the way forward is to focus more on learning and teaching situations while maintaining a focus on the quality of learning. This is not to say that we think the quality of learning is less important. As you will see, we believe it is of the utmost importance, as books such as those mentioned above have convincingly demonstrated. What we believe is needed, and what we hope to supply here, is some way of achieving that quality. Our approach is to address the relations between aspects of the students' experience of learning. These aspects include students' perceptions of their learning situation, their approach to learning, their prior learning experiences and their learning outcome. To do this, we draw heavily on the ideas in the recent text, *Learning and Awareness* (Marton and Booth, 1997).

This is also a book for those interested in what may underlie a range of teaching approaches, including teaching for distance learning, teaching in a culturally diverse context, and the uses of technology in teaching. Its content is related to, but not as specifically focused as *Rethinking University Teaching: A Framework for the Effective Use of Educational Technology* (Laurillard, 1993).

And finally, this is a book for those interested in developing research into their own teaching. Not only does it make extensive use of the published research into teaching and learning, describing both methods and results in some cases; it also contains some details on the questions and approaches which researchers of teaching and learning may find useful. A feature of the collection of examples, and of the book, is that it treats the qualitative and quantitative research results and approaches as complementary. Both have contributed to the ideas in this book in ways that could not have been achieved using either one alone.

The first chapter provides an overview of this research and of the book. It sets the scene concerning variation in student learning and gives an indication of the directions we will take in pursuing the improvement of teaching and learning. Chapter 2 introduces and describes a theoretical model which forms the binding for the theme of variation throughout the book. We define what we mean in our use of the key concepts: experience, variation, awareness, foreground/background, and a relational view. This chapter also briefly outlines where the perspective of this book fits into the broader perspectives of research and practice in higher education.

Chapters 3–6 have a similar structure. Each chapter is self-contained, but is structured in terms of a foreground/background relation where the aspect of the model dealt with in each chapter is in the foreground, and is seen against the background of the model as a whole. The student learning research related to the focus of each chapter is presented, and the principles of practice for teaching which emerge from that research are listed and discussed. Each chapter concludes with examples, including classroom-based research, which illustrate the application of those principles.

Chapter 7 focuses on teaching. It reports on recent research on the experience of teaching, linking teachers' conceptions of teaching to their perceptions of their situation and their approach to teaching. We also tie together the learning and teaching elements in the book through the research relating teaching approach to students' learning approach.

In the final chapter we draw together the messages from the earlier chapters and summarize the implications of the arguments we have presented for student learning, for teaching and for academic development in higher education.

Michael Prosser
Keith Trigwell

Acknowledgements

Numerous people have contributed in a variety of ways to the evolution of this book. The collection and refinement of our ideas and research results such as those in the following chapters have accumulated over a substantial period. Inspiration has come from many sources, including from many people who are also good friends, and through many pleasant and stimulating discussions, both formal and informal. We have received intellectual, financial and emotional support to get these ideas together, and production support to get them into this form. Altogether we have identified six groups of people whose contributions to this book we wish to acknowledge.

The first group are the researchers and practitioners who have collaborated with us in trying our and their own ideas in real teaching contexts. We have joint publications with many of them and some of those publications are referred to in the following chapters. They are: Jane Blackwell, Chris Cope, Katherine Crawford, Jane Davey, Mark Garner, Sue Gordon, Michael Jackson, Rosemary Millar, Jackie Nicholas, Anna Reid, Karen Scouller, Ian Sefton, Ray Sleet, Philip Taylor, Paul Walker, and Caroline Webb.

Then there is the family support group. Kaye Nolan managed the bulk of the index, and with Olympia and Ingrid Walker shared the excitement of the journey, commented on drafts, and coped with disrupted holidays and apparently unproductive writing days.

David Boud helped us develop the courage to take on this task and to approach a publisher. He is part of a group of research colleagues: John Bain, John Biggs, Shirley Booth, John Bowden, Gloria Dall'Alba, Noel Entwistle, Elaine Martin, Ference Marton, Erik Meyer, Paul Ramsden, and Jörgen Sandberg who have been a huge source of inspiration. With them we have argued and discussed. From them we have learned and we have borrowed.

Our work colleagues, Helen Edwards, Denise Kirkpatrick, Brian Low, Jackie Lublin, Jo McKenzie, Erika Martens, Anna Reid, and Fiona Waterhouse gave us some space, some academic support and some feedback.

With respect to production, we acknowledge the patience of John Skelton and Linda Watkins of Open University Press as we struggled to meet deadlines, and then the support of the organization when we finally delivered the manuscript.

Finally we acknowledge both the people of the Australian Research Council (1988–1998) and their referees who have regularly and generously made funds available to us to conduct much of the research reported here, and the research assistants who were funded by this Council to work on those projects.

1

Learning and Teaching in Higher Education

A scenario

Antony Capos failed to pass a core mathematics subject in his first year at university. Melissa Durimah achieved a pass with distinction in the same subject. They were taught the same syllabus by the same university teachers. They went to the same lectures and tutorials and completed the same assignments. They had similar entry scores on the university entrance examination. Both claim to have worked hard throughout the year, and there was no reason to question those claims. So why are their results so different? What was it about their experiences that might help understand these differences? How could the university teachers of this subject find out about the differing experiences, and if they knew, could they have affected this outcome?

We address these and related questions in the remaining pages, and in the process give university teachers some insight into the learning world of their students. For example, let's look more closely at some of Melissa's descriptions of her experience. She says,

> I am doing mathematics for the purpose of improving a logical method of thinking rather than for the course specific subject matter . . .

She goes on to elaborate on this,

> Well more than anything I say that it is probably a thinking process which is not something you get from any other subject and that is probably the reason I am doing it . . . More than anything as a way of thinking . . . Well I think I try to see what is being taught as part of the bigger picture, to see how every thing comes into place and I find if I can get a broad sort of overview of things then it probably helps me to understand the work a bit better, because I can see where it is heading, where it is going to fall into place. I think someone who is not so good at mathematics might struggle to see where it is heading, and they're just sort of interested in getting hold of one thing at a time.

In relation to the way she went about her study she said,

> [I] do as many different types of questions as I can. Try to see how the topic being studied is related to other topics I have studied – get the full picture . . . when I go through and do my notes first I like to get an understanding of the principles behind the topic . . . I don't go back time after time and do the same sort of question. When I am revising I go back and do the same sort of thing again, but when I am trying to learn it, then each type of question I might do only one or two.

In contrast, Antony says,

> I feel mathematics is the process of using different techniques to solve various problems. In my experience this has only involved numbers yet I feel it may be helpful for the wider range of future subjects.

He confirmed this conception, describing mathematics as,

> Oh numbers and problems and getting an actual answer to a problem.

On his approaches to studying, he wrote,

> I usually read summaries and try to memorise formulas when necessary. Also answering questions and doing past papers is what I do . . .

This was supported by the comment,

> I used to do past papers and plenty of problems and writing down formulae and stuff in the hope that I'll be able to recall them in an exam . . . I'm probably just trying to memorise things which, I don't know if that's a good idea, but . . .

And why wouldn't Antony try to memorize things? Wasn't much of his secondary schooling in mathematics geared to memorizing? Wasn't he encouraged repeatedly to complete a variety of problems? Wasn't he 'forced' to do mock university entrance papers? Didn't he get a good grade at the end of secondary school? And didn't he gain entry into this sought-after university mathematics subject? Yes. But this was also Melissa's experience and the approach she describes to her university studies is quite different.

The central theme of this book is the differences in the ways individual students experience learning. We will argue that most of the differences are evoked by the learning situation experienced by the student. Students like Antony and Melissa may enter a similar learning context, but their previous experiences may mean that they see their resulting situations in quite different ways. Their approaches to learning and the quality of what they learned are quite different. What does this mean, and what does it mean for teaching?

An explanation

Some of the most exciting and relevant research to have been reported on learning in higher education in the past 20 years not only offers an explanation of what may be happening to Antony and Melissa, but it also offers university teachers a way of addressing quality of learning issues. It suggests that for all students there are better and worse ways to learn. It also suggests to university teachers that by altering the learning context it may be possible to improve learning by encouraging that approach.

In a nutshell, the research describes students as approaching their learning in two qualitatively different ways (Biggs, 1987a, b; Ramsden, 1992; Marton *et al.*, 1997). In one approach (a deep approach) students aim to understand ideas and seek meanings. They have an intrinsic interest in the task and an expectation of enjoyment in carrying it out. They adopt strategies that help satisfy their curiosity, such as making the task coherent with their own experience; relating and distinguishing evidence and argument; looking for patterns and underlying principles; integrating the task with existing awareness; seeing the parts of a task as making up the whole; theorizing about it; forming hypotheses; and relating what they understand from other parts of the same subject, and from different subjects. Overall they have a focus on the meaning in the argument, the message, or the relationships, but they are aware that the meanings are carried by the words, the text, or the formulae. This is the approach adopted by Melissa in her mathematics subject.

In the other (surface) approach, students see tasks as external impositions and they have the intention to cope with these requirements. They are instrumentally or pragmatically motivated and seek to meet the demands of the task with minimum effort. They adopt strategies which include a focus on unrelated parts of the task; separate treatment of related parts (such as on principles and examples); a focus on what are seen as essentials (factual data and their symbolic representations); the reproduction of the essentials as accurately as possible; and rote memorizing information for assessment purposes rather than for understanding. Overall they would appear to be involved in study without reflection on purpose or strategy, with the focus of that study being on the words, the text, or the formulae. This is the approach described by Antony.

While these approaches are not characteristics of the student (for example Melissa may adopt a deep approach to this mathematics subject and later a surface approach to tasks in another of her subjects) they are strongly related to the quality of the student's learning outcome. Antony failed to pass the subject, Melissa achieved a distinction pass. Antony failed to grasp the significance of mathematics and to see the potential uses of mathematics in other areas. Melissa saw mathematics as abstract reasoning processes that can be utilized to explore and solve a range of problems. Research conducted by a group at Gothenburg University in Sweden showed that qualitative differences in outcomes were closely associated with qualitative differences in approaches to learning (Marton and Säljö, 1997). This work has been replicated and extended in many studies since (as we will see in Chapter 2). Without exception, the results show that deep approaches to learning were more likely to be associated with higher quality learning outcomes. Learning outcomes, or ways of understanding which include the more complete ways of conceiving of something, are of a higher quality than those involving more limited conceptions. Students who are able to see relations between elements of their understanding in a subject and are aware of how that understanding and those relationships can be applied in new and abstract contexts have a higher quality learning outcome than students who cannot.

The significance of this result cannot be overstated. The way students approach their learning is related to the quality of their learning outcome. Students who adopt a surface approach to learning are unlikely to achieve the quality of understanding of their subject that would be expected of a university student. This result is in contrast to results from other forms of higher education research on student learning, which do not show such consistent or useful relations.

But the significance and the usefulness of the research results do not stop there. The results also suggest that students' awareness of their learning environment is related to the approach to learning they adopt. That is, approaches to learning are relational. Ramsden (1992) reports on studies of the relations between students' perceptions of their learning environment and their approach to learning. They show that students who perceive the nature of the assessment as encouraging memorization and recall, and who perceive the workload demands of a subject as high, are more likely to adopt a surface approach. A deep approach is found to be associated with perceptions of high-quality teaching, some independence in choosing what is to be learned, and a clear awareness of the goals and standards required in the subject (Trigwell and Prosser, 1991b).

This suggests that to improve the quality of students' approaches to learning and their learning outcome, university teachers may first need to determine students' perceptions of the assessment, their workload, the clarity of goals and standards, the teaching they receive and the learning choices they receive. Adjusting the context to afford changes in students' perceptions may be an important strategy in improving learning. Differences in these perceptions may relate to differences in approaches to learning. Melissa describes her experience of mathematics teaching as the encouragement of group discussions to help students explore what other students may be thinking. Antony believes that the assessment can be completed using rehearsal, memorization and recall and his approach is geared to that end.

And there is a third dimension to the relevance and usefulness of this research. Students' approaches to learning (deep and surface) have been found to be associated with their conceptions of learning and their conceptions of what they are learning. Students who conceive of learning in a topic as, say, a quantitative increase in knowledge, or as memorizing, are unlikely to be those who adopt a deep approach to the learning of that topic. Conversely students who have a more complete conception such as seeing learning as the abstraction of meaning, or an interpretive process aimed at understanding reality, are more likely to be those who adopt a deep approach to learning of that topic (Marton and Säljö, 1997: 56). Antony sees learning mathematics as involving rehearsal of number-based problems: he is working with a limited conception of learning. He sees mathematics as the study of numbers and their applications in other subjects and the physical world: he is working with a limited conception of mathematics. Without being able to conceive of learning as being more than a quantitative increase in knowledge gained through rote memorizing and rehearsing, Antony will have extreme difficulty in adopting practices that lead to high-quality learning. Without a conception of mathematics as a complex logical system which can be used to solve complex problems, Antony will have extreme difficulty in adopting practices that lead to high-quality learning (Crawford *et al.*, 1994, 1998a). Conceptions of learning and of the subject being learned may also be factors that limit the approach students can adopt to learning.

Melissa and Antony, on starting their university studies, had different prior experiences of learning mathematics, and different conceptions of the nature of mathematics. Even in the same learning context those differences in prior experiences mean that different learning situations are constituted for each student and different perceptions of their learning situation are evoked. Antony perceives his situation as supporting a surface approach to learning. Melissa sees hers as encouraging a deep approach. What do the university teachers know about the student's perceptions, and what do they do? We pursue those questions in the next section and in depth in Chapters 3–7.

This research into student learning from a relational perspective underpins the message in this book. It builds on the seminal studies of the ways students approach learning tasks (Marton and Säljö, 1997) and conceive of what learning is (Säljö, 1979). It is presented in detail elsewhere by Marton *et al.* (1997) and Ramsden (1992). We also describe this research in more detail in Chapters 2–6, taking as our point of departure a perspective of variation between individual students. We explore the relations between students' conceptions of learning, their perceptions of the learning environment, their approaches to learning and learning outcomes in higher education.

Teaching

Within the range of student learning variation experienced by university teachers, Melissa and Antony would be placed towards the extremes. In this book we are attempting to provide an explanation for that variation, and through that explanation a means to address the issues arising from it.

Students such as Melissa and Antony come to the learning and teaching contexts university teachers establish with certain prior experiences of studying. When they enter those contexts, the situation they are in evokes, or brings to the foreground of their awareness, particular aspects of that prior experience. For example, Antony's new university mathematics learning situation may evoke an awareness of a memorized list of secondary school formulae; an awareness that he hated calculus; an awareness that he has the ability to pass; an awareness of a range of largely unrelated mathematical concepts and ideas; an awareness that mathematics was mainly about the manipulation of numbers and formulae; an awareness that by working with his friends and by rehearsing the range of problems presented in the subject, he had been able to pass; and an awareness that the university subject seemed to have fewer imposed deadlines, goals and expectations than his secondary school course. These aspects of his prior experience are evoked by the situation in which he now finds himself. Antony passed a previous examination involving basic mathematics, but this does not mean that the new situation will evoke the same awareness that led to that prior experience. We know that the prior experiences that are evoked are particularly important to the quality of learning in the new situation, and we know that the established context, and the way it is perceived, is similarly important. So what does this say to us about the way we might practise teaching and help students learn?

The answer to this question is the subject of this book. It is addressed through a range of sub-questions that a teacher who is trying to answer the question might ask. Each sub-question is, in itself, a part of the answer to the overall question. For example:

- What is the nature of students' prior orientations to learning and how does this vary?
- What is the nature of students' varying views on what is meant by learning and understanding and the subject matter when they begin their courses?
- What sorts of things do students focus on, or are aware of, when engaged in studying their courses?
- How does what they focus on, or are aware of, relate to how university teachers have designed and constructed courses?
- What effect does this variation in perception have on the quality of the students' learning?
- How do students go about their study? How do university teachers find out how they go about their study? What can university teachers do to affect the way they go about studying?
- What do students learn? How do university teachers find out what they learn?
- Do they learn a greater or less amount about something, or do they understand about something in different ways?
- What can students do with what they learn? What aspects of what they learn do they take beyond the subject?

Just as students experience learning in different ways, university teachers experience teaching in different ways. Their perceptions of their teaching context, the way they approach their teaching, and the outcomes of those approaches vary between individuals in the same context, as well as between contexts. While this type of variation has been the focus of much student learning research in the last decade, similar research on teaching has been given little consideration in the improvement of both learning and teaching despite the fact that it would appear to have profound implications for that practice.

In the previous section, we expressed our belief (supported by the research described there and in the following chapters) that there are better and worse ways for students to approach their learning – a deep approach being better than a surface approach. Research of a similar nature also suggests that there are better and worse ways for university teachers to approach their teaching, and better and worse ways to encourage that approach to teaching. Each of the questions above focuses on aspects of a student's learning. Seeking the answers to these questions is a part of the better approach to teaching. The answers themselves provide the data university teachers need to address the final question, 'What can university teachers do to improve the quality of student learning?.' The principles for teaching practice arising out of the approach taken in this book, and the examples used to illustrate those principles, lead university teachers towards and then beyond this final question.

In reaching the point of being able to address the final question, university teachers will have conducted a range of investigations into their students' learning experience. This information is not just a source of data for the improvement of learning and teaching; it constitutes a resource from which research publications can be produced.

Researching teaching

Earlier in this chapter, we wrote about the excitement and relevance of the research that underpins this book. Its appeal stems from two related factors. First, all the data gathered come from students or teachers in their natural setting. They are not learning and/or teaching out of context. Second, the data are students' and university teachers' self-reports of their experiences, not the observations of the behaviours of students and university teachers by researchers. In addition to this, the results suggest that there is something the university teachers can do about learning – not by trying to change the student, but by trying to change the context experienced by the student. This is a much more attractive prospect for most university teachers.

In this analysis we have used research that is derived from and appeals to university teachers and students. In so doing it bridges the gap between educational research and teaching practice in higher education. Much of the type of research described could be conducted by university teachers in their own context.

The point of departure of this book is that it also addresses some of the ways that university teachers can find out about their students' learning experiences. It contains examples of the action research that has been conducted by university teachers to explore these experiences. And it contains information on those research approaches – sufficient for university teachers interested in researching their teaching/learning context to get started.

Take, for example, the study which has provided the data for the analyses involving Melissa and Antony. While the students' names are fictitious, the data are derived from a study of the experience of first year mathematics students in an Australian university. In three reports on the study, the authors supply information on students' conceptions of mathematics, perceptions of their learning situation, their approaches to learning mathematics, and their learning outcomes and relations between these variables (Crawford *et al.*, 1994, 1998a, b). Because of the depth and inclusiveness of this study, we have used its results throughout the book. It began as a qualitative study based on students' written responses to open-ended questions. We describe the nature of the questions put to students. A small group of students were then interviewed in depth to add to and support the written data. The qualitative methods used to analyse these data are described. Quantitative methods, including correlation, factor and cluster analyses were used to demonstrate relations between variables. The results are presented in a manner that demonstrates the applications of these methods to this type of research.

The improvement of learning and teaching is dependent upon the development of scholarship and research in teaching. Research that is both applicable and accessible to higher education lecturers is presented in this book. It is offered as a source and an incentive: a source of information for scholarship and an incentive for university teachers to make their contribution.

In the following chapters we describe and illustrate a practical model for developing university teaching. It builds on research in student learning to demonstrate the relations between what university teachers do and think, what students do and think, and the quality of the student learning outcomes. The model links students' prior experiences with their perceptions of the learning context, their approaches to learning and their learning outcome. A major focus is on the variation within each of these areas, and how the variation in one area relates to the variation in another.

Summary of Chapter 1

In this chapter we have given a summary overview of the whole book and indicated why it may be of value to a university teacher. We have indicated that this is a book on teaching from a relational perspective. That is, students' perceptions of their learning situation evoke prior learning experiences that relate to their learning approach and their learning outcome. We have foreshadowed that practical implications for teaching, course design and research will be integrated into each of the later chapters and will form the basis of the value of the book to the practice of learning and teaching, and to scholarly pursuits into learning and teaching.

We saw how two mathematics students, Melissa and Antony, on starting their university studies, had different prior experiences of learning mathematics, and different conceptions of the nature of mathematics. In the same learning context those differences in prior experiences meant that different learning situations were constituted for each student and different perceptions of their learning situation were evoked. Antony perceived his situation as supporting a surface approach to learning. Melissa saw hers as encouraging a deep approach. Antony failed the subject, and Melissa achieved a distinction pass.

2

A Model for Understanding Learning and Teaching in Higher Education

Introduction

In the first chapter we provided a summary overview of the book as a whole: the focus on individual variation, the relations between students' prior experiences, their approaches to learning and the quality of their learning outcomes. We emphasized the special place of students' perceptions of their learning situation in our argument, and how university teachers might use this information in teaching. We did not present the model or any of the theoretical ideas on which this book is based. That is the task of this chapter. The model links aspects of the student's experience of learning, and the theoretical ideas are derived from a phenomenographic perspective. Essentially these ideas suggest that the world, as experienced, is non-dualistic. That is, students' and teachers' experiences are not constituted independently of the world of learning and teaching in which they are engaged, but they and the world of learning and teaching are constituted in relation to each other. In this sense the world of learning and teaching is an experienced world. From this perspective students' and teachers' experiences are always experiences of something. Students do not experience learning, they experience the learning of something. Teachers do not experience teaching, they experience the teaching of something (Marton and Booth, 1997).

In proposing a model to help describe and understand the ways learning and teaching are experienced, we are acutely aware that any such model will necessarily simplify the phenomenon being modelled. We are proposing a model as an aid to the analysis of a very complex phenomenon – teachers' and learners' experiences of learning and teaching.

While these ideas provide the background against which the rest of the book should be read, we acknowledge that they may not be equally accessible or of interest to all readers. To accommodate this variation, we have concluded the chapter with a substantial summary which captures the essential elements of these ideas, and a brief description of the model used as the unifying theme in the rest of the book.

The chapter addresses several questions:

- What are the theoretical models that have been used to provide meaning and coherence to the practice of learning and teaching in higher education?
- Is teaching fundamentally about transferring information from the teacher to the learner, or is it, as we would contend, about creating contexts which make learning possible?
- If it is about the latter, what does that mean, and what does it say about the way in which teachers should think about, and approach learning and teaching?
- Do university teachers and learners experience learning and teaching situations in different ways, and if so, what are these different ways?

We will be arguing that learning and teaching are fundamentally related, that good teaching needs to be defined in terms of helping students learn, that it is the learning of students that needs to be the focus of good teaching, not the teaching activities of teachers. We will argue that good teaching is about bringing the teachers' perceptions and understanding of learning and teaching (their awareness of learning and teaching) into closer relationship with the students', and that good learning involves a focus on the meaning and understanding of the material students are studying.

We will contend that university teachers and students engaged in a learning and teaching activity all experience that same learning and teaching context in different ways. We believe that good teaching is about three things. First, it is about teachers developing a coherent and well-articulated view of what they are trying to achieve and how they are planning to achieve that outcome. Second, it is about teachers discovering the variation in the ways students perceive that planned learning context. And third, it is about working towards bringing their students into relation with, and understanding of, that articulated view.

This perspective is in contrast to views that good teaching in higher education is about presenting and structuring content or about developing good teaching *skills*, or about flexible delivery or about giving students choice. These are all important characteristics of good teaching, but should not be the primary focus of attention in efforts to improve teaching. They should be seen as the background, against which students' perceptions and student learning is the foreground or focus.

The presage–process–product model of learning and teaching

The origins of the learning and teaching ideas in this book lie in the presage–process–product model of student learning (Biggs, 1978; Prosser

Figure 2.1   Presage–process–product model of student learning

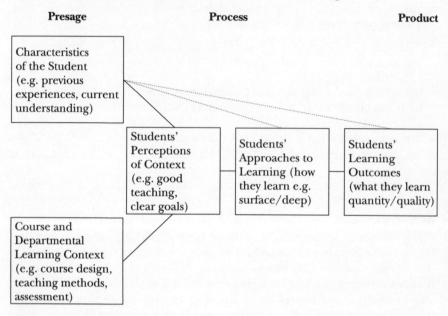

Source: Prosser *et al.*, 1994a.

et al., 1994a). One version of such a model is shown in Figure 2.1. In this model students' perceptions of the learning and teaching context are seen to be an interaction between their previous experiences of learning and teaching and the learning and teaching context itself. They approach their studies in relation to their perceptions of the context, and that approach is related to the quality of their learning outcome. This is a summary of the scenario outlined in Chapter 1. Similar models have also been proposed for teaching (Biggs, 1989).

Models such as these have greatly facilitated our understanding of teaching for student learning, but we believe the models also raise many questions. For example, on the interpretation of the interactions within the models, are the various aspects of the model constituted independently? Are they causally related? Do the models describe an extended period of time or do they describe a momentary act? Addressing these questions leads to new models such as the one on which this book is based.

Fundamental to the responses to questions like these is the epistemological and ontological beliefs of those interpreting the model. The set of beliefs from which we have approached the learning and teaching questions in this book are known as constitutionalism, of which phenomenography is one form. The essence of this view is that meaning is constituted through an internal relationship between the individual and the world. Learning is about experiencing the object of study in a different way, where the experience is a relationship between the person experiencing and the object experienced. This is fundamentally different from other perspectives of learning, such as cognitivist, individual constructivist and social constructivist perspectives. At the risk of grossly oversimplifying these perspectives, we will provide a brief interpretation of the model from each of the perspectives.

From the cognitivist or information processing perspective, sensory data is thought to come in to the student from the outside, be stored for a short time, processed internally and then put in longer term storage and/or an output is generated to the outside world (Gardner, 1987). In terms of the presage–process–product model, the various parts of the model would be considered to be independently constituted and to describe a causal chain from presage to product.

From the individual constructivist perspective, knowledge is constructed internally, and tested through interaction with the outside world (von Glasersfeld, 1995). From this perspective Biggs (1993a) has argued for a systems theory interpretation of the presage–process–product model in which the various parts of the model are independently constituted, but are in continuous interaction with one another. This model then does not describe a causal process, but a continuously interacting system. The process of knowledge construction is driven internally through processes of assimilation (integrating new knowledge into existing knowledge structures) and accommodation (changing knowledge structures).

From a Vygotskian social constructivist perspective, knowledge is thought to develop internally, but in a process driven by social interaction with the outside world (Wertsch, 1985). From this perspective, the context, and particularly the social context, is of prime importance. It is the context which brings about knowledge development within individual students.

For each of these perspectives there is a separation between the individual and the world. Knowledge is brought in from the outside or constructed on the inside. Each of these perspectives is dualistic; there are two elements: the student and the world.

The point of departure of a constitutionalist perspective from each of these is that a constitutionalist perspective is non-dualistic. From a constitutionalist perspective on learning there is an internal relationship between the individual and the world. The individual and the world are not constituted independently of one another. Individuals and the world are internally related through the individuals' awareness of the world. The world is an experienced world. There is not an internal structure of the mind which is composed of, or can be modelled in terms of, independently constituted parts. For analytical reasons we discuss perceptions, approaches and outcomes as separate entities, but they should be considered to be simultaneously present in the students' awareness and are not independently constituted. Marton and Booth (1997) have recently presented a comprehensive description of learning and awareness from this perspective which includes an analysis of why this perspective is appropriate for our current understanding of learning.

In adopting this constitutionalist perspective, we argue that in any act of learning and teaching, prior experiences, perceptions, approaches and outcomes are simultaneously present, although in some contexts, one or more of these aspects may be more to the foreground of awareness, while other aspects may be more to the background. Thus, from this perspective, the presage–process–product model does not describe a chain of causal processes extended over time, but an analysis of individuals' awareness of the learning and teaching acts in which they are engaged.

In the remainder of this book, research into learning and teaching of a relational nature, which is consistent with this constitutionalist perspective, is interpreted from this perspective. We introduced the results of some of this research as it related to the studies of Melissa and Antony in Chapter 1. It includes phenomenographic studies of conceptions of learning and the extensive studies which have explored the relations between conceptions, approaches and outcomes in learning and teaching. This research approach is built on the non-dualist internal relation between individual students and the world, and is informed by the belief that the context forms an integral part of the investigation of any phenomenon or relationship. It is in this sense that it is relational. We present here the research relevant to the learning argument we are making. It addresses five questions. What are the qualitatively different ways students approach learning? What is the nature of the relations between approaches to learning and learning outcome? How are learning approaches related to students' perceptions of their learning environment? What are students' conceptions of learning? How do conceptions of learning relate to approaches to learning? For a more detailed analysis and overview of this relational research, we suggest Ramsden, 1992; Marton and Booth, 1997; Marton *et al.*, 1997.

An overview of relational student learning research

Question 1: What are the qualitatively different ways students approach learning? As we saw in Chapter 1 the research on student learning suggests that students may approach their learning in two qualitatively different ways. In a deep approach, students aim to understand ideas and seek meanings. They engage with the learning task, trying to relate new things to other things that they know. In a surface approach, students see tasks as being imposed on them and they have the intention to cope with these requirements. Overall they would appear to be involved in study without reflection on purpose or strategy (Biggs, 1987a, b; Ramsden, 1992; Marton *et al.*, 1997). The structure of the awareness of students adopting a deep approach is broader and more inclusive than for students adopting a surface approach. It could be said to be more complete. It includes a wider range of interconnected aspects of understanding and they are able to bring to the foreground of their awareness more aspects that are relevant and useful in learning new things and developing new understandings.

Question 2: What is the nature of the relations between approaches to learning and learning outcome? Approaches to learning are strongly related to the quality of the student's learning outcome. Research first conducted by a group at Gothenburg University in Sweden shows that deep approaches to learning were more likely to be related to higher quality learning outcomes (Marton and Säljö, 1976). Students who, in reading a text, used a deep approach were the students who were most likely to be able to describe what the text was about. Results of this sort have been replicated and extended in many studies since (e.g. Biggs, 1979; van Rossum and Schenk, 1984; Prosser and Millar, 1989; Meyer *et al.*, 1990; Trigwell and Sleet, 1990; Trigwell and Prosser, 1991a, b; Crawford *et al.*, 1994; Prosser *et al.*, 1996; Crawford *et al.*, 1998a; Entwistle, 1998; Tang, 1998).

Question 3: How are learning approaches related to students' perceptions of their learning environment? Further investigations of these phenomena by Entwistle and Ramsden revealed that the students' approaches to learning are also related to their awareness of their learning environment. That is, approaches to learning are relational. Ramsden (1992) reported that there are five key learning environment factors which relate to students' approach to learning. Building on these studies of the relations between students' perceptions of their learning environment and their approach to learning, it is now consistently being shown that students who perceive the workload demands of a subject to be high, and who perceive the nature of the assessment as encouraging recall of facts and bits of information, are more likely to adopt a surface approach. A deep approach is found to be related to perceptions that there is choice in what is to be learned, that teaching is of a high quality, and that there are clear goals and standards for what is to be learned (Trigwell and Prosser, 1991b; Prosser *et al.*, 1996; Trigwell *et al.*, 1998).

The fourth major research question involved students' conceptions of learning. Säljö (1979) reported five qualitatively different conceptions of learning (1–5) among a group of Swedish adult learners. Learning was seen as:

1. a quantitative increase in knowledge
2. memorising
3. the acquisition, for subsequent utilisation, of facts, methods, etc.
4. the abstraction of meaning
5. an interpretive process aimed at understanding reality.

(Marton and Säljö, 1997: 55)

A sixth conception (learning as developing as a person) was added by Marton *et al.* (1993) in a study which also found evidence of the first five conceptions. Students report a similar range of conceptions of the subject matter they are studying. For example, in their study of first year mathematics students, Crawford *et al.* (1994) found five different ways (A–E) of conceiving of mathematics:

A. mathematics is numbers, rules and formulae
B. mathematics is numbers, rules and formulae which can be applied to solve problems
C. mathematics is a complex logical system: a way of thinking
D. mathematics is a complex logical system which can be used to solve complex problems
E. mathematics is a complex logical system which can be used to solve complex problems and provides new insights used for understanding the world.

(Crawford *et al.*, 1994: 335)

Question 5: How do conceptions of learning relate to approaches to learning? Students' approaches to learning (deep and surface) have been found to be related to their conceptions of learning and the subject matter. Students who conceive of learning in a topic in a *limited* way (such as a quantitative increase in knowledge, or as memorizing) are unlikely to be those who adopt a deep approach to the learning of that topic. Conversely students who have a more *complete* conception (learning as the abstraction of meaning, or an interpretive process aimed at understanding reality) are more likely to be those who adopt a deep approach to learning of that topic (van Rossum and Schenk, 1984; Crawford *et al.*, 1994; Marton and Säljö, 1997). Conceptions of learning and of the subject being learned are part of a student's prior experience. They may be part of a student's awareness when he or she is focusing on an approach to learning.

This relational research on the four aspects of awareness of interest here – prior experiences, perceptions, learning approaches and outcomes – and the relations between them forms the empirical support for the student learning model described in the next section.

A model for understanding variation in learning

The inner box in Figure 2.2 represents an individual student's experience of learning. It describes the learning *situation* of an individual student in a teaching/learning context. When a student enters a learning context (the 'world' outside the inner box) the interaction between the student and this context constitutes a unique learning situation for this student (represented by the inner box and its contents). The situation will be different for each student even though they may be in the same context. The reason for this is that the situation is constituted in the interaction between the student and the learning context – including any other students studying the same subject, the teacher and the milieu. So, for example, for an individual student entering an architecture lecture theatre, a situation is constituted in the interaction between the individual student on the one hand, and the lecture theatre, the lecturer, other students etc. on the other. Each student will be aware of aspects of his or her situation. For some students, aspects of

Figure 2.2 A constitutionalist model of student learning

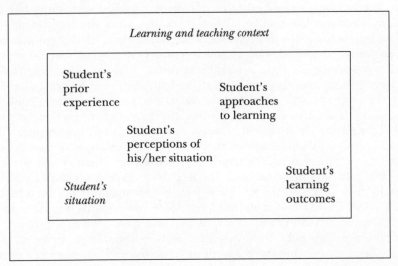

awareness brought to the foreground will be substantially greater and broader than it will be for other students.

Each student will have a unique perception of his or her situation. Such a perception cannot be described 'objectively' – i.e. independently of the individual student and the context. In this book, we will show that an individual student's perception is related to that student's prior experience of other situations, and to his or her approach to learning and their learning outcome (Figure 2.2), and it is likely to be different for each student. This is the basis of our explanation of individual variation.

In Chapters 3–6, we use this variant of the presage–process–product model as the basis of discussions of variation in aspects of student learning. Marton *et al.* (1995) have used the concept of 'temporality' in analysing the structure of students' conceptions of learning. The basic idea is that in any act of learning, students simultaneously engage in three successive phases – acquiring, knowing and applying. The same idea from a similar theoretical perspective is used here to analyse the temporal structure of students' experiences of their learning situations. It reconceptualizes the presage–process–product model which relates prior experience, perceptions of the learning environment, approaches to learning and learning outcomes.

From the constitutionalist perspective, we consider students' prior experiences, perceptions, approaches and outcomes to be simultaneously present in their awareness. By this, we mean that a student such as Melissa studying mathematics will, at any time, be aware of a great many things or phenomena that relate to mathematics (and many that don't). She will have a greater focus on some of those things than on the others (some will be central, in the foreground; others less so, more in the background (Marton and Booth, 1997). She will have many aspects of her experience of learning present in her awareness. Even when focusing on the way she will approach a learning task, she will be aware whether or not she has studied something like this before; what examination result she is seeking; what the lecturer may be expecting; how she felt last time she studied this topic; what she is planning to do during the lunch break; how her sick grandparent may be feeling, and so on. Her prior experiences, perceptions of her situation, approaches to learning and outcomes of learning will all be present in her awareness.

These aspects will also be *simultaneously* present in the student's awareness. The structure of individual students' experiences of learning is conceived of, for analytical reasons, as simultaneously consecutive (that is, temporal) and not extended over time. So, for example, a student with some prior experience of learning in a particular situation will perceive his/her situation in relation to his/her prior experiences, and adopt a certain approach to learning. All aspects of this situation will be a part of the student's awareness at all times, but some components may be more to the foreground than others at any instant. We have tried to represent this awareness in Figure 2.2 by having all aspects (without boundaries) present in the box representing the student's situation but still maintaining a degree of consecutiveness (from left to right). In Chapters 3–6 we will represent a focus on one of these aspects over the others by highlighting that aspect.

By now it may be apparent that with respect to the learning of an individual student, we are using the words 'situation' and 'context' in very specific ways. We use *context* to describe the 'learning world' that does not include the student. It could be the teaching package prepared by the teacher or it could be the teaching. It could be the science laboratory or the engineering workplace. A *situation* is what is constituted when a student enters the context. It is the relation between the context and a student and is unique to each student. It is, for example, the interaction between the student and the laboratory.

Each student will have a perception of the context and a perception of his or her situation in that context. These could be different. For example, a student may perceive that the workload set up by the teacher in a laboratory class is reasonable for the nature and level of the topic, but may consider that for him or her, with his or her prior experiences of learning, the workload is excessive. Some authors in this field have used the word 'environment' where we would use one of either context or situation. In reporting on their work we may use environment when we are unclear of their specific intent. University teachers are able to change learning and teaching contexts, but with respect to the message in this book, what is important is to find out, and if necessary attempt to change, the student's perception of his/her learning situation. A key way of trying to bring about such changes is through changes to the context.

We will now consider how this general model might describe cases of individual student learning. The focus of this book is on variation: variation within and between students in their approaches to learning, variation in the quality of learning outcomes, variation in perceptions of learning

Figure 2.3 Analysis of the experience of learning

Student's prior   2.3A
experience
is of limited
conceptions and
surface approaches surface
                   approach
                   adopted
  situation
  perceived as not
  affording a deep
  approach   lower
                   quality
                   learning
                   outcome
Situation (A) Context
affords a deep approach
	Student's prior 2.3B
	experience
	is of limited
	conceptions and
	surface approaches surface
	                   approach
	                   adopted
	  situation
	  perceived as
	  affording a surface
	  approach lower
	                   quality
	                   learning
	                   outcome
	Situation (B) Context
	affords a surface approach

Student's prior   2.3C
experience is
of more complete
conceptions and
deep approaches   deep
                  approach
                  adopted
  situation
  perceived as
  affording a deep
  approach   higher
                  quality
                  learning
                  outcome
Situation (C) Context
affords a deep approach
	Student's prior 2.3D
	experience is higher
	of more complete quality
	conceptions and learning
	deep approaches outcome
	                 deep
	                 approach
	  situation or surface
	  perceived as approach
	  affording a
	  surface lower
	  approach quality
	                  learning
	                  outcome
	Situation (D) Context
	affords a surface approach

Note: Conceptions (of learning) refer to the conceptions of Marton *et al.* (1993), which are a modification of Säljö's (1979) conceptions. Limited conceptions refer to Conceptions 1–3 (page 15), focusing primarily on reproduction; more complete conceptions refer to Conceptions 4–6, focusing primarily on meaning.
Adapted from Trigwell and Prosser, 1997.

situations. The power of this model in explaining variation is illustrated in Figure 2.3 which shows an analysis of some simplified examples of individual students' learning experiences. It includes analyses of five different experiences of learning in four different learning situations. The analysis is consistent with the results of the research on student learning referred to above and in Chapter 1.

Figure 2.3 portrays simplified examples of five different experiences of learning. Figure 2.3A shows a situation (A) in which the context affords a deep approach to learning by the student, but the student enters the context with prior experiences involving limited conceptions of learning and surface approaches to learning. (Contexts which afford a deep approach to learning are ones in which, for example, the goals for learning are clear, the teaching takes account of students' prior experiences, students have some independence in what and how they learn.) In this situation of limited prior experiences, the student perceives his or her situation as not affording a deep approach, the student adopts a surface approach and the learning outcome is of a lower quality. All these aspects (prior experience, perception, approach and outcome) are experienced as simultaneously successive (temporal) elements in the student's experience of learning.

While Figure 2.3A describes a situation in which the student's prior experiences and the context are not matched, Figures 2.3B and 2.3C describe situations (B and C) in which they are matched. In Figure 2.3B, the prior experiences are of a surface nature (limited conceptions of learning and surface approach to learning) and the context affords a surface approach. In Figure 2.3C, the prior experiences are of a deep nature (more complete conceptions and deep approach to learning) and the context affords a deep approach. The associated learning outcomes are of lower and higher quality respectively.

Figure 2.3D describes a somewhat different situation. This is one in which the context affords a surface approach, and a student whose prior experiences have been in terms of a deep approach. This student is likely to perceive his or her situation as affording a surface approach, and may adopt a surface approach. However it is also possible for such a student to transcend (or not be limited by) his or her situation and to adopt a deep approach. The completeness (or inclusiveness) of the student's prior conceptions of learning and approaches to study makes this possible for this student in this situation, but not for students with prior experiences involving limited (or less inclusive) conceptions and approaches to learning.

This analysis may help explain the experiences of students in the same or different learning contexts. Such an analysis and the model from which the analysis derives (Figure 2.2) are used in the next four chapters as the basis of a detailed discussion of variation in learning, and the implications for teaching that arise from such an analysis. In Chapter 7 we focus on teaching, and variation in teaching. To aid that discussion we have used a similar reconceptualization of the presage–process–product model and the concept of temporality to help analyse and understand individual teachers' experiences of teaching. The research supporting this model is summarized in the next section and is described in detail in Chapter 7.

Relational research into university teaching

There has been very little relational research into university teachers' conceptions of teaching, and even less into their perceptions of the teaching

Figure 2.4 A model of the experience of teaching

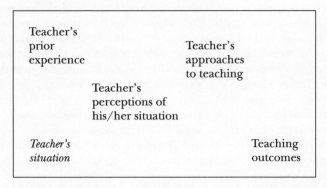

context, their approaches to teaching, outcomes of teaching and relations between these aspects of the experience of teaching. But what has been reported, as we show in this section, supports the teaching counterpart shown above (Figure 2.4) of the model developed to describe the variation in student learning.

We are aware that in the last eight years just over ten investigations have been reported on university teachers' prior experiences. Most have been on conceptions of teaching (see Kember, 1997 for an overview). Five have been conducted from a relational perspective (Dall'Alba, 1991; Martin and Balla, 1991; Samuelowicz and Bain, 1992; Martin and Ramsden, 1993; Prosser *et al.*, 1994b). They all yield similar results, showing variation from limited to more complete ways of conceiving what teaching is about. The range constituted by Prosser *et al.* (1994b) is typical of the variation found. The more complete conception involves helping students change their conceptions of the subject matter, while the limited conceptions involve transmission of the subject information or teacher's understanding.

The more complete conceptions of teaching are thought to be related to an awareness of more aspects of teaching. For example, teachers working with this conception may see the purposes of teaching as increasing knowledge through the transmission of information, helping students acquire the concepts of the discipline, developing their conceptions and changing their conceptions. Those who work with the more limited conceptions may not see the purpose of teaching as being any more than an increase in student knowledge through the transmission of information.

We are aware of only one study describing teachers' perceptions of their teaching situation in the literature (Prosser and Trigwell, 1997a), and from a relational perspective we are aware of only one report of teachers' approaches to teaching (Trigwell *et al.*, 1994). Both studies reveal variation in these aspects of the experience of teaching, and both studies show the expected relations between these aspects and teachers' prior experiences.

In a study of teachers' approaches to teaching in first year university physics and chemistry subjects we found five qualitatively different approaches, each with a focus on the strategies teachers adopt for their teaching and the intentions related to the strategies. There are two qualitatively different groups of approaches within the range. The first group have a teacher or content focus with the intention of transmitting information or the content to the students. These approaches are in contrast to those in the second group, where the focus is on the student, and the intention is to develop or change the student's conceptions of the material being learned (Trigwell *et al.*, 1994).

Teachers who had prior experiences of teaching involving the more complete conceptions of teaching were found to be more likely to adopt approaches to teaching in the second group (student-focused) while the more limited conceptions were related to teacher-focused transmission approaches (Trigwell and Prosser, 1996a). Relations have also been observed between these approaches to learning and teachers' perceptions of their teaching context. In a separate, but related, exploratory relational study we found systematic relations of the sort found for student learning (Trigwell and Prosser, 1997). The results suggest that if teachers perceive that they have some control over what is taught and how it is taught, then they are likely to adopt more of a student-focused approach to teaching. The same approach is also related to teachers' perceptions that the workload is not too great, that student diversity is not too great, and that class size is not too large. An information transmission/teacher-focused approach is related to perceptions that the teaching unit does not have a strong commitment to student learning, and that the teacher has little control over what is to be taught.

What is the outcome of teaching? From the perspective of the model described in this section, it is a part of the teacher's experience of teaching. It might involve an expanded awareness of a range of issues related to that teaching experience. For example, the teacher may be more aware of how to stimulate discussion in small groups; be more aware of the feeling of students who have never given an oral presentation; be aware that one of the fundamental concepts of the discipline is conceptually too difficult for most of the students; and be aware of a group of students who might be at risk. Research investigating teaching outcomes of this sort is yet to be reported.

From a more practical perspective, student learning could be considered to be the outcome of teaching. The relation between teachers' approaches to teaching and students' approaches to learning has been explored in two recent studies (Trigwell *et al.*, 1998; Trigwell *et al.*, 1999). In both studies it was found that the classes of those teachers who report using more of a student-focused teaching approach contained students reporting higher quality approaches to learning, while classes of teachers using more of an information transmission/teacher-focused approach contained students who reported using more surface approaches to learning.

These results support the model as conceived in Figure 2.4 and help explain the experience of university teachers in the same or different teaching contexts, and the variation in teachers' approaches to teaching, their perceptions of their teaching situation, and their prior conceptions of teaching. As with students and their learning situations, each teacher will have a unique perception of his or her teaching situation. These perceptions, their prior experience, approach to teaching, and teaching outcomes will be simultaneously present in their awareness at all times, but some components may be more in the foreground than others.

Both teachers and students see and experience phenomena in the world in relation to other phenomena. We see things as they vary from, and are similar to, other things. If we are not aware of the variation in the way that learning and teaching can be conceived, then we cannot become aware of our own way of conceiving them. Becoming aware of the variation in the way our colleagues and others conceive of learning and teaching and approach learning and teaching is a key step in developing our own awareness of our own way of conceiving and approaching learning and teaching.

It might be argued at this point that we are providing an oversimplified account of learners' and teachers' experiences of learning and teaching. We would respond that in our account we are focusing on what we see to be the key aspects of the structure of the variation in these experiences. We are not attempting to provide a full account of these experiences. Other perspectives on learning and teaching are able to provide this. But we do argue that the aspects of the experiences that we focus on are powerful aspects in the sense that they are ones that are most likely to relate to the quality of the students' learning outcomes – the improvement of which is the major focus of this book.

From the theoretical perspective described above, we argue two points through the remaining pages of this book. First, that good teaching is about teachers becoming aware of their own conceptions of learning and teaching, their approaches to teaching, and their teaching outcomes. Second, that in good teaching a major task that is to a large extent currently being overlooked is to ascertain the perceptions students have of their learning situation, and to work towards developing learning and teaching contexts which students experience in similar ways to that intended by the teacher. This involves putting the focus on the individual students and their experience – a student-focused approach.

Summary of Chapter 2

Students do not have a similar experience of the same world. In Chapter 1 we saw how two students, Melissa and Antony, studying the same mathematics subject at university, had quite different learning outcomes. We suggested that an important aspect in understanding this variation was in the students' varying perceptions of their learning situation. Even though the context was the same for both students, their prior experiences varied and their placement in the same context evoked different aspects of their prior experiences. Differences in perceived learning situations are related to varied approaches to learning and assessment results. Similarly, teachers do not have the same experience of the world. There is variation in their approach to teaching, their perceptions of their teaching situation, and their prior experiences of teaching. Their students do not necessarily experience the world in the way university teachers have intended them to experience it.

These variations in experience are the focus of this book. Through the investigations of the varying experiences of teachers and learners, we have been able to offer some ways of understanding the variation in outcomes of learning, and focus on approaches to teaching that are related to high quality of learning.

In this chapter we have outlined a conceptual underpinning for a student learning model which helps us to understand this variation. We have defined what we mean by a constitutionalist perspective, and used it to develop the model below (also Figure 2.2, and at the beginning of the next four chapters). A similar model has been developed for teaching. In the student learning version of this model we consider the learning situation (inside the box) for students entering a learning context as involving the students' prior experiences, their perceptions, their approaches and their learning outcomes, all interrelated and all simultaneously present in their awareness.

Student's prior experience	Student's approaches to learning
Student's perceptions of his/her situation	
Student's situation	Student's learning outcomes

The relations between the elements of awareness are not sequential or causal, but are conceived of as simultaneously consecutive. So, for example, a student with some prior experience of learning in a particular situation will perceive his or her situation in a certain way because of his/her prior experiences, and adopt a certain approach to learning. All aspects of this situation will be a part of the student's awareness at all times, but some components may be more to the foreground than others at any instant.

Here we mean that a student like Antony studying mathematics will, at any time, be aware of a great many things or phenomena that relate to that topic (and many that don't). He will have a greater focus on some of those things than on the others (some will be central, in the foreground; others less so, in the background). Ways of conceiving some phenomena will be in the foreground of his awareness and some others will be in the background.

He will be able to bring to the foreground of his awareness ways of conceiving some phenomena, and others will recede to the background (Marton and Booth, 1997). He will have many aspects of his experience of learning present in his awareness. Even when focusing on the way he will approach a mathematics learning task, he will be aware whether or not he has studied something like this before; what the assessment will involve; what the lecturer may be expecting; how he felt last time he studied this topic; what he is planning to do that evening; that he had forgotten to return an overdue book to the library and so on. His prior experiences, perceptions of his situation, approaches to learning and outcomes of learning will all be present in his awareness.

We have used this perspective on the model to try to understand the variation in individual acts of learning in terms of the individual learner's awareness of certain aspects of the phenomena or context in which he or she is engaged. We have argued that, according to this model, variation in students' perceptions of their situation with variations in prior experiences will evoke or bring to the foreground aspects of awareness that lead to variations in approaches to learning, and to variations in the quality of the learning outcomes.

When looked at from this theoretical perspective, a major task of teaching is to ascertain the perceptions students have of their learning situation, and work towards developing learning and teaching contexts which students experience in similar ways to that which the teacher designs.

In Chapters 3–7 we use the quantitative and qualitative relational research literature, and the models, to support and develop this argument. We suggest a range of teaching practices that are consistent with this argument and indicate how university teachers can use the research in their teaching, and in the process add to that research by investigating their own students' learning.

In each of these chapters we attempt to establish a context affording a deep approach, using the model to illustrate structures of awareness. We are all aware of many things at the one time. Some things are more to the foreground of our awareness than others. Part of a teacher's role is to assist students to bring the relevant aspects to the foreground of their awareness. In a learning context students will be aware of aspects of their experience including aspects of their current situation. In Chapter 3 we aim to bring students' prior experiences to the foreground of the awareness of readers. But it will be done with the other elements (perceptions of the student's situation, approaches to learning and learning outcomes) as part of the background of awareness. In Chapter 4 perceptions are brought to the foreground with the other elements as the background, and so on through Chapters 5 and 6. In Chapter 7 the focus shifts to teaching, and conclusions from each of these analyses are drawn together in the final chapter.

3

Students' Prior Experiences
of Learning

Student's prior experience		Student's approaches to learning
	Student's perceptions of his/her situation	
Student's situation		Student's learning outcomes

Introduction

In Chapter 2 we outlined the conceptual base upon which this book is structured. We showed how students' prior experiences of learning and teaching are fundamentally important to what they focus on in their studies. That is, their experiences are fundamentally important to the way they perceive their learning situation and approach their studies in that situation. In this chapter we propose to focus on the variation in students' prior experiences. We will do this by providing an example illustrating students' prior experiences. We will then outline some of the research into the range of prior experiences students bring to their studies, including such things as prior understanding and prior conceptions of learning. We will then identify and discuss some principles of practice for learning and teaching based upon this variation, and describe some examples of classroom teaching drawing upon these principles. Finally, we will suggest some examples of classroom research that university teachers can engage in to help them better understand the nature and variation in their students' prior experiences.

In the process, we will attempt to address in detail questions such as:

- What is the nature of students' prior orientation to learning and how does this vary? Do students have different views on what is meant by learning and understanding when beginning subjects and courses? If so, does such variation matter?
- What is the effect of different levels of background understanding on what and how students study and how they understand the material they are studying? What are the effects of different levels of prior academic ability?
- What can university teachers do to ameliorate the effects of poor prior experiences? What are some of the principles that can be developed for good practice, and what are some examples of good practice that university teachers can use to guide their own practice?

In addressing these questions we will be arguing that students who undertake subjects and courses with an awareness of poorly developed background understanding, or who have conceptions of learning and understanding as being about reproduction of rote learnt material, or whose previous experience of studying the sort of material in their subjects is of a surface nature, are likely to be adopting surface approaches to their studies. They are likely to be perceiving the learning context as affording such approaches, and consequently to have poor quality learning outcomes.

This perspective is in contrast to views that students are either a blank slate to be written on when they enter subjects, or that the quality of prior understanding, and not students' awareness of their own prior understanding, is what is important. It is also in contrast to views that students who have a deficit in particular study skills need some remedial programmes to learn these skills. Our view is that the motivation or intention students have when undertaking subjects is as fundamentally important as, or more important than, the particular skills they have.

In taking account of this student variation in their teaching, university teachers need to help their students to be aware of the effects of prior experiences on how they approach their studies, and to offer students an appropriate academic orientation to their subject.

Experiencing the variation in students' prior experience

We wish to begin by providing an example of the sort of variation in prior experiences we are talking about.

In Chapter 1, we introduced Melissa and Antony and the study of the experience of learning first year university mathematics (Crawford *et al.*, 1994). A part of that study, on prior experiences of studying mathematics, elicited the following range of responses to the question, 'Think about the maths you've done so far. What do you think mathematics is about?'

Maths is the study of numbers and the application of various methods of changing numbers.

Mathematics is the study of numbers and their applications in other subjects and the physical world.

Mathematics is the study of logic. Numbers and symbols are used to study life in a systematic perspective and require the mind to think in a logical and often precise manner.

Maths is an abstract reasoning process which can be utilised to explore and solve problems.

Techniques for thinking about observable, physical phenomena in a quantitative way and also for thinking more abstractly with little or no relation to the directly observable universe.

(Crawford *et al.*, 1994: 335)

In the same study, in response to the question, 'Think about some maths you understand really well. How did you go about studying that? (It may help to compare how you studied this with something you feel you didn't fully understand)', we received this range of responses:

I liked calculus because I could remember formulas which is how I used to study. I would rote learn all the formulas and summarise all my theoretical notes.

The way I go about studying for mathematics is by doing a lot of questions and examples. Firstly I would study the notes and learn formulas, then I put all of that to use by doing heaps of exercises.

To understand a topic well it was important to gain an understanding of the basic concepts involved, backed up by some problem solving on the topic. However, concepts which were not fully comprehended could become well understood through extra work on related questions, i.e. it is essential to do a wide range of questions on a topic to fully understand it.

After listening to an explanation of how a particular maths works the most essential features of repetition to develop speed (this usually consists of boring menial tasks) and an equal component of very difficult problems which require a great deal of thought to explore that area and its various properties and their consequences.

Read the relevant theory and try to get the same 'wavelength' as the person who actually discovered it. Before I attempt any problems I try to think where you can use the concept: i.e. what the concept was invented for. Then I attempt problems (on my own).

(Crawford *et al.*, 1994: 337)

These quotes suggest that students have a range of prior conceptions of mathematics, varying from a focus on mathematics being about numbers and their manipulation to mathematics being about ways of understanding our world. They also show that students have a range of prior orientations to the study of mathematics varying from doing lots of problems with little or no reflection on the theory or ideas upon which the ideas are based, to trying to understand those theories and ideas upon which the problems are based. What does this tell us about the nature of the prior experiences these students have had of studying mathematics, and what implications this may have for the way they study mathematics in their first year university subject? Given this variation in their prior conceptions of mathematics and ways of studying it, will they focus on different things in their university study of mathematics – will they perceive the subject in different ways?

In another study in first year university sociology (Prosser and Webb, 1994) students were asked to explain their idea of what constituted an essay in sociology. One student responded:

> I found this essay like – in sociology you can write about your own thoughts and no one can say this is right or wrong. It's your opinion and your opinion can't be wrong . . . Other essays like in ancient history and psychology, most of it is quotes and it's facts really . . . it was on experiments in animals [psychology] and so they were all facts, but this is more, sociology is more opinions and arguments, they're different . . . but I think generally just a basic idea of what you feel and a list of your points of what you are trying to explain and continue on what you are feeling and link all your ideas together in one essay.
>
> (Prosser and Webb, 1994: 128)

Another responded:

> . . . everyone sort of looked on it from their own way and that's what I like to, discover a way of you know how I'm going to deal with it. Also because . . . you could bring in examples and go to different books . . . just different examples which I like bringing into essays, rather than just facts . . . Well, I mean the standard thing is to argue about, about something which means um . . . to try to prove something or disprove another thing and to show the pro and cons . . . actually create an argument for this particular question . . . understand something a lot better, a lot deeper which then you can link up with other things . . . to systematically logically present all the evidence for what I was trying to show.
>
> (Prosser and Webb, 1994: 128)

Here we see students entering a first year sociology subject with conceptions of what constitutes an essay in sociology ranging from reproducing a list of points which are tied together, to being about an argument designed to address a particular issue or problem. Again, what do these quotes tell us about the way these students conceived of the task they were undertaking, and what would such conceptions mean for the quality of the essay produced? Given this variation, would they be focusing on different things in their reading and in their lectures and tutorials?

In these two examples we hope to have illustrated the sorts of variation in prior experience evoked in different students by the same context – that is, the subject or course in which they are enrolled.

Research describing the variation in students' prior experience

The nature of the prior experiences evoked in students when beginning a particular subject, task or activity is many and varied. There can be variation in prior conceptual understanding of the subject matter being studied, prior ways of understanding the nature of the subject being studied, prior approaches to, and experiences of, studying that subject matter.

Before looking at specific aspects of this variation, it may be worth reviewing an early study from the student learning perspective that discussed the issue of background knowledge and interest of students and their approaches to study. The results of the study begun in 1976 were reported by Entwistle and Ramsden in 1983. In this report they state that:

> Of course background knowledge and level of interest are not necessarily productive of a deep approach; they provide favourable conditions for it. As might be expected, background knowledge is most often related to level of approach in the science and technology departments: when knowledge is hierarchically structured and operation learning is favoured, an understanding of new concepts is often only possible if the previous stages have been fully grasped (c.f. Biggs, 1978). Level of interest is more commonly related to deep approaches in arts and social science tasks; this result is also understandable in the light of what has already been said about the greater informality of teaching and learning, and the more opportunities for choice, in the arts subjects.
>
> (Entwistle and Ramsden, 1983: 175)

This passage:

• introduces the idea of approaches to study being related to both background knowledge and interest;
• indicates variation in the relationship due to field of study;
• foreshadows the idea of the importance of departmental teaching context and student perceptions of that context.

The general issue of prior understanding of and interest in the topic being studied is a rather complex one. Indeed, Tobias, in a substantial review of the research relating interest and prior understanding, concludes that the two are inextricably related and cannot be separated (Tobias, 1994), and which is of greater importance probably depends on the context and the discipline being studied.

In the next section we will begin our review of the implications of variation in background understanding and interest by examining some of the research into the nature of students' prior conceptual understanding of key concepts and ideas and how that relates to the way students approach their studies. In later sub-sections we will examine how the variation in prior understanding of the nature of the subject matter being studied, and the variation in prior conceptions and approaches to learning relates to students' approaches to study.

Variation in prior conceptual understanding of key concepts and ideas

We begin this analysis of the variation in students' prior experience and interest by looking at the variation in students' prior conceptual understanding of key concepts and ideas in the subject matter they are about to study. The issue of the variation in prior conceptual understanding of the subject matter students are about to study is the one which is readily acknowledged as being of major importance to the learning outcomes. For example, David Ausubel, a distinguished cognitive psychologist, stated in 1978:

> If I had to reduce all of educational psychology to just one principle, I would say this: the most important single factor influencing learning is what the learner already knows. Ascertain this and teach him (sic) accordingly.
>
> (Ausubel *et al.*, 1978: 163)

Ausubel's view of the nature and role of prior conceptual understanding is, however, fundamentally different to ours. Ausubel believed that students entered learning and teaching situations with a stable structure of prior understanding, which was more or less correct, and that subsequent meaningful learning resulted from students integrating new knowledge into their present knowledge. Our view is that when students enter a learning and teaching context, it evokes, or brings to awareness, understanding based upon previous learning experiences in specific learning and teaching situations. That is, that prior conceptual understanding, in this sense, is relational. It is a relation between the students and the learning and teaching situation they presently find themselves in. It is not a stable structure they bring from their previous subject or studies. Given a changed learning and teaching situation, those previous understandings may not be evoked. Thus, for example, when Prosser and Millar (1989) found that none of their interview sample of first year university physics students were able to explain successfully the motion of a car travelling at constant speed along a straight road in terms of Newtonian mechanics, this does not mean that given a change of situation or a change of task those same students would not be able to explain such motion successfully. Indeed, over half were able to explain successfully the motion of an ice puck on ice from a Newtonian mechanics perspective – a different task but same situation.

So what is the nature of students' prior conceptual understanding and how does that relate to how and what students subsequently learn and understand? The following examples of research will show that students do undertake subjects with a substantial variation in their understanding of key ideas to be taught in the subject, and that this variation relates to how they approach their studies in the subject. We will show that students with poor prior conceptual understanding are more likely to adopt surface approaches, while students with well-developed conceptual understandings are more likely to adopt deep approaches.

A substantial amount of research suggests that students enter higher education courses not just knowing more or less about the subject, but more importantly, with qualitatively different conceptual understandings of key concepts and ideas to be taught and learnt in that subject. For example, in the physics study referred to above, the range of explanations given for the forces acting on the car travelling at constant velocity ranged from one in which the external forces acting on the car were in equilibrium, to one in which there was a net force in the direction of motion. The former is a Newtonian explanation while the latter is less desirably non-Newtonian. In this study, none of the 14 students at the beginning of the subject were able to provide the Newtonian explanation, although all had achieved well in physics at secondary school. At the end of the topic on Newtonian motion, four were able to provide a Newtonian explanation. This is consistent with the earlier study by Johansson *et al.*, 1985 in Sweden, in which 15 of 22 students were able to explain the motion in Newtonian terms at the start of their university subject in physics, while at the end, 16 were able to do so. In both cases there was little apparent change from the beginning of the subject until the end. Such results are common in university science subjects (West and Pines, 1985).

There has, however, been far less research in other fields of studies. In the social sciences Dahlgren, in a much-cited study of economics students' responses to the task to explain 'Why does a bun cost one crown?', identified two qualitatively different explanations, representing two qualitatively different conceptions (Dahlgren, 1997). They were:

A. The price is dependent on the relationship between the supply and demand for buns.
B. The price is equal to the (true) value of the bun.

(Dahlgren, 1997: 33)

According to Dahlgren, Conception B represents the more everyday way of thinking about price, while Conception A is the more economically appropriate way. In his longitudinal study he found substantial variation in their conceptions of price, both on a pre-test and on a post-test, with little change from pre-test to post-test. It is clear, however, that in his study students entered the subject with an everyday but not economically valid conception of price, and left the subject with a similar conception.

So how does this variation in understanding of key ideas at the start of a subject relate to students' experiences of studying in the subject and their subsequent understandings? In his 1987 summary of the research on student learning from the perspective adopted in this book, Entwistle states:

Previous knowledge and conceptualisation clearly have an important influence on approaches and outcomes, as do the balance and level of intellectual abilities, but the research described here, by its methodology and focus, has de-emphasised this whole area.

(Entwistle, 1987: 24)

Since then we have been engaged in a substantial project in the physical and biological sciences in higher education looking at just this issue. Here we will focus on the physics, and in particular, the study of electricity in a first year university physics subject (Prosser *et al.*, 1996). We used open-ended written questions and concept maps to obtain data about students' conceptualization of key ideas in electricity before and after the topic. We also used subject-specific versions of Biggs's Study Process Questionnaire (Biggs, 1987b) and Ramsden's Course Experience Questionnaire (Ramsden, 1991) to obtain data about the way 141 students perceived their subject situation and the way they approached their studies in the subject.

The analysis of these data identified four groups of students. The first group includes 36 students with well-developed prior conceptual understanding who perceived the learning context as affording a deep approach to learning, who adopted a deep approach and who had higher quality learning outcomes in terms of a well-developed post-conceptual understanding. The second group (55 students) may be characterized as a group who had poorly developed prior conceptual understanding, who did not perceive the context as affording either a surface or a deep approach, who did not adopt either a surface or a deep approach and who had poor post conceptual understanding. The third group (20 students) had very poor prior conceptual understanding, perceived the context as affording both surface and deep approaches and reported adopting both approaches (disintegrated perceptions and approaches), and had very poor post conceptual understanding. The final group (20 students) had poor prior conceptual understanding, perceived the context as affording a surface approach and not a deep approach, adopted a surface and not a deep approach and had poor post-conceptual understanding.

These results and our model suggest that students with well-developed prior conceptual understanding are likely to be aware of those aspects of the context affording a deep approach, to adopt a deep approach and to have well-developed post understanding. On the other hand, students with not so well-developed prior understanding are more likely to be aware of those aspects affording a surface approach, to adopt a surface approach and to have poorly developed post understanding. The first and last groups are consistent with the model. However, it is particularly interesting to note that those students with the least developed prior and post understanding were those Meyer *et al.* (1990) describe as having disintegrated perceptions and approaches. These students seem to be unaware of, and not be able to differentiate between, those aspects of the context affording different approaches.

So what do these examples suggest about student learning? They suggest that students undertake subjects in higher education not just with a more or less well-developed conceptual understanding of the key concepts and ideas we wish students to learn, but with qualitatively different conceptual understandings of those key concepts and ideas. The research also suggests that we are not particularly successful at changing students' understanding from the limited to the more complete conceptual understandings. We have also seen that there is a relationship between the quality of students' understanding on entering subjects and the approach to study they adopt within those subjects. Given the close relation between students' approach to learning and quality of understanding at the end of their subjects, the issue of what to do about this variation at the beginning is one of substantial importance to the quality of students' learning outcomes. We will return to this later in the chapter. For now, we wish to examine some examples, not of students' prior conceptual understanding of key concepts and ideas, but of their prior understanding of the nature of the subject matter they are studying and the relation that may have to their approaches to study.

Variation in prior understanding of the nature of the subject matter being studied

In the previous section we looked at some examples of the literature on students' prior conceptual understanding of key concepts and ideas in the subject they are studying. In this section we wish to focus on their prior conceptual understanding of the nature of the subject matter they are studying. To do this we will return to the two examples described on pages 27–9 – the first year mathematics study introduced in Chapter 1 and the study of a first year sociology subject (Prosser and Webb, 1994). We will also show how this variation relates to the way students approach their study and consequently to the quality of their learning outcomes.

In the sociology subject, the study focused on students writing their first essay in sociology. The two quotes shown on page 29 represent two qualitatively different ways of conceiving of or understanding what an essay is in sociology. The first quote represented a view that an essay was composed of a 'collection of points, each related to the topic, but not contributing to a whole view of the topic' (Prosser and Webb, 1994: 128). This was termed a multistructural conception of an essay (after Biggs and Collis, 1982). The second quote represented a view that an essay was '. . . an argument. Issues were included because they were a coherent part of the cases being argued in the essay, not just because they related to the question' (Prosser and Webb, 1994: 128). This was termed a relational conception of an essay (again after Biggs and Collis, 1982). In the study, 13 of the 19 students interviewed were classified as probably adopting a multistructural conception of an essay, while only 6 were classified as adopting a relational conception.

This study illustrates an interesting example of how a particular subject or situation can evoke a particular conception or way of thinking. The quote representing the multistructural conception showed that this student conceived of the essay in sociology as being different from that in psychology, for example. But given this variation in understanding of what the essay was about, the question is, does it have any relation to the way the students went about writing the essay and, more importantly, does it relate to the quality of the essay produced? The answer to both these questions is definitely yes. On the whole, students with prior conceptions described as multistructural subsequently adopted a surface approach to the writing of the essay and students with prior conceptions described as relational subsequently adopted a deep approach to the writing of the essay.

The above example looked at the variation in students' understanding of the nature of the task in which they were involved – the task of essay writing. The next example from the research literature looks at the variation in students' prior conceptual understanding of the nature of knowledge in the field in which they are studying. In a longitudinal study of students studying business administration and engineering in Sweden, Dahlgren and Pramling (1985) asked the question of students, 'What do you actually mean by knowledge?' in the context of their studies. They identified three groups of responses. In the first group were students who did not seem to link knowledge with reality – they spoke about theoretical knowledge – termed a *separationist* understanding. In the second group were students who conceived of knowledge as being either theoretical or practical and the relationship between the two being *sequential*. The third way of understanding knowledge is that knowledge is about reality – an *integrated* way of understanding. In their study they found that at the start of their studies, 9 of the 20 business administration students expressed the sequential view of knowledge, while 9 of the 15 engineering students expressed an integrated view. It may be concluded from this that there is substantial variation in the way students entering higher education conceive of knowledge in the field in which they are studying.

Having seen examples of variation in students' understanding of the nature of tasks in which students are being engaged and in the nature of knowledge in the subject in which they are studying, the next example is one which looks at students' prior conceptual understanding of the nature of the subject matter they are studying. The mathematics subject in which the students were enrolled was designed to be the first subject in a three-year mathematics course. Students were surveyed with an open-ended response questionnaire at the start of the subject. The quotes shown on page 28 represented the following ways of thinking about mathematics by these students at the start of their first year university mathematics subject:

A. Mathematics is numbers, rules and formulae
B. Mathematics is numbers, rules and formulae which can be applied to solve problems

C. Mathematics is a complex logical system; a way of thinking
D. Mathematics is a complex logical system which can be used to solve problems
E. Mathematics is a complex logical system which can be used to solve complex problems and provides new insights used for understanding the world.

(Crawford et al., 1994: 335)

Seventy seven per cent of the students at the start of that subject – after completing mathematics at secondary school – gave responses representing the first two ways of conceiving mathematics. That is, 77 per cent thought mathematics was basically about numbers and how they might be applied in problems. Only 23 per cent had a more complete understanding – that is that mathematics is about a way of thinking about complex problems and insights into understanding the world. If students believe at the start of their mathematics subject that mathematics is basically about numbers, their manipulation and application, what are they likely to focus on as the subject progresses? Our answer is that without substantial support to develop a more complete understanding of what mathematics is about, they will focus on those aspects of the subject which deal with numbers. It might be interesting to note that the students who thought mathematics was basically about numbers achieved at substantially lower levels in the end of term assessment compared to those with the more complete understanding. We will return to this study again in the next section, where we will see that there is a relationship between the way these students approached their studies of mathematics in secondary school and their understanding of what mathematics was about at the start of their university subject.

Having identified the variation in the way these students conceived of mathematics at the start of their subject, how does this relate to the way they approached their study in that subject? In a follow-up study, Crawford *et al.* (1998a) developed a questionnaire designed to measure the two fundamentally different ways of understanding mathematics (i.e. either a focus on numbers or a focus on logic, problems and the real world). In the study the questionnaire was administered at the beginning of the students' first year of mathematics and again at the end of that year. As well, a revised version of the Biggs's Study Process Questionnaire was administered both times, and a revised version of Ramsden's Course Experience Questionnaire was administered with the second survey. A cluster analysis of the results identified two groups of students. In the first group were students with a relatively poor prior understanding of what mathematics was about; who reported adopting relatively surface approaches to studying mathematics at secondary school; who reported adopting relatively surface approaches to their study of mathematics in their first year at university; who perceived the context as supporting surface approaches; and who subsequently had relatively poor understanding of what mathematics was about and had relatively poor achievement results. The second group were opposite in all respects. They had a relatively well-developed understanding of what mathematics was about at the start of the subject; they reported having adopted relatively deeper approaches to their mathematical studies at secondary school; they adopted relatively deeper approaches at university; perceived the same context as affording a relatively deeper approach; had relatively well-developed understanding of what mathematics was about at the end of the year and had relatively high achievement (see also Chapter 4).

This study again highlights the importance of students' prior understanding of the nature of the subject matter they are studying – not just of the key ideas and concepts being taught in the subject.

In this section we have expanded our vision of what constitutes students' prior conceptual understanding from a focus on key concepts and ideas to what they conceive the subjects or major task to be about. Students enter courses not only with ill-formed understandings of key ideas that university teachers often assume they understand, but with very ill-formed ideas of what their programmes, subjects and major tasks are about. As we have indicated in this section, and will explore more deeply in later chapters, these ill-formed ideas have substantial associations with how the students approach their studies and with the quality of the learning outcomes. In many respects these aspects of their prior understandings can have a more profound impact on the subsequent learning than do some misunderstandings of some of the key concepts and ideas.

Variation in prior conceptions of, and approaches to, learning

In the previous sections we have discussed examples of research which have looked at the variation in students' prior conceptual understanding of key concepts and ideas, and of the nature of the subject matter and task in which they are engaged. In this section we will broaden this issue even further by showing that students enter university subjects with substantial variation in the way they conceive of learning and in the way they have previously approached their learning. Again the issue is not that they have greater or lesser experiences of the same things, but that their prior experiences are qualitatively different.

Conceptions of learning

The classic, and among the most often cited, study of students' prior experiences of learning and understanding is that by William Perry at Harvard University in the United States of America (Perry, 1970). He conducted a longitudinal study of university students' intellectual development, and identified nine stages of development from one representing an absolute view of knowledge (there is one correct or right answer), to a relativist view (all answers are equally valid), to finally a committed view or understanding (accepting that while there may not be any absolute answers, a commitment to a particular way of seeing and understanding the world needs to be accepted). Perry conceived this to be a developmental scheme in which most, but certainly not all, students enter university with absolutist views of knowledge and understanding, and in which many leave not having changed or developed those views.

A somewhat later study (and one equally well cited) of students' conceptions of learning, or ways of understanding, was conducted by Roger Säljö in the late 1970s (Säljö, 1979). In that study, previously introduced in Chapter 2, Säljö interviewed a group of adults about what learning meant to them. He identified the following range in the way they responded:

Learning was seen as:

1. a quantitative increase in knowledge
2. memorising
3. the acquisition, for subsequent utilisation, of facts, methods, etc.
4. the abstraction of meaning
5. an interpretive process aimed at understanding reality.

(Marton and Säljö, 1997: 55)

While these ways of conceiving of learning do not form a developmental sequence – having not been identified in a longitudinal study – they are nevertheless hierarchical in that the later conceptions incorporate and build upon the former. As well, there is a qualitative shift between the third and fourth ways of conceiving of learning. The first three have an external focus – with little or no focus on meaning for the learner – while the last two have a focus on meaning for the learner.

These qualitatively different conceptions have since been replicated by Marton *et al.* (1993) with students studying at the Open University in the United Kingdom. In that study, Marton *et al.* identified a sixth conception which they termed 'Changing as a person'. The question to keep in mind at this stage about these sorts of differences is whether, and how, such differences relate to the way students approach their learning and to the learning outcomes. It would seem logical to suggest that if students conceived of learning to be about rote memorization only, then there is little likelihood that they would focus on meaning and understanding in their study. If on the other hand, learning is conceived of as the abstraction of meaning, then it may be expected that students will approach their studies in ways in which meaning can be extracted.

We will now turn from looking at how students conceive of learning to their prior orientations and approaches to learning.

Prior orientations and prior approaches to learning
From the perspective on learning adopted in this book and the model at the beginning of the chapter, we argue that when students enter a learning

and teaching context, their situation within that context evokes an immediate response from them about how they are going to approach tasks in that situation. This immediate response we would call a prior approach to learning. It is not necessarily the approach students once engaged in the task will adopt; it is their immediate, initial response. This is in contrast to their prior orientation to learning, which may be considered to be a reasonably stable culmination of their previous experiences of studying generally. For example, a student may enter a subject having generally adopted a deep approach to studying that subject matter in secondary school, but on entering university may feel very anxious about his/her ability to cope in a new situation, and so immediately adopts a surface approach. In this case we would say that the student's prior orientation to learning was deep, but prior approach to learning was surface. It then remains to be seen what approach the student adopts for various tasks during the course – this we would term his/her approach to learning those tasks in the subject. The way students approach their learning during the subject and its relationship to their learning outcomes will be the focus of Chapters 5 and 6. In this chapter we wish to look at their prior orientation and prior approaches to learning.

The research into students' orientations and approaches to learning from the student learning perspective adopted in this book seems to have had two separate origins. One is more qualitative and focuses on the relational response of students to particular learning tasks (Marton, Säljö), the other more quantitative and focused on students' more stable orientations to learning (Entwistle, Biggs). We will look first at an example of the qualitative perspective and then at an example from the quantitative perspective.

In studies of students' processes and outcomes in reading academic textual materials in the mid 1970s, Marton and Säljö (1976) identified two qualitatively different ways in which students read those texts. One of those ways 'focused on the text itself or on what the text was about', while the other focused on 'the author's intention, the main point, the conclusion to be drawn' (Marton and Säljö, 1997: 43). As we saw in Chapter 1 they termed these two ways of approaching the reading of the text, surface and deep. Since then, a great deal of qualitative research into the way students approach learning tasks has confirmed the fundamental difference between attempting to reproduce the material being read and understanding that material (Chapter 5). From the perspective of this research, an approach is defined in terms of the relationship between the student and the particular task with which he/she is engaged. It is not a stable learning style, as was dramatically shown by Laurillard (1997) referring to one of the seminal studies in this field. In her interview study of 31 undergraduate science students she found that 19 of them used different approaches on different occasions on different tasks, while 12 used the same approach. While these two studies refer to students' approaches to particular tasks, the following example looks at student prior orientation to the study of particular subject matter.

On pages 27–9 we illustrated the variation in students' prior experiences using a number of statements by students about their study of mathematics. As mentioned previously in this chapter, the responses are by students to an open-ended written survey conducted at the start of their first year university subject. The quotes about how they went about studying mathematics previously – representing what we would call their prior orientation to the study of mathematics – were illustrative examples of the following categories:

A. Learning by rote memorisation, with an intention to reproduce knowledge and procedures
B. Learning by doing lots of examples, with an intention to reproduce knowledge and procedures
C. Learning by doing lots of examples with an intention of gaining a relational understanding of the theory and concepts
D. Learning by doing difficult problems with an intention of gaining a relational understanding of the entire theory, and seeing a relationship with existing knowledge
E. Learning with the intention of gaining a relational understanding of the theory and looking for situations where the theory will apply.
(Crawford *et al.*, 1994: 337)

The first two of these categories represent examples of surface prior orientations to studying mathematics, while the latter three represent deep prior orientations. They describe how the students have studied mathematics before beginning their studies at university. In that study, 82 per cent of 294 responses were classified in categories A and B. That is, 82 per cent of the students reported surface prior orientations to the study of mathematics. Only 18 per cent reported deep prior orientations to study.

Several things should be noted about these descriptions. First of all, they are contextualized within the discipline – they represent examples of surface and deep orientations to the study of mathematics. They are not contextualized within a particular learning and teaching situation – they represent students' responses to a range of situations in their previous study of mathematics. Each category is constituted in terms of an underlying intention and strategy. That is, for this study, an orientation was defined in terms of congruent intentions and strategies. As well, they are hierarchically inclusive, at least in terms of the strategies, in the sense that, for example, doing difficult problems to extend understanding (D) may very well involve some memorization (although probably not rote memorization).

That study also reported a close relationship between prior conceptions of mathematics and prior orientations to the study of mathematics. Students who understood mathematics to be about numbers and their applications almost invariably reported a surface prior orientation to the study of mathematics, while students who understood it to be about complex problem solving and help in understanding the world almost invariably reported a deep prior orientation to that study. This suggests that students' conceptions of the nature of the subject matter they study are closely related to their orientations to the study of that subject matter. Indeed we would argue that conceptions and orientations are internally related, that is, that they are defined in relation to one another, and are not separable. If university teachers find that at the beginning of their subjects students conceive of the subject matter in certain ways, and have orientations to the study of that subject matter consistent with the way they conceive it, then part of the process of influencing the way they approach their study of that subject matter must include helping them develop their understanding of what that subject matter is about.

This study represents one of the few examples of a qualitative approach to research being used to look at students' prior orientations to learning. Most of the research into orientations has been based upon quantitative methods using inventories. Two such approaches were developed independently by John Biggs working in Australia and Noel Entwistle working in the United Kingdom. Biggs developed his Study Process Questionnaire comprising three scales with two sub-scales in each scale. The three scales are now called a surface approach, deep approach and achieving approach (initially he termed them reproducing, internalizing and organizing; Biggs, 1978). Each of these is composed of an intention or motive sub-scale and a strategy sub-scale. Biggs initially conceived of these approaches as being reasonably stable learning styles of students (1987a). More recently, however, he has disavowed this cognitivist perspective, and has argued that orientations and approaches are contextually situated (1993b), in many ways similar to the perspective adopted in this book.

Entwistle's original Approaches to Study Inventory was composed of four main scales, each with several sub-scales. The four scales were called meaning orientation (incorporating a deep approach, relating ideas, use of evidence and intrinsic motivation sub-scales), reproducing orientation (incorporating surface approach, syllabus-boundedness, fear of failure and extrinsic motivation sub-scales), achieving orientation (incorporating strategic approach, disorganized study methods, negative attitudes, achievement motivation sub-scales), and finally learning style (incorporating comprehension learning, globetrotting, operation learning and improvidence sub-scales). The first three scales bear remarkable similarity to Biggs's three scales – incorporating both intention and strategy sub-scales. Indeed Entwistle (1988) has commented on the similarity, noting, 'the similarity between these two sets of factors is all the more remarkable when it is realised that Biggs was describing students in terms of a different inventory and within a different educational system' (Entwistle, 1988: 29).

The general structure of the meaning, reproducing and achieving scales with related intention and strategy components has been replicated in many studies using these inventories. We will return to the use of these inventories in later chapters. But for now we wish to note that both qualitative and quantitative research into students' prior orientations to study have produced similar qualitative variations.

Principles of practice for learning and teaching resulting from the variation in prior experiences

Having reviewed some of the student learning literature on students' prior experiences of learning, and how these relate to the way students subsequently approach their study of a particular topic, we wish to distil some of the key principles for practice that we see emerging from this literature. Before doing so, we reiterate that students come to learning and teaching contexts with certain prior experiences of studying. When they enter those contexts, the situation evokes from them, brings to their awareness, particular aspects of that prior experience. The aspects that are evoked – for example, prior conceptual understanding of key concepts and ideas, prior understanding of the nature of the subject matter they are about to study, prior conceptions of learning of that subject matter and prior approaches to that learning – are related to the context and the situation in which the students find themselves. Just because, for example, a student has passed a previous examination involving the writing of an essay in a particular situation or discipline, this does not mean that a new situation will evoke that same prior experience. But we do know that the prior experiences that are evoked are particularly important to the quality of learning in the new situation.

So what does this say to us about the way we might practise our teaching and help our students learn? The principles are:

1. Students enter our learning and teaching context with substantial qualitative variation in their prior experiences of learning and teaching.
2. These prior experiences of learning and teaching are related to specific prior situations in which those experiences occurred.
3. A new learning and teaching situation they find themselves in evokes certain aspects of these prior experiences, the aspects evoked being related to the congruence between the previous situation and the new situation.
4. The aspects evoked have a subsequent substantial impact on what and how students learn in the new situation.

These principles are consistent with the perspective on student learning underlying this book, and are, we believe, consistent with the experiences of many university teachers in higher education, although it is not the way many may have thought about learning and teaching. They help explain why students, who have exhibited certain competencies and understandings in their previous studies, on entering new learning and teaching situations do not seem to bring with them these competencies and understandings. They also explain how some students are able to draw upon their previous experiences, while others seem to be unaware of them. They also provide pointers, or a basis for the consideration of action, which can be taken by university teachers to enhance the quality of their teaching and their students' learning.

We now wish to provide some illustrative examples of classroom-based research and practice which is consistent with this perspective on students' learning and with these principles.

Examples of classroom research and practice related to the learning and teaching principles

In considering the implications for classroom research and practice of the research focused on in this chapter, the major issue is how to bring to the foreground of students' awareness their previous experiences of learning the subject matter they are about to learn, and how to help them see how those experiences relate to the subject and situation they are about to study. As discussed so far, these experiences relate to their prior conceptual understanding of the material they are to study, their prior approaches to and conceptions of learning similar material, and their prior understanding of what the material they are about to study is about.

In the first three examples relating these principles to classroom teaching, the university teachers took as explicit aims for early activities in their classes:

- to provide relevance to the learning by focusing the students' awareness on the conceptual aims and the learning demands of the subject. Through participation in activities which demonstrate the limitations of their understanding of the content matter and learning itself, the students can be made aware of the need to apply learning approaches which lead to a more complete understanding of the content;
- to promote awareness in the students of the different ways they, and their fellow students, conceptualize the subject matter and their learning. The development of more complete conceptions can be encouraged through contemplation of this variation;
- to allow the lecturer to become aware of the way students conceive of the subject matter and of their learning, as a precursor to providing teaching approaches designed to improve understanding.

The three examples refer to cases of student learning in computer programming, student learning in physics and student learning in political science.

Student learning in computer programming

This case concerns second year undergraduate students taking a computer programming subject featuring the COBOL programming language (Cope *et al.*, 1996). The students had previously completed two other programming subjects involving the C++ language and two subjects on information systems (IS) development.

In a previous study, Booth (1992) had investigated students' conceptions of computer programming. She found three conceptions of computer programming forming a hierarchy based on logical inclusiveness. The three conceptions were computer programming as a computer-oriented activity, a problem-oriented activity, and a product-oriented activity. Product orientation logically includes the problem orientation and both include the computer orientation.

In the programming subjects already completed by the students in this case, the emphasis was on programming as a computer-oriented activity. The students entered this subject with prior conceptions of programming as being a computer-oriented activity. This subject was intended to change the students' perception of computer programming to that of a problem-oriented activity.

The subject was designed to emphasize problem solving rather than rote memorization of language syntax. Students need to apply a deep learning approach in order to succeed, so their prior conception of learning is important. As previously discussed in this book, Marton *et al.* (1993) identified a hierarchy of six different conceptions of learning: a quantitative increase in knowledge; memorizing; the acquisition of facts which can be retained for use when necessary; the abstraction of meaning; an interpretive process aimed at understanding reality; and developing as a person. Only students holding the last three conceptions are likely to adopt a deep learning approach.

The first teaching activity of the subject was vitally important in conveying to the students the subject's aims and conceptual learning demands. The activity was based on a phenomenographic perspective of learning, and was designed to help students address their prior conceptions and orientations to learning. Students were required to describe in written or pictorial format, on large sheets of paper, their conceptions of computer programming and of learning. Student responses were consistent with the hierarchies of conceptions of computer programming and learning outlined previously.

Computer programming was seen, for example, by one student as 'screenfuls of long complicated code' and 'large programs requiring hours of debugging' and by another as 'sitting in front of a terminal for hours' and 'too many commands and functions to remember', clearly computer-oriented activities. Others described 'solving puzzles' and 'finding a problem then writing a solution', clearly problem-oriented conceptions. Also included were 'a means to an end' and 'producing something useful for someone to use on their computer', conceptions involving product orientation.

Conceptions of learning were concentrated at the lower level conceptions identified by Marton *et al.* (1993). Examples were 'remembering', 'cramming', 'regurgitation', 'listening, reading, watching etc. and committing it to memory for later use'. Some conceptions at the higher levels included 'understanding or improving your understanding of something', 'being open to new ideas' and 'correctly interpreting information'.

The large sheets of paper were laid out around the room and the students read each other's responses. Small group discussions were then initiated to consider the differences and similarities between the responses. Each group reported back to the lecturer who summarized the findings. The students were clearly surprised by the variation in conceptions. A facilitated class discussion then took place on the existence of this variation and the lecturer's purpose in using this approach.

This case shows how one teacher structured a learning and teaching situation to help refocus students' attention on the aims of the subject. This was done by structuring an exercise in which students could see variation in the way they and their fellow students conceived of or understood the nature of computer programming at the start of the subject. This variation came out of or was evoked from the students' prior experiences of computer programming. The variation related strongly to their experience of computer programming. While this case was developed in a workshop situation, the example described in the next case was developed for a large lecture situation.

Student learning in physics

The example described in this case was designed with two aims. First, to help focus students' awareness on what was being aimed at in this subject and how that varied from what they might have expected. Second, to help students become aware of the variation in the way they and their fellow students understood and conceived of a major principle which was to be learnt and understood by the students.

The topic being taught was Newtonian mechanics. It was being taught in the first year of a university physics major stream. Most if not all students had studied Newtonian mechanics at secondary school, and felt that they had a reasonable understanding of it. The problem was that while most students are able to solve textbook problems involving Newtonian mechanics, their understanding of the fundamental concepts on which it is based is poorly developed (Prosser and Millar, 1989).

In the second lecture of a series of 27 lectures on the topic, the students were asked to engage in a 'buzz group' (Bligh, 1971) and then plenary discussion focused on their understanding of the fundamental concepts. In the buzz group students were asked individually to draw a diagram of all the forces on a car going up a hill at a constant speed. They were asked to compare their diagram with the student next to them and to arrive at an agreed diagram. They were given five minutes for this task. It was a task which they felt they were able to achieve.

At the end of the five minutes, the lecturer asked pairs of students at each end of the back row, middle row and front row to describe their diagrams. The diagrams were drawn on the board without comment by the lecturer. The students were then asked to examine the diagrams and to identify the major differences between them. It soon became clear to the students that the diagrams were fundamentally different, and that there was substantial variation within the lecture group on the nature and relative sizes of the forces acting on the car. Subsequently, similar activities were engaged in by the students throughout the teaching of the topic.

An evaluation of the topic in this case, based on interviews with 24 students at the beginning and the end of the topic, showed that at the end of the topic there was substantial variation among the students in what they focused on during the teaching of the topic (Prosser and Millar, 1989). For a substantial number of students, while they found activities such as the buzz sessions interesting, they were not the focus of their attention. These students showed little change and, in some cases, regression in their understanding of the fundamental concepts. Those students for which these activities were focal showed substantial change and improvement. A more detailed account of this development is given in Chapter 4.

In summary, the teaching task here was first to help students focus their attention on their lack of understanding of the fundamental concepts and the importance of understanding in the study of physics at university, and second to help them see the range of understandings held by the group of students on the fundamental concepts.

These two cases have focused on variation in students' prior conceptual understanding of key concepts and on their understanding of the nature of the subject matter they were about to study. The next case describes an example of variation in students' understanding of the nature of the tasks they are to engage in.

Student learning in political science

This case comes from an activity developed by Michael Jackson, and used by him in a first year government subject (Jackson and Prosser, 1985, 1989). The activity aims to help students develop their awareness of the nature and structure of essays in political science. It helps students examine their prior conceptions of essay writing and change these conceptions. In this case, students are asked to read (in the lecture theatre) extracts from two essays written by students about the portrayal of power in Golding's *Lord of the Flies*. These are shown in Figure 3.1.

They are also given a checklist on which to rate the two examples. The checklist is shown in Figure 3.2. A show of hands is then used to identify the proportions of the class rating the extracts in particular ways. It is soon seen by the students that other students have perceived the extracts differently to the way they have.

This case provides another example of helping students focus on the conceptual and learning demands of the subject, helping students see the different ways in which essays can be conceptualized and helping the lecturer become aware of the ways in which his/her students are conceiving of essays in political science.

Figure 3.1   Political science essay extracts

ESSAY EXTRACT A

Power is a complex phenomenon which includes authority and coercion. A power struggle lies at the centre of William Golding's novel *The Lord of the Flies*. The principal characters in this book are Ralph and Jack. Jack is quick to claim the leadership and with it power by declaring that he can sing C sharp (p. 23). However, Ralph wins the election for the chief. Ralph's size, attractive appearance, and stillness made him seem like an adult to the little ones and his accidental use of the conch to attract attention made him seem like the man with the megaphone that the boys can remember before the crash (p. 24).

Ralph shares power with Jack by letting him command the choir after the election. In fact, the election did not resolve the conflict over leadership, but only defined the context within which it would occur.

Ralph's goal was rescue. He tried to govern according to that goal. Piggy advised him much as a political scientist employed by a politician would. (Is Piggy's fate what happens to students of political science?) Ralph is a weak leader. When his plans are challenged, when his leadership is challenged he appeals to the conch.

Jack manipulates the boys' desire for play (p. 140). In time, he leads them to the murder of Simon (p. 168). By then everyone is in Jack's power, except Piggy and Ralph. Jack was ever ready to enforce his rule with power, whereas Ralph was not.

While the recollection of their lives before the crash was strong with the boys, it was only natural that they would follow Ralph. His manner and the system he tried to establish was consistent with their previous lives. Because his intentions were logical and responsible, they naturally cooperated.

Jack exploited the weakness of human nature by leading the boys into play hunting, and finally murder. He capitalised on the boys' excitement at doing things that were forbidden in their previous lives. Equally, he was able to exploit their fear of the beastie, because he understood that fear. He understood it, because he shared it. Jack's forceful personality kept the pressure on all the time. . . .

ESSAY EXTRACT B

The thesis of this essay is that Piggy and Ralph, the two central characters in Golding's novel *The Lord of the Flies*, stood in a relationship of reciprocal influence. Reciprocal influence exists when two (or more) actors influence each other. Influence exists when A cause B to perform

Figure 3.1   (cont'd)

an act X, or adopt an attitude X, that B would not otherwise have done or adopted but for the intervention of A. To argue this thesis, I will analyse the elements of power available to Ralph and Piggy. These elements can be categorised as skills, willingness, and resources. It is because neither Piggy or Ralph had much in the way of skills, willingness, and resources that they combined their efforts. In order to highlight the relationship between Ralph and Piggy, the skills, willingness, and resources of other characters will also be referred to.

The analysis of the skills, willingness, and resources of Ralph and Piggy can be outlined using a table to indicate their scores on these elements.

Table: Elements of power

Elements	Piggy	Ralph
Skills	–	0
Willingness	0	+
Resources	+	++

+ *A high degree of the element*
0 *Average degree of the element*
– *Absence of the element*

Lacking in the skill of exercising influence, Piggy made himself a victim from the start by needlessly revealing his dreaded nickname. This revelation indicated the poor judgement he showed on other occasions, such as when he clung to the conch as though it were a lump of power. In more general terms, he does succeed in establishing a relationship with Ralph, although this cannot be described as being through skill but rather by accident.

In comparison, the skills that Ralph possesses meant that he was able to influence the boys, even though he neither realised what the skills were nor developed them. Here he is in contrast to Jack who perceived which skills and resources could be used to influence the boys and set out to develop those that he could, for example he learned how to hunt despite his fear.

Similarly, Piggy and Ralph had different degrees of . . .

Source: Jackson and Prosser, 1985, 1989.

Figure 3.2   Checklist for analysing the essay extracts

CHECKLIST

Choose the best answer for each of these items:

		Essay A	Essay B
1. This type of essay is	a) a descriptive type	▭	▭
	b) an analytical type	▭	▭
2. The field of this essay is	a) literature	▭	▭
	b) politics	▭	▭
	c) psychology	▭	▭
3. The essay is about	a) *Lord of the Flies*	▭	▭
	b) power	▭	▭
	c) Piggy, Ralph and Jack	▭	▭
4. The essay's thesis (or main point to be argued)	a) is clear	▭	▭
	b) is not clear	▭	▭
5. The structure of the essay	a) is clear	▭	▭
	b) is not clear	▭	▭
6. The writer substantiates the points with evidence from	a) primary sources (the original document)	▭	▭
	b) secondary sources (writings about the original document)	▭	▭
7. The way the ideas flow from one point to the next	a) is clear	▭	▭
	b) is not clear	▭	▭
8. The essay answers the question	a) what is power in *Lord of the Flies?*	▭	▭
	b) describe the characters of Piggy and Ralph	▭	▭

Source: Jackson and Prosser, 1985, 1989.

Having described three examples focusing on classroom teaching, we will now turn to some examples which have a stronger focus on classroom research. But first a few comments on the conduct of classroom research from the student learning perspective. For university teachers wishing to research their students' prior experiences of studying the subject matter they are about to study, there are two fundamental questions, and some related questions, that need to be asked. They are:

- What is it I want to find out about?
- How can I go about finding out?
  - What data do I wish to collect?
  - How can I collect those data?
  - How can I analyse those data?
  - How can I interpret or make sense of the analysed data?

The most important of these – and the one most often overlooked – is the first, because it is the answer to the first which will guide the answers to the second. For example, suppose a classroom researcher wishes to find out about the way students had previously approached their studies of his/her subject. One appropriate way would be to use Biggs's Study Process Questionnaire (Biggs, 1987b). But if the questionnaire was used in its original form, it is much more likely to tap students' general prior orientation to study generally than their previous approaches to the study of the present subject matter. In this case the research would have been driven more by the availability of a well-developed and researched questionnaire than by carefully thinking through what it was that the researcher wanted to find out.

Continuing this hypothetical example: suppose the researcher had used a properly revised and contextualized version of the Study Process Questionnaire, how would he/she analyse the data and make sense of the analysed data? One way is to calculate the mean scores on the scales of the questionnaire. But what do the students' mean scores tell us? Suppose the mean score on the surface scale was 3.4 and on the deep scale was 3.7. Does this mean that the students' previous experience of studying the subject matter was deep? We would very much doubt that the data could be interpreted this way. The results of such a questionnaire cannot tell us whether their previous experience was deep or surface. To find out about that, the researcher would probably need to use an open-ended written questionnaire, asking students to describe how they had previously approached their studies, or better still to engage in a series of interviews with a well-selected sample of students.

So what could the results of the administration of the questionnaire have told us? Well, for example, if the research question had been 'Have students who enter a subject with previous high achievement studied the subject more deeply than students with previous low achievement?', then a correlation between a deep approach scale and previous achievement scores would be appropriate.

This example highlights the primary importance of identifying what it is you wish to find out about, and having carefully clarified that, thinking about how you will then find out about it. Of course, after having identified what you want to find out about, and having sought ways of finding out about it, you may decide that your original questions were inappropriate and you may wish to revise the question. That is, there is a relationship between the what and the how – just as there is in student learning.

Now let us turn to some examples of classroom-based research into students' prior experiences. We will describe one example of possible research from each of the major areas addressed previously. The first is an example of classroom research into students' prior conceptual understanding of key concepts and ideas.

Classroom research into prior conceptual understanding of key concepts

In a study of students' prior understanding of the concept of photosynthesis in a first year university biology subject (Hazel *et al.*, 1996) students were asked to respond in written form to the following open-ended question at the start of the subject:

The Blackwood River in Western Australia had been infected with a rapidly-growing green alga. In terms of photosynthetic reactions, describe what happens when light falls on the algae, what happens at night, and any differences between these two situations.

Responses were analysed using a method derived from the phenomenographic tradition adapted for use with written responses[1]. The analysts' first task was to try to identify the qualitatively different ways in which the students responded to the question. There were four analysts involved. They selected a sample of about 20 responses, and each analyst developed his/her own set of ways in which he/she judged the students had responded. The analysts met, compared and contrasted their categories, looked for logical structure within the set of categories, and went away and recategorized the 20 statements. They met again, compared their categorizations, revised their categories, analysed the structure, selected another 20 statements, categorized those, compared categorizations and finally categorized the remaining statements. An example of the results for the analysis of this question is shown in Figure 3.3.

We mentioned previously that part of the analysis was to look at the structural relations between the categories. In this example, the structure is inclusive in that the later categories incorporate the former categories. For classroom-based research, this sort of structure is quite useful. It shows how more complete understandings can be related to limited understanding, and provides university teachers with a structure which they can use to make sense of students' seemingly non-sensical responses.

The next two examples focus on ways in which classroom teachers can research their students, prior understanding of the subject matter being studied and their prior approaches to studying the subject matter they are about to study.

Figure 3.3   Categories of description for students' conceptions of photosynthesis

Category 0 (n = 36)
Not on photosynthetic reactions
Students do not address the central issue of the question – 'In terms of photosynthetic reactions . . .'. Instead, students give isolated and often incorrect responses, e.g., 'When light falls on alga, CO_2 is produced', or they discuss some general aspects of algae or of pollution but do not discuss photosynthetic reactions.

Category 1 (n = 192)
Photosynthesis involves energy interconversion
Students may discuss the conversion of light energy into chemical energy, may use specific energy terms such as Glucose or ATP, may use an equation form of expression. Students do not discuss the two key stages in the process, Light and 'Dark' reactions.

Category 2A (n = 21)
Photosynthesis involves energy interconversion and key Light and 'Dark' reactions recognised but undefined
Light and 'Dark' reactions recognised. There may be confusion between 'Dark' reactions and what happens at night.

Category 2B (n = 7)
As for 2A. With a limited biochemical explanation
Further explanation is offered of one or both the key reactions. Examples would be mentioning Photosystems I and II, or the flow of electrons, or light initiating splitting of water and transfer of energy, or a description of the 'Dark' reaction that clearly describes carbon dioxide fixation.

Category 3A (n = 4)
The process as a whole. Photosynthesis involves energy interconversion and key Light and 'Dark' reactions recognised, defined and described in both day and night settings
Here there is clear recognition of Light and 'Dark' reactions, recognition that the Light reaction only occurs in the presence of light, and its products are required by the 'Dark' reaction. The 'Dark' reaction (Calvin cycle) does not require light, but will not occur at night because it is dependent on the products from the Light reaction (as energy source). Photosynthesis cannot occur in the dark, at night.

Category 3B (n = 2)
As for 3A. With a biochemical explanation
The biochemical explanation might explain one or both of the key reactions and their relationship, e.g. light energy conversion in Photosystems, splitting of water and release of H, flow of electrons and capturing of chemical energy into ATP and NADPH which are being used as energy sources in fixation of carbon dioxide in the 'Dark' reaction, resulting in the production of sugar.

Source: Hazel *et al.*, 1996.

Classroom research into prior understanding of the nature of the subject matter being studied

In a study of first year university physics students' prior experience of studying physics, students were asked to respond to an open-ended question (from Prosser *et al.*, 1995):

> If you had a friend who had never studied physics before and they asked you to tell them what the study of physics involves, what would you say?

The responses were analysed using a phenomenographic approach aimed at identifying a structured set of categories of description describing the variation in the way the students had responded. The process was similar to that described in the previous example. The categories, typical responses and the distribution of responses are shown in Figure 3.4.

These categories again form a hierarchical structure through logical inclusiveness, with categories 1a and 1b being relatively limited views of what the study of physics is about, and with categories 2 and 3 being increasingly complete. The distribution of responses again suggests that the majority of students have a relatively limited view (60 per cent in categories 1a and 1b).

We see from this study that students entered this first year subject with a range of understandings of the subject matter they were about to study. They responded to the open-ended question in the first week of their university study, reflecting back on their previous study of physics. The categories describe their prior experience of studying physics as evoked by the situation that students found themselves in, in their first week of university study. The categories represent the relation between these first year university students and the task of responding to the open-ended question in their first week of study. They provide information to the classroom teacher about the aspects of the first year subject that these students are likely to focus on, at least in the early stages of studying in the subject.

The next example is drawn from the same study, but focuses on the range of prior approaches to studying the subject matter.

Classroom research into prior approaches to learning the subject matter being studied

In the same study as that described above (Prosser *et al.*, 1995), the first year university physics students were asked to respond in writing to the following question: 'How do you go about learning physics? Say what you actually do rather than what you think you should do?'

The categories of description covering the range of responses are shown in Figure 3.5. Again the categories form a logically inclusive hierarchy, with category 3 being more complete and inclusive of categories 1 and 2.

Figure 3.4 Categories of description of students' prior understanding of what the study of physics is about

Category 1a Response based upon physics being about facts and formulas and/or hard work (n = 37, 14%).
'It involves use of mathematics to work out problems that are present in many areas', 'Learning of formulas, a logical mind.'

Category 1b Response based upon physics being about the study of the physical world (n = 121, 46%).
'The study of the world around us', 'Investigating how the universe works.'

Category 2 Response based upon physics being about the relationship between mathematics and the physical world and/or understanding the underlying principles governing the behaviour of the physical world (n = 91, 35%).
'If you're clever it involves coming to understand principles about the physical world. If you're dumb it involves learning lots of rules and doing lots of questions even though you can't understand why they work', 'A lot of hard work, along with understanding of why some things happen.'

Category 3 Response based upon physics being about an integrated and creative process of developing models and a language to describe observed behaviour of physical systems in the physical world (n = 12, 5%).
'Try to see where phys[ics] fit into life. Doing prob[lem]s to help me understand how and why', 'A process of successive approximation, which attempts, to construct, an internally consistent, and experimentally consistent explanation of the phenomenon of the natural world.'
'It gives no pretence of delivering a "true" representation of the universe.'

Source: Prosser *et al.*, 1995.

In category 1 (Figure 3.5), the focus is on reproduction, while in categories 2 and 3 the focus is on seeking understanding. The distribution of responses suggests that three-quarters of the entering students approached their studies by seeking to reproduce rather than seeking understanding. In this sense, category 1 represents a surface approach to study, while categories 2 and 3 represent deep approaches.

Figure 3.5 Categories of description of students' prior approaches to the study of physics

Category 1 Explanation based upon attendance and/or reviewing notes and/or learning formulae and/or doing exercises (n = 218, 75%).
'Doing the assignments, listening in class, studying for exams', 'I try to look at examples first. Then try some questions to build confidence, then when I feel confident, I do a lot more questions to be good at it.'

Category 2 Response based upon seeking understanding, seeing how principles work, discussing with other students (n = 61, 21%).
'In class I take notes of the important details without being a slave to them. I try to understand the concepts there and then rather than adopting a "she'll be right" attitude. Any areas which intrigue me or of which I have incomplete understanding I will ask questions about', 'Go to lectures and try to understand the concepts behind what is being taught. This may also require some time at home staring at the ceiling puzzling it out until it "clicks". Once this understanding is in place, any problems/exercises should be relatively straightforward. Any difficulties with problems which are then thought through and understood reinforce the overall understanding.'

Category 3 Response based upon relating to real world experiences, reading around the subject etc (n = 12, 4%).
'Examples, applications to the physical world. To learn physics, better, to understand physics needs visualisation of many concepts so experiments and observations substantiate learning. Many areas just need various examples to explain it more clearly but in different context. Thus demonstrating the basics. Problem solving is the key', 'I enjoy reading about physics, e.g. in *New Scientist*, astronomy magazines etc., in books. I also try simulating physical problems on computers – I can't really tell the difference in the time I spend studying physics and just having fun.'

Source: Prosser *et al.*, 1995.

These responses represent the prior experiences of studying physics as evoked by the situation of being in the first week of university study of physics. They do not necessarily describe what these students did in their secondary school study of physics, but they do provide the classroom teacher with indicators of these students' present awareness of how they previously studied the subject matter.

In this section describing some examples of classroom practice and research, we have shown how some university teachers have responded in their classroom practice to the sorts of ideas being presented in this book, and have shown some examples of the sort of research classroom teachers could engage in to help expand their awareness of their students' prior experiences of studying the subject matter they are about to teach. The key aspects of the practice and research are to focus on experience and variation. University teachers need to help their students focus on their previous experience and the variation among the students in that previous experience, and they need to seek to be more aware themselves of the variation that exists in their classrooms and lecture theatres.

Summary of Chapter 3

In this chapter we began by arguing that students' prior experiences of studying the subject matter and their prior understanding of key concepts of that subject matter are vital to their subsequent approaches to study and learning outcomes. We took as our point of departure from previous ways of examining prior experiences and understanding, that it is the prior experiences and understanding that are evoked or brought to the foreground of awareness by the immediate situation that students find themselves in which are important in learning and teaching.

We then described the results of a number of research studies which looked at various aspects of students' prior experiences, including prior conceptual understanding of key concepts and ideas, prior understanding of the nature of the subject matter being studied, and prior conceptions of learning and approaches to the learning of that subject matter. We showed that for each of these there was substantial variation within the student body. We showed that the same situation – a first year lecture theatre for example – can evoke or bring to the foreground of awareness substantially different prior experiences among the students.

We then described several examples of classroom-based research and practice which aimed at helping both students and university teachers become more aware of the variation in students' prior experiences of learning. We argued that the students' learning situation was a particularly salient aspect of the prior experience evoked.

Finally, we return to the three sets of questions asked at the beginning of the chapter. In response to the first set of questions, we have shown that there is variation in students' views on what is meant by learning and understanding when undertaking subjects, and we have characterized that variation in a number of ways. In terms of the second set, we have shown that students enter subjects with different levels of background understanding, and more importantly, we have shown that it is the background understanding and experience that is evoked by their present situation that is vital to the development of high-quality student learning. Finally, for the third set, we have listed a number of principles of practice based upon the variation in background understanding and experience, and described some examples of practice based upon those principles.

Having discussed the nature of, and some examples of research into students' prior experiences in this chapter, the next chapter focuses on the students' perceptions of their learning and teaching situations. We will show that their perceptions of their situation are fundamentally related to the context designed by the teacher and their experiences of similar learning and teaching situations. We will then go on to show in later chapters how these perceptions and prior experiences are related to the approach to learning adopted by the students and to the quality of the students' learning outcomes.

Note

1. Phenomenography is the empirical study of the limited number of qualitatively different ways in which we experience, conceptualize, understand, perceive, apprehend etc. various phenomena in and aspects of the world around us. These differing experiences, understandings etc. are characterized in terms of categories of description, logically related to each other, and forming hierarchies in relation to given criteria. Such an ordered set of categories of description is called the outcome space of the phenomenon or concepts in question. Although different kinds of data can be used, the dominating method for collecting data is the individual interview which is carried out in a dialogical manner. The interviewee is encouraged to reflect on previously unthematized aspects of the phenomenon in question. The interviews are transcribed verbatim and the analysis is carried out in an iterative manner on those transcripts. Distinctly different ways of experiencing the phenomenon discussed in the interview are the units of analysis and not the single individuals. The categories of description corresponding to those differing understandings and the logical relations that can be established between them constitute the main results of a phenomenographic study (Marton, 1992).

We have made extensive use of the results of phenomenographic analyses in this book. University teachers interested in finding out more about this research approach are directed to the articles referred to in this book, as well as to Marton, 1981, 1986, 1992; to Marton and Booth, 1997 for the theoretical basis of phenomenography; and to Prosser, 1993, Bowden and Walsh, 1994, and Trigwell, 1997 for applications and methodology. The internet site http://www.ped.gu.se/biorn/phenom.html contains much current information on this growing approach to research.

4

Students' Perceptions of Their Learning Situation

Student's
prior
experience

Student's
approaches
to learning

**Student's
perceptions of
his/her situation**

*Student's
situation*

Student's
learning
outcomes

Introduction

In the previous chapter we showed that students enter subjects and courses
with a large variation in background and experience. This variation is not
only in terms of varying levels of prior understanding, but also in terms of
how students conceived of learning, how they had previously approached
their learning, and what they thought about – or their experience of – the
nature of the subject matter they are now about to study. We argued that
the situation in which students find themselves evokes certain aspects of
their prior understanding and experience. In other words, while students
may exhibit a certain understanding, skill or competency in one situation,
this does not mean that they can exhibit it in another somewhat different situation. Students may have well-developed mathematical or essay writing skills
in their mathematics or English subjects, but this does not necessarily mean
that they can use these same skills in subsequent physics or sociology subjects.

In this chapter, we wish to extend these ideas by showing that students
focus on various aspects of their learning situation in different ways; that
students in the same situation will experience that situation in different ways;
that their perceptions of that situation vary, and are systematically related to

the prior experiences evoked by the situation; that their perceptions and prior experiences are simultaneously constituted within the situation they find themselves; and that by changing the situation, it is possible to change the prior experience evoked in that situation. This may sound a little strange at first, but it has very far-reaching consequences for the way university teachers teach and structure their subjects and courses.

Key questions to be addressed in this chapter are:

- What sorts of things do students focus on or are aware of when engaged in studying their subjects and courses?
- How does what they focus on or are aware of relate to how university teachers have designed and constructed their subjects and courses?
- What effect does this variation in perception have on the quality of the students' learning?

The perspective adopted in this chapter is, in contrast to commonly accepted views that prior experience and perception are independent of each other, and that sensory data is brought in from outside the perceiver through the senses, and then made sense of by the perceiver. That is, for example, that students sitting in a classroom or lecture theatre take in through their senses various 'objective' aspects of the context such as the goals of the course, how the course is assessed, the nature of assessment in the course, etc., and that this 'objective' information is then processed internally. The view of learning underlying this book is that students do not live in an 'objective' world but in an experienced world. The learning and teaching issue is not that of how university teachers have designed and constructed their subjects and courses, but rather how their students perceive and understand the way they have designed and structured them.

This change in perspective from how university teachers design and structure courses to how students perceive that design and structure means that university teachers need to take a student perspective on teaching, and to think about the variation in students' experience and how it may affect the way students perceive and experience what they are designing and structuring. University teachers need to try to look at their designs through their students' eyes.

Experiencing the variation in students' perceptions of their learning situation

The following pages contain extracts from transcripts of interviews with two first year science students in an Australian university (Prosser and Millar, 1989). In these extracts, both students are discussing their perceptions of the teaching of a physics topic, and the way they went about learning that topic. These students are two of the many who were interviewed. Their interview extracts have been selected for inclusion here as they illustrate the extremes of the variation found in perceptions of the learning and teaching situation and approaches to learning in this context.

The aim of this section is to illustrate the variation in students' perceptions of their learning situation. We suggest you read each transcript, and that you characterize the variation in the way the two students perceive their learning and teaching situation. In Chapter 5 we will return to this example and ask you to focus on the variation in the way the students approached their studies. For now, focus only on the variation in their perceptions of their learning and teaching situation, for example, their perceptions of the teaching they experienced. In both extracts, *I* is the interviewer, *S* is the student.

Student A

I: I just want to ask you a few questions about the way you went about studying physics in first term, right? What sort of things did you do in the lectures?

S: Well, we did a lot of theory, he was writing – the lecturer was.

I: What did you do?

S: What did I do? I copied down the notes that were written up on the board including examples and then went over the notes that night and two or three days later did some problems on the notes we did using the problems in the exercise book and the assignments and I think that was all.

I: Yes, well hold on. We were back at what you did in lectures so you copied everything down –

S: And tried to understand it from what he'd wrote on the board, yes.

I: And why did you do that?

S: Well, I – if I hadn't written down what he'd wrote on the board I don't think I would have retained it at all.

I: Writing it down then meant what?

S: It meant that I had a permanent record that I could go and look up if I had troubles.

I: What sort of things did you do at other times in the University with regards to physics?

S: What around and about?

I: Yes.

S: Other than the problems with the tutorials and the assignments and –

I: You went to tutorials?

S: I went to tutorials and I did all the assignments and –

I: Why do you think you did all those?

S: Because I thought – they were basically the harder ones that were chosen out of the book and I felt they were good preparation for the exam because if I do that I could probably handle anything that was thrown at me.

I: So what do you think they achieved, doing these problems?

S: I think they'd let you know where your weaknesses were in physics.

I: Right, OK. So they helped you understand, you think or –

S: Yes, they helped me understand a lot more about mechanics than I would have got from . . . the [Higher School Certificate] but at the moment I'm still rusty on mechanics because I've forgotten what . . . last term. Not all of it but if I revise . . .

I: Right, OK. Do you think there's more to understanding physics than just doing problems?

S: It was trying to understand the concepts behind it which is a big help. It's not just problems or just theory. It's sort of a mixture of all of them I reckon.

I: What sort of things did you do at home during the term with regard to physics?

S: Problems that I read out of the textbook, followed in the textbook where we were from day to day and prepared the stuff for the lectures just by reading out of the textbook so I knew what we were going to do that day and then I read over it again that night making notes on anything I didn't understand.

I: And if you didn't understand something, did you go and ask?

S: Yes, I asked. I didn't go and see him personally but if I had any problems, say for anything in the lecture, I asked him at the end of the lecture. Or if I had any problems with anything I'd done at home, I'd ask him as well.

I: Right, OK. What sorts of things did you do when you were preparing for exams?

S: I read over all the notes which were taken during the term and including various bits out of the textbook that he'd drawn our attention to. Worked through problems. Revised the assignments to see what sort of things they'd given us in the assignments and if I had any problems I asked him sort of in the last few lectures before the lectures ended I asked him how well I went – not how well – how to do such and such if I had any difficulty.

I: OK. So you summarized and tried to learn everything as best you could. Did you go back and try to do this sort of thing from scratch?

S: No, not at all.

I: And yet he did it in the lectures didn't he?

S: He started off from scratch, yes, but he never actually went back to the basics – once say . . . towards the end of term . . . a really complicated problem or something that was difficult to get to he never really went back to basics. He sort of went back to say . . . not right back to . . .

I: OK. Is there anything you did at the beginning of term that affected the way you went about studying physics at all?

S: Well, it made me try and understand what I did in the interview, I tried to understand what I did but I couldn't really say it had an effect because I can't remember what I did.

I: Right, OK. Well that's all, thanks very much.

Student B

I: Now I want you to just think for a moment about how you went about studying physics this term. What did you do in the lectures?

S: Well in the lectures we had our lecturer sort of he wanted us to understand things and we spent a lot of time, him getting us just to think about things and discussing actual why things happen and if we say something he give sort of – on a few topics like force – he'd give us a check list to sort of actually go through and find out why things are like they are, and if they don't sort of go by the definition of that . . . that you can't really call it a force or whatever you're talking about.

I: And do you participate in that?

S: Yes. We all had our say and he gave us what he calls buzz sessions and you just sort of – he gives a problem and you talk to a few people around you, decide on what you think and then he takes sort of – takes several options and then goes through each option saying and then get people to say what it is or why isn't it and we come up with the answer like that.

I: And why do you think you did that?

S: Well, it's because I think you get a lot more out of it if you discover things with yourself and not just be told a whole lot of facts just to learn. If you actually think about it, come up with the answer yourself when all physics and that was sort of being developed they did it all by themselves and we are sort of being stimulated to think about it . . . the problem and it sort of makes you think about –

I: That's what you think these sessions achieve, they make you think.

S: Yes, well our lecturer made us think for ourselves and not just tell us the answer.

I: Right. And what did that do for you? Did that make you understand it better or –

S: Yes, because it actually – if you come up with the right answer you know why you've come up with the right answer because you thought about it and then if you come up with the wrong answer you know, you can sort of have the answer, and then you can sort of think why the argument that you're putting forward, why that's incorrect.

I: And are you talking about problems like this or are you talking about actual mathematical –

S: Actual algebra didn't really argue that much about . . . just like problems of putting an object in a certain position and arguing where the forces are and things like that and you'd have to argue for and against why the forces are there or why this should happen.

I: And do you think that that's important in understanding physics?

S: I think it's important to understand in yourself not just be told that if a ball's hanging there it's only got two forces acting on it. I think you should understand why. And –

I: OK. What sort of things did you do at home then during the term for physics?

S: Mostly a lot of problems like out of the text book. Re-reading my notes and sort of thinking about where that, where that sort of knowledge or whatever is useful in the real world and how especially because I'm interested in sort of when we talk about concepts and then something's mentioned on where that's used in industry or something like that, that sort of makes me think that what I'm doing is worthwhile and I try and think of other areas that it can be used for.

I: OK. What about for the exam? What did you do?

S: Basically, reading my notes and summarizing my notes, things like that. Write down formulas like read and then put them away for half an hour and do something else and see if I could come back and write them all down again. And problems and things like that.

I: So basically, you were learning it off by heart.

S: Yes, just to actually understand it and like just to know how to do problems you just do sort of different types of force problems over and over again until you sort of can see a problem and you just know how to do it.

I: And you feel that's necessary?

S: It's not just sort of understanding why it's like that, sort of right from the beginning. You shouldn't actually have to learn formulae. You should know how to get them and where they come from.

From these short extracts it is not possible to say anything definitive about their perceptions, but you may have characterized their perceptions of their two learning situations quite differently. Student A describes how the lecturer wrote things on the board (which the student copied) and never went back to basics in his analysis of the problems being discussed. Student B sees the situation differently. He talks of the teacher's attempts to get the students to think about things and discuss things. He uses 'buzz sessions' and he asks students to argue for and against why something may or may not be happening.

Most people who read these transcripts are surprised to learn that these two students were enrolled in the same topic in the same term and that they have the same lecturer and tutor and attended the same sessions. The learning context for both students is the same. The variation in the students' perceptions of their learning situation is remarkable. This example clearly indicates how students in the same learning and teaching context can perceive their situation in that context quite differently.

Research describing the variation in students' perceptions of their learning situations

When students enter into a learning and teaching context, they form certain perceptions of their situation. Those perceptions we would describe as being relational. The context itself may be designed to afford a particular approach to study, but students do not necessarily perceive their situation in the way it was designed. The perception relates particular students to their situation. That is, a students' perception is a relation between the student and his/her particular situation. In a particular class of students, while the context as it was designed may be the same for all students, the students' perceptions of their situation in that context vary. This variation results from the interaction between the students' prior experiences of similar learning and teaching situations and the particular context within which they are placed. Those perceptions in turn are related to the way the students approach their learning in that context. Thus given the same context, different students form different perceptions of their situations within the context, and approach their learning tasks in different ways. Different prior experiences evoke a focus on different aspects of the situation. In lectures, for example, some students may focus on those aspects of the lecture which are affording a more surface approach to study, while others may focus on those aspects affording a deeper approach as shown in the previous example.

This situation, in which a series of lectures was designed to afford a deep approach to study and high-quality learning outcomes, is described in detail in Chapter 6 (page 130). The lectures included some presentation by the lecturers, based around a number of specific activities for students in the lecture theatre. Those activities were designed to tap into students' prior experiences of studying the subject matter and ways in which that subject matter related to students' real world experiences. The problem was, however, that a substantial proportion of the students focused their attention only on the presentation aspects, and constituted those in terms of an information presentation, while having little or no focus on the other activities. Those students perceived the lecture in terms of affording a surface approach, while for many others the focus was on the activities supported by the presentations (Millar *et al.*, 1989).

Seminal qualitative studies of students' perceptions of their learning situation

In an experimental, qualitative study of students' approaches to reading an academic text and their learning outcomes, Fransson (1977) clearly identified this variation in perception and its effects. As part of the study, Fransson established one experimental group in which the context was designed to afford a deep approach to reading the text, while another was established with a context designed to afford a surface approach. In the context designed to afford a surface approach, students in groups of three to five were told that immediately after reading the textual material one of them would have to report what he or she had learnt to the other students in the group.

They were told that the report would be tape-recorded and later analysed in detail. A large number of tape recorders were set up in front of the students. In the other experimental group, students were told that they would be asked to write down what they had learnt and that there would then be a general discussion. As expected, students in the context designed to afford a deep approach described adopting deeper approaches and showed a better understanding of the text than those in the context designed to afford a surface approach.

But of greater interest was the finding that students in the context designed to afford a deeper approach showed substantially more variation in approach and outcome than those in the other context. In interviews with the students in the context designed to afford a deeper approach, it was clear that in spite of the attempt to design such a context, nine of the fourteen students in that group perceived it to be affording a surface approach in that they perceived that the written test would focus on factual recall and not on understanding, while the other five perceived that it would focus on understanding.

While the Fransson study showed explicitly how students' perceptions of a learning and teaching situation may vary dramatically, Ramsden (1979) identified the key aspects of the variation which seem to be related to the way students approach their studies. In that paper he presented several quotes from students talking about their studies and the sorts of things which affected them. The following quotes focus first on students' perceptions of assessment and second on their perceptions of the quality of teaching they received.

First, two quotes on how two students saw assessment:

I look at [the topic] and think to myself, 'well, I can do that if I can be bothered to hunt hundreds of textbooks and do the work' – and you sort of relate that to the value of the work in the course, which is virtually zero because it is so much exam assessment . . . I just don't bother with it until the exams come around . . . my revision is basically for the exams, purely and simply aimed at passing the exams without bothering too much about studying the subject (Natural Science student).

With that essay I was just discussing, that reference group one, I wrote for, with a, the image of a marker in mind, the personality, the person. I find that's important, to know who's going to be marker of the paper . . . you see an essay is an expression of thought, really, but that's not what they're after, they're after a search through the library, I think, and a cribbing of other people's ideas (Social Science student).

(Ramsden, 1979: 420)

Here are extracts from transcripts of two students talking about the quality of teaching from the same study:

If they [tutors] have enthusiasm, then they really fire their own students with the subject, and the students really pick it up . . . I'm really good at and enjoy [one course], but that's only because a particular tutor I've had has been so enthusiastic that he's given me an enthusiasm for it . . . (Arts student).

Recently we were doing Fourier analysis, and the lecturer mentioned in passing that it was really something which they used when they transmit moon pictures back to earth . . . that makes a lot of difference, you can see it being used . . . Another example he quoted was about why when you bang a drum you get lots of sounds rather than when you, say, play a violin you get just one note . . . he said if you look at it this way you can see why . . . and he was right, you could see why, it did make sense (Natural Science student).

(Ramsden, 1979: 420)

It is clear from these quotes that these students had certain perceptions of their learning situation – about what the assessment processes were about and about the quality of the teaching they were receiving. The quotes also show that in terms of the students' experience these perceptions are fundamentally related to how they approach their studies, and in some cases, to the quality of the learning outcomes.

Other key aspects identified in that and another study reported by Entwistle and Ramsden (1983) were students' perceptions of the workload in the subject – whether it was manageable or not, the goals of the subject or tasks in which they are engaged and how clear they were, and a sense of some freedom in learning. These five categories – good teaching, clear goals, appropriate workload, appropriate assessment and freedom in learning – form the dimensions of Ramsden's Course Experience Questionnaire (Ramsden, 1991). That questionnaire grew out of an earlier version by Entwistle and Ramsden (1983) – the Course Perceptions Questionnaire. These two questionnaires have been used in most of the quantitative research from the student learning perspective into students' perceptions.

Before examining the implications of some of the more quantitative research, it may be appropriate to reiterate our argument so far. Students enter any learning and teaching context with certain prior experiences of learning and teaching – prior conceptual understandings, prior understandings of the nature of the subject matter they are studying, successful prior approaches to learning, etc. Their perceptions of their situation in that learning and teaching context evoke certain aspects of those prior learning and teaching experiences. They adopt approaches to study consistent with their perceptions, resulting in variation in the quality of their learning outcomes. So far we have looked in some detail at the issue and nature of the students' prior experiences, and some aspects of their perceptions of their learning and teaching situations. Now we will continue to examine the students' perceptions of their learning and teaching situations before looking at some of the research relating perceptions to approaches.

Figure 4.1 Scales of the Course Experience Questionnaire

Scale	Example of item
Good teaching	Teaching staff here normally give helpful feedback on how you are going
Clear goals	You usually have a clear idea of where you're going and what's expected of you in this course
Appropriate workload	The sheer volume of work to get through in this course means you can't comprehend it all thoroughly (negatively scored)
Appropriate assessment	Staff here seem more interested in testing what we have memorised than what we have understood (negatively scored)
Emphasis on independence	Students here are given a lot of choice in the work they have to do

Source: Ramsden, 1991.

Quantitative studies of the students' perceptions of their learning situation

While the research referred to so far has been mainly qualitative (based upon interviews), much of the research into students' perceptions has been quantitative (based upon quantitatively scored inventories). Entwistle and Ramsden in their 1983 study developed a questionnaire designed to measure students' perceptions of the course in which they were studying. The questionnaire was developed from the interviews with students referred to previously in this chapter. It was composed of eight scales including workload, commitment to teaching, clear goals and standards, and freedom in learning.

Using this questionnaire and their Approaches to Learning Inventory, they were able to identify interpretable relationships between the way students perceived their courses and the approaches to study they adopted in them. Since then, Ramsden has gone on to develop further the Course Perceptions Questionnaire into the Course Experience Questionnaire (Ramsden, 1991, 1992). The scales of this questionnaire with associated identifying items are shown in Figure 4.1.

Relating the students' perceptions of their situation to their approaches to learning

In a recent study of the relationship between different forms of academic leadership, learning and teaching, Ramsden *et al.* (1997) surveyed over

Table 4.1 Factor analysis with varimax rotation of the Subject Perceptions
Questionnaire and Study Process Questionnaire scales

Questionnaire scale	Factor	
	1	2
Subject perceptions		
Good teaching	83	
Clear goals	63	
Appropriate workload		−69
Appropriate assessment		−66
Emphasis on independence	81	
Approaches to study		
Surface approach		81
Deep approach	63	

Source: Ramsden *et al.*, 1997.

8000 students in 51 different subjects with a subject-specific version of the
Course Experience Questionnaire (Subject Perceptions Questionnaire) and
with a subject-specific and cut down version of Biggs's Study Process Questionnaire (with scales measuring a surface approach and a deep approach
to study). The students – all in first year subjects – were asked to complete
the questionnaires in relation to the first year subject which was the focus of
the study. In selecting the subjects, there was an attempt made to have a
reasonable spread across four fields of study – arts and social sciences, law
and economics, health sciences, and natural sciences. Table 4.1 shows the
unpublished results of the factor analysis based upon 8829 student responses.
The factor analysis enables the analyst to identify those variables which
seem to be related to one another, but unrelated to the other variables.

This analysis shows clearly (in Factor 1) that a deep approach to study is
associated with perceptions that the teaching was good, the goals were
clear, and that there was some emphasis on independence. We also see in
Factor 2 that a surface approach to study is associated with an inappropriate
workload (workload perceived to be too high) and inappropriate assessment (assessment perceived to measure rote learnt material). This is consistent with a substantial amount of previous research on this relationship
(Trigwell and Prosser, 1991a, b and Chapter 5). While this analysis has
included students from a range of different subjects, similar patterns are
found when all the students within the same subject complete the questionnaires. That is, within a subject there is a variation in students' scores
on the Subject Perceptions Questionnaire, which is systematically related
to the variation in students' scores on the subject-specific Study Process
Questionnaire.

Another way to look at such results is to group students according to
their scores on the questionnaire scales, rather than looking at associations

Table 4.2   Cluster means for the three cluster solution for the Subject Perceptions and subject-specific Study Process Questionnaire scales for individual students

Questionnaire scale	Cluster 1 (n = 307)	Cluster 2 (n = 362)	Cluster 3 (n = 224)
Subject perceptions			
Good teaching	0.77	−0.20	−0.74
Clear goals	0.73	−0.29	−0.54
Appropriate workload	0.39	−0.10	−0.56
Appropriate assessment	0.24	0.30	−0.65
Emphasis on independence	0.64	−0.18	−0.62
Approaches to study			
Surface approach	−0.20	−0.26	0.62
Deep approach	0.47	−0.58	0.10

Source: Ramsden *et al.*, 1997.

between scale scores. A cluster analysis is a statistical technique for doing this. Table 4.2 shows the results of a cluster analysis of a random sample of 893 of the students completing the questionnaires.

The analysis shows a cluster of 307 students (Cluster 1) with relatively high scores on the good teaching, clear goals, emphasis on independence and deep approach to study scales. It shows another cluster of 224 students (Cluster 3) with relatively low scores on the good teaching, clear goals, appropriate workload, appropriate assessment, emphasis on independence and a relatively high score of surface approach to study scale. The third cluster of 362 students (Cluster 2) is one in which the scale scores are relatively close to the average – apart from a relatively low score on the deep approaches scale.

These results suggest that the one third of the students who perceived that the teaching was relatively good, that the goals were relatively clear and that there was relatively some independence in their learning were adopting a relatively deep approach to their studies. While the somewhat less than one third who perceived that the teaching was relatively poor, that the goals were relatively unclear, that the workload was relatively too high, that, relatively, the assessment was measuring reproduction and that they had relatively little independence in their studies reported adopting relatively surface approaches to their learning. Thus those students who perceived their learning and teaching situation as affording a surface approach were adopting a surface approach, while those who were perceiving it as affording a deep approach were adopting a deep approach.

So far we have analysed the results in terms of individual students, but do these relations between perceptions and approaches hold at the level of subjects? That is, in those subjects in which the students perceive that a deep approach is afforded, do they adopt a deep approach relative to the

Table 4.3 Factor analysis of the Subject Perceptions and subject-specific Study Process Questionnaire scales for individual subjects (n = 51)

Questionnaire scale (mean scores by subject)	Factor	
	1	2
Subject perceptions		
Good teaching	84	
Clear goals	70	
Appropriate workload		−74
Appropriate assessment		−86
Emphasis on independence	81	
Approaches to study		
Surface approach		90
Deep approach	83	

Source: Ramsden *et al.*, 1997.

Table 4.4 Cluster means for the three cluster solution for the Subject Perceptions and subject-specific Study Process Questionnaire scales for individual subjects

Questionnaire scale	Cluster 1 (n = 14)	Cluster 2 (n = 9)	Cluster 3 (n = 28)
Subject perceptions			
Good teaching	−0.99	1.11	0.12
Clear goals	−0.35	0.68	−0.04
Appropriate workload	−0.42	1.21	0.18
Appropriate assessment	−0.02	1.16	0.38
Emphasis on independence	−1.01	1.12	−0.15
Approaches to study			
Surface approach	0.42	−1.38	0.14
Deep approach	−1.17	0.84	0.38

Source: Ramsden *et al.*, 1997.

subjects in which they perceive a surface approach is afforded? Table 4.3 shows the results of a factor analysis using the subject as the unit of analysis.

The results of the analysis of the relationship between variables for subjects is very similar to that for individual students. The analysis shows that the deep approaches scale is associated with the good teaching, clear goals and emphasis on independence scales. As well, the surface approach scale is associated with the appropriate workload and appropriate assessment scales. The results of the cluster analysis of the same data are shown in Table 4.4.

This analysis shows a cluster of 14 subjects in which the students perceived that the teaching was relatively poor, that the goals were relatively unclear, the workload was relatively high and that there was relatively little emphasis on independence. In these subjects, the students' mean scores on the surface approach scale was relatively high and on the deep approach scale was relatively very low. In the second cluster of nine subjects, the students perceived that the teaching was relatively very good, that the goals were relatively clear, that the workload and assessment were relatively very appropriate, that there was relatively a very high emphasis on independence. In those nine subjects the students' mean scores on the surface approach scale was relatively very low and on the deep approach scale was relatively high. Finally, as in the analysis for individual students, there was a cluster of 28 subjects in which the scores were relatively close to the average score on most scales.

These results, with the subject as the unit of analysis, are very similar to those where the individual student is the unit of analysis.

In summary, students on entering a learning and teaching context form certain perceptions of the context and their situation within the context. They may well perceive that the context affords one particular approach to study, but that their situation affords another. Students focus on those aspects of the context which are appropriate to their perceived situation. Thus, for example, a student who enters a learning and teaching context and perceives his or her situation in that context as affording a surface approach (maybe perceiving that the workload is very high) and who has little or no experience of similar situations is likely to adopt a surface approach, while a student who enters the same context and who perceives that his or her situation in that context is affording a deep approach (maybe perceiving that there is choice in what to study) and who has experienced a similar situation previously may well adopt a deep approach. Thus for individual students in the same context, the situations they find themselves in can be quite different, with varying perceptions of their situation relating fundamentally to varying approaches to studying. It is not the perception of context but the perception of their situation in that context which relates fundamentally to their approaches to study.

Recent studies of students' disintegrated perceptions of their learning situations

But is the relationship between perceptions and approaches as coherent as has been portrayed so far? For several years, Erik Meyer and his colleagues at the University of Cape Town have been analysing the relations between perception and approach in terms of their relationship with student achievement, and have found that the coherent relationship between perception and approach breaks down in the case of failing students (Meyer *et al.*, 1990). Instead of the coherent patterns described above, they found no coherent pattern in the relationships between perceptions and approaches for failing students – Meyer described these incoherent patterns as disintegrated perceptions and approaches. Subsequently Entwistle reanalysed some of his data, and found the usual patterns for the successful students *and* the disintegrated patterns for the unsuccessful students (Entwistle *et al.*, 1991). Entwistle and his colleagues described the incoherent patterns as 'bizarre and uninterpretable'. The following quote exemplifies this disintegration well.

> The successful students show the expected pattern of relationships, even more clearly than in the analysis of the whole sample (Entwistle and Tait, 1990). The first factor links meaning orientation with those features of an academic environment expected to facilitate a deep approach to learning, while the second factor links the reproducing orientation with surface features . . . Among the failing students, however, the expected pattern does not materialise. The first two factors represent bizarre and uninterpretable combinations of loadings. The first factor is particularly strange as it is defined in terms of high posit- ive loadings on all four of the orientations, in spite of the fact that two are essentially the converse of the others. The second factor makes more sense in relation to the orientations, showing reproducing associ- ated negatively with meaning, but that is then linked to both deep and surface facets of lectures and examinations.
>
> (Entwistle *et al.*, 1991: 252)

We have confirmed these patterns in some of our recent work focusing on student learning in first year physics classes (Prosser *et al.*, 1996, 1997). In the study we surveyed the students at the beginning of their first term of study and again at the end. We used an open-ended response task and a concept mapping task to obtain information about students' conceptual understanding of the topic they were studying before and after the topic, and subject-specific versions of Biggs's Study Process Questionnaire and Ramsden's Course Experience Questionnaire to obtain information about the way the students approached their studies and perceived their learning situation. The study was based upon 63 responses to 65 questionnaires distributed before and after a physics subject in one university and 81 re- sponses to 82 questionnaires distributed at a second university.

In seeking to confirm these patterns we analysed how individual students' perceptions of their learning situation related to their prior conceptual understanding, their approaches to study and their conceptual understand- ing at the end of the subject. A cluster analysis was conducted with the aim of identifying sub-groups of students. The cluster analysis identified four groups. The results are summarized in Table 4.5 which also shows the mean achievement scores of the students in each cluster in the two universities.

As we saw in Chapter 3 the analysis identified four groups of students. The first group includes 36 students with well-developed prior understand- ing who perceived the learning context as affording a deep approach to learning, who adopted a deep approach and who had a well-developed understanding and a relatively high mean assessment result at the end of the subject in both universities. The second group (55 students) may be characterized as a group who had poorly developed prior understanding, who did not perceive the context as affording either a surface or a deep

Table 4.5 Cluster means for the four cluster solution for the prior understanding and outcome measures, the approaches to studying and the perceptions of the learning environment for the physics study

Variable	Cluster 1 (n = 36)	Cluster 2 (n = 55)	Cluster 3 (n = 20)	Cluster 4 (n = 20)
Prior understandings				
Phenomenographic	0.46	0.20	−1.43	0.04
Concept map	0.80	−0.41	−0.47	0.17
Approaches and perceptions				
Surface approach	−0.22	−0.39	0.47	1.01
Deep approach	0.46	0.01	0.36	−1.18
Perception affording surface approach	−0.56	−0.09	0.29	0.96
Perception affording deep approach	0.49	−0.10	0.45	−1.06
Outcome (understanding)				
Phenomenographic	0.82	0.05	−1.50	−0.10
Concept map	0.90	−0.34	−0.62	−0.08
Outcome (achievement)				
University 1 mean	0.51	−0.16	−0.92	0.26
n	18	15	10	10
University 2 mean	0.62	0.01	−0.72	−0.43
n	18	40	10	10

Note: Hierarchical Cluster Analysis using Ward's method, n = 131
Source: Prosser *et al.*, 1996, 1997.

approach, who did not adopt either a surface or a deep approach and who had poor learning outcomes. The third group (20 students) had very poor prior understanding, perceived the context as affording both surface and deep approaches and reported adopting both approaches (disintegrated perceptions and approaches) and had very poor learning outcomes. The final group (20 students) had poor prior understanding, perceived the context as affording a surface approach and not a deep approach, adopted a surface and not a deep approach and had poor, though not the poorest, learning outcomes.

These results and our student learning model suggest that students with well-developed prior understanding are likely to be aware of those aspects of the context affording a deep approach, to adopt a deep approach and to have well-developed understanding at the end of the subject. On the other hand, students with less well-developed prior understanding are more likely to be aware of those aspects affording a surface approach, to adopt a surface approach and to have poorly developed understanding. The first and last groups are consistent with the model. However, it is particularly interesting to note that those students with the least developed prior and post understanding were those Meyer *et al.* (1990) describe as having disintegrated perceptions and approaches. These students seem to be unaware of, and not be able to differentiate between, those aspects of the context affording different approaches. They are the least successful in terms of achievement. We pursue this topic further when we discuss approaches to learning in Chapter 5.

So, in summary, it seems that students enter learning and teaching contexts in higher education with varying perceptions of the context and their situation. Those perceptions are related to the quality of their prior understanding, the approach to study they adopt during their studies, and the quality of the learning outcomes and achievement. Some students perceive the situation as evoking both surface and deep approaches. They are described as having disintegrated perceptions and approaches, and the research suggests that these students are the lowest achieving students with the poorest quality learning outcomes.

Principles of practice related to the variation in students' perceptions of their learning situation

Having reviewed some of the salient literature on how students perceive their learning, and how those perceptions relate to their prior experiences, approaches to study and learning outcomes, we now wish to extract some key principles of practice for learning and teaching. We have argued that the situation students find themselves in evokes certain prior experiences of learning, perceptions of the present learning context and approaches to learning in that context. Aspects of their situation that most successful students are aware of are that the teaching is good, the goals are clear and they have an awareness of independence in their study. They are more likely to be adopting a deep approach. Less successful students perceive the workload to be too high and the assessment to be measuring reproduction. They are more likely to be adopting a surface approach. For unsuccessful students, it seems that no such coherent relation exists. These students seem to have incoherent perceptions and approaches. It seems as though such students are unable to differentiate between those aspects of their situation affording a deep approach or a surface approach. They seem to be unable to differentiate between meaning and reproduction.

Thus it seems that three broad groups of students have emerged. One group are very successful, with good prior and post conceptual knowledge, perceptions affording a deep approach and the adoption of a deep approach. Another group, who may survive, have some prior and post understanding, perceive their situation as affording surface approaches and adopt a surface approach. The third group, who tend to be unsuccessful, have very poor prior and post understanding and have disintegrated or incoherent perceptions and approaches.

From this analysis emerge four principles upon which good practice should be based.

1. Students have substantial qualitative variation in the way they perceive their learning and teaching situation.
2. This variation in perceptions is related to their prior experiences of study and present approaches to study.
3. In a new learning and teaching context, different students focus on or perceive different aspects of their situation in that context.
4. The aspects focused on or perceived are related to their approach to study in integrated or disintegrated ways, the nature of this relationship being fundamentally related to their post-conceptual understandings and achievement.

These principles which are meant to underlie or inform practice are consistent with the perspective on student learning upon which this book is based. They help explain for practising teachers why students sitting in the same classrooms can, at times, appear as though they are sitting in different classrooms. They can explain why the results of student evaluations of teaching can be variable both within and between classes. They can help explain why students adopt varying approaches to study, and how these varying approaches may relate to students' learning outcomes. Finally, they can provide the basis for considerations of action that university teachers can take to improve their students' learning.

So from this perspective, good teaching is teaching that tries to see the learning and teaching context from the student's perspective. It helps students understand the context in which they are situated and it helps students understand why the material is being taught, and what it is they should learn.

Examples of classroom research and practice related to the learning and teaching principles

Having identified a number of principles from the research into the students' perceptions of their learning situations that inform practice, we will now describe an example of practice based upon these principles. This involves the redesign of a large first year university subject in political science. We then look at two examples of classroom-based research.

Student learning in political science

In redesigning the first year subject in political science, Michael Jackson judged that the original subject focused too much on comprehension and retention of information and too little on application and analysis (scholarly analysis) (Jackson and Prosser, 1989). In order to help focus students' attention on the new objectives, a number of problem-based learning activities in small groups were introduced in place of many of the traditional

Figure 4.2   Structure and rationale for redesign of political science subject

The first 15 minutes of the first lecture were used to state that this course would be based upon small group learning and problem solving. Then the first problem for group work was set and small groups were formed [in a lecture theatre with about 105 students]. While small group teaching need not be the exclusive teaching method in a course, to be effective it needs to be introduced at the start. This modest precept is more important than it may first appear. Characteristically, an open-minded teacher who is quick to value the intellectual activity of students wants them first to learn a good deal of content before they begin to think for themselves.
. . .

On the first day the purpose of the group problem work was to introduce the technique. The problem set was simple, something that required no preparation and something with a clear goal. Groups were asked to answer the question 'What is politics?' in no more than three propositions. . . . The statements of each buzz group (Bligh, 1971) were jotted down. The teacher then asked a student from each group to bring the group's statement to the teacher. These were the basis of a short plenary followed by questions. . . . Nearly all the subsequent lecture periods represented variations on this structure.
. . .

A number of printed problems were used as means for students to learn what scholarly analysis is (see, e.g. May and Bemesderfer, 1972). These problems were often the basis of group work in the lecture hall and the tutorial room. Sometimes they were assigned as homework to be prepared before a class meeting where further small group work occurred. At other times they were handed out and finished in a fifty minute class period.

Over the year there were about 15 of these problems. For the first five, after the students had worked through the problem, models of scholarly analysis and popular responses were provided. These, too, were the basis of group work. The first two times each was labelled, but the last three groups had to decide which was which and state two reasons.

Source: Jackson and Prosser, 1989.

lectures and tutorials. Indeed, about 60 per cent of the lecture time and 75 per cent of the tutorial time was devoted to problem-based, small group activities. In redesigning the subject, Jackson was aware that it was vital that he help students develop an understanding of the new aims of the subject, given their previous experiences of studying. The structure of, and the rationale for, the redesigned subject is described in Figure 4.2.

For our present purposes, the main points to note in this description are the teacher's:

* continued concern about how the students perceived or understood the reasons underlying the redesign of the subject – their perceptions of what the subject was about;
* continued focus on getting students to work on those problems during classroom teaching time, seeing how other students responded to the problems, and in the process helping them change their perceptions of what the subject was about.

The teacher was aware that an important aspect of the success of the innovation lay in helping students change their perceptions of what the subject was about. This required continuous efforts to bring the students' perceptions to the foreground of their awareness as the subject was being studied. It was not enough to state what the subject was about in the subject description and in the first lecture, but required a continuous process of helping students change from seeing the subject as being about comprehending and retaining information to seeing it being about problem solving and scholarly analysis.

We now turn to two examples of classroom-based research into the students' perceptions of their learning and teaching situations.

Classroom-based research into student perceptions of a mathematics subject

This first example of classroom-based research has been previously referred to in Chapters 1 and 3. In those chapters we described the results of the initial qualitative study of the experience of first year mathematics students in some detail and referred to the subsequent quantitative study. Here we will describe the quantitative study in some detail, as we will be returning to it again in later chapters.

In this section we will focus on the part of the study which explored how the students' perceptions of their learning and teaching situation were related to their prior experiences of studying mathematics, their approaches to studying mathematics and their experience and understanding at the end of the subject. Perceptions were collected using a revised version of Ramsden's Course Experience Questionnaire – here called the Perceptions of Studying Mathematics Questionnaire. Defining items for the five sub-scales are shown in Figure 4.3.

In the initial qualitative study, Crawford *et al.* (1994) described a range of conceptions of mathematics held by the mathematics students included in the study. Based upon these descriptions a Conceptions of Mathematics Questionnaire was developed. That questionnaire was composed of two sub-scales: a fragmented conceptions sub-scale accommodating mathematics conceptions A and B (page 35) and a cohesive conceptions sub-scale

Figure 4.3   Defining items of the mathematics questionnaires

Scale	Item
Conceptions of Mathematics	
Fragmented conception	Mathematics is figuring out problems involving numbers
Cohesive conception	Mathematics is a logical system which helps explain things around us
Approaches to Studying Mathematics (based upon Biggs, 1987b)	
Surface approach	I think it is only worth studying the mathematics that I know will be examined
Deep approach	I find that studying mathematics is as interesting as a good novel or movie
Perceptions of Studying Mathematics (based upon Ramsden, 1991)	
Good teaching	The staff make a real effort to understand the difficulties we may be having with our work
Clear goals	The standard of work for this course is always clear
Inappropriate workload	The workload in this course is too heavy
Inappropriate assessment	Assessments in this course test rote memory rather than understanding
Independence	There is opportunity for us to choose aspects of the course which we want to concentrate on

Source: Crawford *et al.*, 1998a.

accommodating mathematics conceptions C, D and E (Crawford *et al.*, 1998a). The five mathematics conceptions were detailed in Chapter 3, pages 35–6, and defining items for these two sub-scales are also shown in Figure 4.3. A revised version of Biggs's Study Process Questionnaire – here called the Approaches to Studying Mathematics Questionnaire (Figure 4.3) – and the students' assessment results were used to collect approach and outcome data.

The data for this quantitative study were collected from 274 first year university mathematics students. They completed the Conceptions of Mathematics Questionnaire and the original version of Biggs's Study Process Questionnaire at the start of their first term. The Biggs's Study Process Questionnaire was included to obtain information about the students' general orientations to study before commencing their university studies. The Approaches to Studying Mathematics Questionnaire, the Perceptions of Studying Mathematics Questionnaire and the Conceptions of Mathematics Questionnaire were administered in the first week of the second term.

The results of a cluster analysis of the data aimed at identifying groups of students with common experiences is shown in Table 4.6.

The analysis identified two clusters or groups of students. We previously described these clusters in Chapter 3 as follows:

Table 4.6 Cluster means for the two cluster solution for students' experiences of studying mathematics data

Variables	Cluster 1 (n = 147)	Cluster 2 (n = 127)
Prior experiences		
Prior fragmented conception	.31	−.46
Prior cohesive conception	−.39	.45
Prior surface orientation	.34	−.44
Prior deep orientation	−.56	.59
Prior academic ranking	−.29	.35
Perceptions and approaches		
Surface approach	.44	−.45
Deep approach	−.54	.57
Good teaching	−.37	.37
Clear goals	−.23	.24
Inappropriate workload	.30	−.32
Inappropriate assessment	.12	−.13
Independence	−.26	.26
Post experiences and understandings		
Post fragmented conception	.34	−.41
Post cohesive conception	−.27	.27
Achievement	−.34	.40

Source: Crawford *et al.*, 1998a.

In the first group were students with a relatively poor prior understanding of what mathematics was about, who reported adopting relatively surface approaches to studying mathematics at secondary school, who reported adopting relatively surface approaches to their study of mathematics in their first year at university, who perceived the context as supporting surface approaches, and who subsequently had relatively poor understanding of what mathematics was about and had relatively poor achievement results. The second group were opposite in all respects. They had a relatively well-developed understanding of what mathematics was about at the start of the subject, they reported having adopted relatively deeper approaches to their mathematical studies at secondary school, they adopted relatively deeper approaches at university, perceived the same context as affording a relatively deeper approach, had relatively well-developed understanding of what mathematics was about at the end of the year and had relatively high achievement.

In terms of the focus of this chapter – the students' perceptions of their learning situation – the study shows how these perceptions relate to the students' prior experiences of studying mathematics, their approach to study and their post experiences and achievement. It shows that students who perceive that their situation affords a deep approach to study tend to have had good prior experiences of studying mathematics, to have adopted a deep approach to their study of mathematics, to have good subsequent experience and achievement. Those students who perceive their situation as affording a surface approach tend to have had poor prior experiences, to have adopted a surface approach and to have poor post experiences and achievement. This example also shows how quantitative methods and quantitatively based questionnaires can be used together to study students' experiences of studying.

Classroom-based research in student perceptions of a multiple-choice examination

Our final example is drawn from a study of students' experiences of studying for a multiple-choice examination (Scouller and Prosser, 1994). It focuses on student perceptions of the type of learning being assessed by multiple-choice examinations and its relation to their general study orientations and to their proposed study strategy in preparing for the examination. The study was based upon a sample of 190 first and second year university students enrolled in the faculties of science and nursing. Students were surveyed by questionnaire about three weeks before their multiple-choice examinations. The survey included Biggs's Study Process Questionnaire measuring students' surface, deep and achieving general orientations to study, a purpose-developed Student Perception of Mult-iple Choice Questions Questionnaire measuring perceptions of whether the multiple-choice questions measured 'surface' or 'deep' learning, and a purpose-developed contextualized Study Strategies Questionnaire measuring whether students intended adopting surface or deep strategies in preparing for the multiple-choice examination.

A factor analysis of the results showed, among other things, that a percep-tion that multiple-choice questions measure understanding rather than re-production was associated with an intended deep study strategy, and that a surface general orientation to study was associated with perceptions that multiple-choice questions measure both understanding and reproduction. This suggests that students with surface orientations to study have disinteg-rated perceptions of the role of multiple-choice examinations. This ex-ample of classroom-based research highlighted to the teacher that there is substantial variation in the way students perceive multiple-choice examina-tions, and that these perceptions are related to the way students approach their study for multiple-choice examinations.

These two examples of classroom-based research show examples of how university teachers can begin to research their students' learning using the concepts, ideas and instrumentation being described in this book. As we have already discussed, the important issue in designing such research is to decide on what it is that is the focus of the research: the object of study. These two examples show how classroom teachers, with support from their academic development unit, were able to adopt and adapt instruments from research to focus on issues of concern to them. In both cases, the university teachers were able to see for themselves the variation in perceptions and how this variation related to the way their students approached their study. An example of how university teachers make use of data on the student's perceptions of their learning situation is described in Chapter 6.

Summary of Chapter 4

In this chapter we have argued that the way students perceive their learning and teaching situations is central to the quality of their learning. Different students focus on different aspects of the learning and teaching context, their learning and teaching situation being different for each student. For example, some students may experience their situation as involving a heavy workload while other students may feel it is not too heavy.

What constitutes a perception is central to the argument in this book. From what has been written so far, we can distinguish several aspects of what constitutes perceptions. For example, a student can describe his/her perceptions of the context and the same student can also describe his/her perception of his/her situation within that context. These two things may be quite different. For example, in describing the context students may perceive that the workload in general is not too heavy, but given their situation, they perceive that their own workload is too heavy. Students approach their study in terms of their perceptions of the *situation* in which they find themselves, not their perceptions of the context. While the context may be the same for all students (and there may be variation in their perceptions of the context) the situation is different for each student. There is necessarily a variation between students in their perceptions of their situation.

In this chapter we have seen that within the same class, there is a substantial variation in the way students perceive the quality of teaching, clarity and meaning of the goals, the amount of work required, the nature of assessments, etc. We have also seen that within the same class these perceptions are systematically related to the approaches to learning adopted by students. That is, the variation in perceptions within classes is related to the variation in approaches to study. The variation in perception is not an error in measurement. We have interpreted this variation in perception theoretically in terms of the variation in each student's situation in the same learning and teaching context. There is a variation in what is in the foreground and what is in the background of students' awareness and this variation relates to how students are situated in the context. Thus in our original example of students discussing their experiences in a lecture theatre we see that for some students what was at the foreground of their awareness was the lecturer's presentation of the material at the blackboard. For other students what was at the foreground of their awareness was the small group discussion and activities in the lecture theatre. While the lecture context was the same for all students, the situation varied between students; what they focused on and what was at the foreground of their awareness varied; and the way they approached their learning varied.

Thus university teachers, in designing learning and teaching contexts and in engaging in their teaching, need to be continually aware that each student is situated differently within that context and will perceive his or her situation differently. It is not sufficient to develop a context which affords a deep approach to study. University teachers need also to determine how their students are perceiving their situation within that context.

Finally, we return to the questions asked at the beginning of this chapter. In response to the first question, we have shown that there is a variation in what students focus on in their subjects, and that that variation is constituted in terms of both the students' past experiences and the present learning context. As far as the second question is concerned, we have discussed those aspects of the context that students focus on, in particular issues about the quality of the classroom teaching, perceptions of aims and objectives, and perceptions of workload and assessment among other things. Finally in response to the third question, we have shown that how students focus on something or are aware of something relates to the way they approach their studies, and consequently to the quality of their learning outcomes.

In this chapter we have focused on the students' perceptions of their learning and teaching situations. In the next chapter we will focus on, and expand our discussion of, the approaches students adopt for their studies and the variation in those approaches.

5

Students' Approaches to Learning

Student's
prior
experience

**Student's
approaches
to learning**

Student's
perceptions of
his/her situation

Student's
learning
outcomes

*Student's
situation*

Introduction

In this chapter we look at the approach individual students take to learning,
and how teachers and administrators might influence that approach.
While approaches to learning are the focus, they are viewed from within a
learning context and from the perspectives of the topics of the previous
two chapters (the students' prior experiences and their perceptions of
their learning situation). We also address the misconceptions which now
surround student approaches to learning, particularly the meaning of deep
and surface approaches to learning. We are interested in students' approaches to the learning of university subjects because those approaches
are related to the quality of what they learn. To improve the quality of
student learning, some consideration must therefore be given to improving
the quality of the approaches students take to their learning.

As we saw in Chapter 1, students' approaches to learning are defined as
incorporating both the way they go about their study (strategy) and their
reasons for adopting that strategy (intention). In that overview we saw how
students' learning approaches are related to their perception of their situation and to their prior learning experiences. In Chapter 2 we introduced
the model (reproduced above) that portrays these relations for a student in

a particular learning context, suggesting that the model helps understand the variation in students' approaches to learning in the same context.

Chapters 3 and 4 introduced the student learning research on students' perceptions of their learning situation, and on their prior learning experiences. The implications for teaching of that research were discussed, and the research linking students' learning approaches to their perceptions of their learning situation and to their prior experiences was also introduced.

Our focus here is on what, from the student learning perspective, is considered to be the crucial element in understanding the teaching/learning process: students' approaches to learning and the variation in those approaches to learning. We address questions that teachers trying to improve student learning may have, such as:

- How do students go about their study? Does it matter how they go about it? How do I find out how they go about their study? What can I do to affect the way they go about studying?
- What does the variation in students' approaches to learning mean and what does it say about the way I should think about teaching?
- What are the principles of practice which derive from a consideration of the variation in students' approaches to learning? What teaching practices exemplify these principles?

To address these questions we will look at the variation in students' approaches to learning. We will be drawing upon information from earlier chapters and on information on how approaches relate to the quality of students' learning outcomes. As illustrated in the model above, approaches to learning will be seen here as foreground in relation to a background of students' perceptions of their learning situation, their prior experiences and their learning outcome.

We will argue that in their learning of a topic, most students are likely to adopt elements of either a deep or surface approach to learning. Those who adopt surface approaches to learning are more likely to have learning outcomes of a poorer quality than those who adopt deeper approaches. We will reintroduce the recent research suggesting that some students who perceive the situation as affording the adoption of both or neither approach constitute a very high-risk group. We will also reinforce the arguments in previous chapters that students who think of learning and understanding as being about reproduction of rote learnt material, who enter our subjects with a poorly developed prior understanding, or whose previous experience of studying the material in our subjects is of a surface nature, are likely to be students who perceive the learning context as affording such approaches, and are more likely to adopt surface approaches to their studies. And in doing so, we will address some of the misconceptions about deep and surface approaches to learning.

To illustrate some of the relations found between the students' perceptions of their learning situation, the variation in their approaches to learning

Table 5.1 Relations between individual students' academic achievement and their study orchestration/perception of the learning situation

Orchestration/perception category	Academic achievement category		
	Fail	Pass	Total
Undesirable	11	3	14
Average	6	6	12
Desirable	0	14	14
Totals	17	23	40

Source: Meyer *et al.*, 1990.

and the quality of their learning outcome that will be described in this chapter, we return to the quantitative study we introduced in Chapter 4.

Meyer *et al.* (1990) observed that individual engineering students who were classified as having, in their terms, an undesirable perception of their learning situation and approach to study orchestration, were much more likely to fail their subject than students with a desirable approach to study orchestration and perception of their learning situation (Table 5.1). A desirable approach to learning and perception of learning situation is described as one in which the student perceives the context to be affording a deep approach and in which he or she adopts a deep approach to learning. The undesirable category is associated with surface perceptions and approaches to learning.

What follows from these results and a considerable amount of related research is that when viewed from the perspective of learning outcomes, surface approaches to learning are undesirable. What also follows is that teachers and administrators have a role to play in changing the learning context to one which students perceive as affording a deep approach to learning.

These perspectives are in contrast to views that there is no preferred way for a student to approach his or her learning, and that the role of a teacher is to offer to students a variety of experiences so that they each might, for some time at least, find a match between their learning style and the approach of the teacher. Our view is that approaches to learning are *not* stable characteristics of students. Students' approaches to learning do change with changing perceptions of their learning situation and their perceptions of it can be changed by university teachers and administrators.

Pages 88–90 of this chapter contain a brief overview of the seminal research work on students' approaches to learning from the 1970s, in which the qualitatively different ways students go about learning were first identified. Recognition of the importance of these ideas continues to grow, as do the research results supporting and further developing the results of the earlier studies. With this growth has come an increase in the number of critics and the amount of criticism of these ideas. As the foundations of this research are now relatively well known, we have shifted the focus of this chapter away from lengthy reports of the seminal research towards more recent studies which are clarifying some areas of controversy.

The final sections address teaching and classroom-based research into the variation in students' approaches to learning. These sections include some principles of practice for teaching derived from variation in approaches to learning, and examples of the ways teachers have applied those principles. They include some insight into the nature of the classroom-based research being conducted by teachers into the fascinating question of the variation in student approaches to learning.

Experiencing the variation in students' approaches to learning

As with the previous two chapters, we include here a section on experiencing the variation in students'. approaches to learning. In the same section in the previous chapter, we asked you to read several pages containing extracts from transcripts of interviews with two first year science students in an Australian university (Prosser and Millar, 1989). In those extracts, both students are discussing their perceptions of the teaching of a physics topic. They also talk about the way they went about learning that topic, so the two interview extracts also illustrate the variation found in approaches to learning in this context.

Again we aim in this section to offer an experience of the variation in the approaches students take to learning. We suggest you reread each transcript on pages 60–3, and that this time, instead of focusing on students' perceptions, you:

- try to characterize the variation between the approach each student describes; and
- speculate on the differences in the quality of learning you imagine may result from the approach of each student.

From these short extracts it is not possible to say anything definitive about these approaches, but Student A describes how he needs lecture notes for revision because he would not have retained the information otherwise, and that he geared his study to examination preparation. While he describes an intention to understand, he means being able to do things without necessarily understanding the meaning behind those things. This extract contains several elements of a surface approach to learning. Student B describes having to think things through and to understand by discovering it himself. He also links what he is learning to examples from other contexts. Student B could be described as having adopted more of a deep approach to the learning of the subject during lectures, but he does appear to switch to a surface approach when preparing for examinations. There is considerable variation between the two approaches to learning described.

As we noted in Chapter 4, most people who read these transcripts are surprised to learn that these two students were enrolled in the same topic in the same semester and that they have the same lecturer and tutor and attended the same sessions. The variation in these students' perceptions of their learning situation is remarkable and, as discussed in the last chapter, it is one of the factors that relates to the variation in their approaches to the learning of the topic.

In terms of learning outcome, Student A gave two examples of not being able to remember things he had learned previously or even earlier in the same term. Student B talks of 'knowing when you know something' and having an understanding that derives from knowing the basics. He has been trying to add relevance to what he is learning through links to industry and real problems. If you noted some or all of these differences you have identified the variation in students' reported approaches to learning.

Research describing the variation in students' approaches to learning

In this section we will present more detail on the two qualitatively different learning approaches adopted by students, as exemplified in the transcript extracts used above. We will give an overview of the research which led to the ideas of deep and surface approaches to learning, and to the research which has extended, questioned and, to some extent, helped clarify some areas of confusion resulting from the earlier studies.

Our point of departure from previous reports of this research is in the way approaches to learning have been used and defined. By this we do not mean differences between approaches to learning and learning styles (though of course we do see these as different and we return to these differences later). The approaches to learning literature describes three different perspectives of approach to learning, and they tend to be used interchangeably (Chapter 3). They are:

- an approach to learning in a current learning task. Here the task is in the foreground of the students' awareness and it is in relation to that task that an approach is adopted;
- an approach adopted in a prior experience of learning in a similar task; and
- a prior orientation to learning (a general study process).

From our model of learning and the perspective of this book, only the first of these is used here as an approach to learning. As we saw in Chapter 3, we consider the last two of these to be a part of the background of awareness of the student in the present learning context, aspects of which are evoked by their learning situation, and which relate to the learning approach adopted. As a result we have already addressed them in Chapter 3. In the remainder of this chapter we will focus on the students' approach to a current learning task.

The main point we will stress in this section is that an approach to learning is how an individual student goes about studying in a particular context. It is evoked by that situation (a relationship between the context and the student) and so it is not fully either a characteristic of the student or the context. The implications of this point will be illustrated later in the chapter.

Seminal studies of student approaches to learning

Research results from studies which identified the variation in students' approaches to learning of the type illustrated above first appeared in the literature from three sources in the mid-1970s. In the United Kingdom at Lancaster University, Noel Entwistle led a group which explored student learning by interview and questionnaire across a wide range of disciplines (Entwistle and Ramsden, 1983). In Sweden, at Gothenburg University, Roger Säljö, Ference Marton, Lars Owe Dahlgren and Lennart Svensson developed new ways of studying the way students approached reading tasks, initially in education (reported in Marton and Booth, 1997). In Australia, at Newcastle University, John Biggs investigated the motives and strategies of tertiary students and described three processes that students used in studying (reported in Biggs, 1993b).

While there were substantial differences between the aims and results of the three different research projects, as we will see later, the results they reported had one thing in common. All three studies identified two qualitatively different ways that students approach learning or had approached learning, whether it be approaches to a small reading task or to a whole degree programme. The labels for those approaches, as we have used throughout this book, have now been widely accepted as surface and deep approaches to learning.

The Gothenburg research group first used the terms surface and deep approach to learning to describe the very different ways that students went about learning tasks. Marton and Booth (1997) describe the origin of this work as emanating from the comments of the external examiner of Marton's PhD thesis. After reading Marton's study of artificial learning tasks, the examiner asked whether his results told the education community anything about how their own students were actually learning. Two elements of this comment were taken seriously by Marton, and have resulted in an approach to research in student learning which has played a major role in bridging the gap between educational research and the practice of university learning and teaching.

The first element is whether the results told the community anything about actual (as distinct from laboratory) learning. This element led Marton and others to focus their research on real learning (learning in the context in which learning would normally occur). The second element is about how the students learn, not from the point of view of the researcher, but from the students' own views of their approach. In the next chapter, we will dwell on the importance of an awareness of variation in learning outcome in providing feedback to students about their learning. It is something of a sweet coincidence that feedback from an external examiner (and Marton's willingness to pursue the question) has led to research which gives all practising teachers some insight into a range of teaching/learning issues, including the important process of feedback on assessment items.

The approach adopted by Marton and his colleagues amounted to a 'shift in focus, away from measuring the quantity of stuff learned and the psychological means of achieving greater quantity more efficiently, to examining the quality of what students learned and the educational implications. What eventually happened as a result was another shift, away from viewing the learner from the outside to one which tried to see learning from the learners' point of view' (Marton and Booth, 1997: 15).

Having found in one of their earliest experiments that a group of students who were engaged in a reading task had described *what* they had read in four qualitatively different ways, Marton and Säljö looked for reasons for the variation in what the individual students involved in the experiment said about their way of going about that reading task. Marton and Säljö identified two approaches which different students adopted for that task: a surface approach which was characterized by a focus on the words in the text and a deep approach where the focus was on the meaning of the text. The most complete descriptions of the text were achieved only by students who had adopted a deep approach, whereas the least meaningful outcomes came only from students who adopted a surface approach.

The strength of this relationship (since replicated in numerous qualitative and quantitative studies as we will see in Chapter 6), in combination with the contextual dependence of approach to learning, is at the heart of the reason for this book. It has excited many educationalists (including university teachers) by offering real prospects of their being able to do something to improve learning.

While this work of Marton and Säljö was firmly embedded within the student learning perspective (analyses of students' reports of their own learning experience), Biggs's research perspective had its origins in information processing derived from cognitive psychology. In investigating whether the mediation of students' study behaviour might increase correlations between students' personality factors and academic performance, he identified 10 scales of study behaviour. Subsequent analysis yielded three study processes, each containing a combination of learning motives and learning strategies. As we saw in Chapter 3, Biggs developed the Study Process Questionnaire (SPQ) from the analysis of this data from students, describing the three approaches to learning as reproducing (surface), internalizing (deep) and achieving. Because the motive–strategy combination was to be interpreted in a relational way (i.e. within an academic context) and because the dynamic of the internalizing strategy was on coding for meaning and that for the reproducing strategy was on rehearsing for accurate reproduction, Biggs later adopted the surface/deep terminology and has acknowledged that the subsequent developments to the SPQ were more strongly influenced by the student learning perspective (Biggs, 1993b).

Unlike the task level focus of the studies by the Gothenburg group, the focus of Biggs's investigations was the students' experience of what they had done or were predisposed to do when studying generally. This level of investigation, in its time and scope, in our terms, is that of a prior learning orientation rather than an approach, and has been discussed in Chapter 3.

Entwistle investigated student learning from within a student learning perspective, but frequently incorporated aspects of related paradigms. With Ramsden (Entwistle and Ramsden, 1983) he identified, through interviews with students, three orientations to learning (meaning, reproducing and achieving), which combine elements of the context-related approaches to learning as espoused by Biggs and by Marton and Säljö with aspects of the personality of the student. Entwistle notes that consideration of student learning on the basis of personality suggests too static a picture, as learning is necessarily reactive to the learning context.

> Students' approaches are affected by their prior educational and personal histories, which produce habitual patterns of studying. However, the content and context of a task evoke strategies which are specific to that particular situation. Both consistency, up to a point, and a certain variability, have thus to be incorporated into descriptions of student learning.
>
> (Entwistle, 1998: 73–4)

Again, this work, in our terms, is more akin to prior orientations to learning.

Deep and surface approaches to learning

Each of these seminal research studies contributed to an understanding of the qualitative variation in student learning. Approaches to learning in a range of tasks, topics, subjects and courses have now been explored from the student's perspective, and while there are some differences between what constitutes a deep approach in different disciplines (for example between chemistry and design) or between what constitutes a surface approach in different tasks, the robustness of the fundamental qualitative differences has been a feature of almost all of the studies. It is important to note at the beginning of this section that part of the reason for this robustness is that the metaphor of surface and deep approaches to learning picks up on the key aspects of variation in approach – it does not aim to describe fully students' approaches to learning.

The characteristics of these fundamental differences in approaches to learning are described below. A student who adopts such an approach would describe himself or herself as employing some or all of the elements associated with that approach (from Biggs, 1987a, b; Ramsden, 1992; Marton and Booth, 1997; Marton *et al.*, 1997).

The motivation associated with a deep approach to learning is to understand ideas and seek meanings. In adopting this approach students have an intrinsic interest in the task and an expectation of enjoyment in carrying it out. They adopt strategies that help satisfy their curiosity, such as making the task coherent with their own experience; relating and distinguishing evidence and argument; looking for patterns and underlying principles; integrating the task with existing awareness; seeing the parts of a task as making up the whole; theorizing about it; forming hypotheses; and relating understanding from other parts of the same subject, and from different subjects. Overall they have a focus on the meaning in the argument, the message, or the relationships but they are aware that the meanings are carried by the words, the text, the formulae.

Individual students (as described in the model at the beginning of this chapter) in a particular learning context, who perceive their situation as evoking a deep approach to learning, are more likely to be aware of more aspects, or different aspects, of their learning situation. They are aware of their prior experiences of similar situations, they are aware that what they are doing may relate to other things they have done. For example, an examination paper sitting on a table in a large hall is a 'learning context'. A student who enters the hall, opens the exam paper and begins to read it with a view to responding to questions, enters the context and a learning situation is constituted. The student may perceive the question to be from a certain syllabus area, but also to be related to a project he/she is conducting in another subject, and respond by including links between the subjects. This response is possible because the student has taken a deep approach to the learning of the materials in these two subjects.

In adopting a surface approach to learning, students see tasks as external impositions and they have the intention to cope with these requirements. They are instrumentally or pragmatically motivated and seek to meet the demands of the task with minimum effort. They adopt strategies which include: a focus on unrelated parts of the task; separate treatment of related parts (for example principles and examples); a focus on what are seen as essentials (factual data and their symbolic representations); the reproduction of the essentials as accurately as possible; and rote memorizing information for assessment purposes rather than for understanding. Overall they would appear to be involved in study without reflection on purpose or strategy, with the focus of that study being on the words, the text, or the formulae.

An individual student in a particular learning context who adopts a surface approach to learning is aware of fewer aspects, or a narrower range of aspects, of his/her learning situation. For example, for this student entering this examination room a different situation is constituted through an awareness of different prior experiences. He or she may respond to the question from his/her memory of the lecture notes or the textbook within the constraints of the syllabus, but will have a more limited response. This student's approach to the subject tasks is associated with a more limited awareness of his/her learning situation.

While these are considered to be the major qualitatively different approaches to learning, several other approaches have been described in the literature. Biggs, and Entwistle and Ramsden describe achieving or strategic approaches which can be used in conjunction with a deep or surface approach and where the focus is on maximizing effort. Eisenberg (1988) described the situation in which students adopt neither approach as nonengagement. We have not discussed these approaches further here, as neither are considered part of the qualitative variation which is the focus of this chapter.

Varying interpretations of approaches to learning

There is now widespread support for the concept of variation in the quality of learning approaches arising out of research and development in classrooms throughout Europe, Hong Kong, Australia, Canada and elsewhere. National programmes of reform have been developed and funded around the associations between approaches to learning and the quality of the learning outcome (Gibbs, 1992). Books on teaching in higher education written from this perspective are increasingly requiring reprinting (Gibbs *et al.*, 1984–8; Ramsden, 1992; Marton *et al.*, 1997). The original research report on qualitatively different approaches to learning is one of the most widely cited sources in educational psychology (Walberg and Haertel, 1992). With the increased use and popularity of these ideas has come some variation in interpretation, and some doubts about definitions, validity and uses are beginning to be expressed (e.g. Christensen *et al.*, 1991; Webb, 1997).

As noted above, from the model of learning used in this book, approaches to learning are defined in relation to the learning of a task. From this perspective, two of the fundamental relationships emanating from the study of student learning are:

- that surface approaches to learning alone are inappropriate and should be discouraged as they are consistently associated with poorer quality learning outcomes; and
- that the learning approaches adopted by students are evoked by the relationship between the student and their perceptions of the context: they are not a characteristic of students. If the context is changed, there is the likelihood the student's approach will change.

Some of the questions directed at this view of learning have been associated with these two relationships. Both are discussed in more detail below.

Rote learning, memorizing and rehearsing

Many university teachers argue that surface approaches to learning are appropriate because they equate memorizing and rehearsing with rote learning. But as we will argue, this view is invalid because memorizing and rehearsing are not necessarily the same as rote learning.

As noted in the definitions above (page 91) the essential differences between a surface approach to learning and a deep approach to learning are in the learning intention or motive component of the approach. Rote learning (a mechanical act without thought of the meaning) is by definition a part of a surface approach because there is no intention to seek meaning. It can involve memorizing and rehearsal without thought of meaning, and they too would be part of a surface approach. But students can also rehearse and memorize with the intention of seeking meaning. A good example of the use of rehearsal strategies with different intentions is in two of the orientations to learning reported by students in the first year mathematics study. In one description (Orientation B, page 40) students learn by doing lots of examples, with the intention to reproduce knowledge and procedures. In the other description (Orientation C), students learn by doing lots of examples with an intention of gaining a relational understanding of theory and concepts.

Memorization has been the topic of much recent research which, like the rehearsal example above, indicates that students engage in two types of memorizing: meaningless memorizing (rote memorizing) and meaningful (deep) memorization (Watkins and Biggs, 1996). Marton *et al.* (1996) describe the former as mechanical memorization and the latter as memorization with understanding. Marton, Watkins and Tang (1995) describe them as memorizing (words) and memorizing (meaning) respectively, where the word in parentheses is the object of the act.

Memorizing can be described as a learning strategy and it could therefore appear in the student's description of what was either a surface or deep approach. Within a deep approach, memorizing may be appropriate as a strategy involving the linking of the memorized material to other components of the study area, with the overall intention to achieve understanding. In other circumstances (within a surface approach) meaningless memorizing as a strategy to recall information for assessment purposes may appear to be appropriate from the perspective of the student, but is indefensible when viewed by academic teachers using the model of learning in this book. Given the two bullet points above it would be professionally incumbent on a teacher to attempt to change the context so that such a strategy was not seen to be appropriate from the perspective of a student.

Meaningful or deep memorizing has also been identified in recent studies as an integral part of a deep approach to learning by many students within a Confucian-heritage culture (Tang, 1991; Watkins and Biggs, 1996). This observation has explained aspects of the paradox that students from this learning culture appear to adopt a surface approach to learning, but still out-perform many of their colleagues from other learning cultures. In the process of meaningful memorizing, these students repeat the text being memorized several times which may be outwardly suggestive of rote or surface approaches to learning. However, the text is repeated in a way that deepens understanding. The process of repetition contributes to understanding because different aspects of the text are in focus with each repetition, which is different to the mechanical memorizing that characterizes rote learning (Marton and Booth, 1997: 39).

The paradox arises (as it does for students in science and engineering subjects in most learning cultures) from a (limited) conception that meaningful or deep memorizing is a part of a surface approach to learning. Our observations that many science and engineering students adopt deep memorizing strategies is supported by Entwistle (1998) who observed similar strategies in students revising for examinations.

Rather than questioning the idea of qualitative variation in student approaches to learning, these studies are contributing to the expansion and the enhancement of the descriptions of the different approaches. For example, Marton *et al.* (1995) describe four ways of experiencing learning:

- committing the words, the text, the formulae to memory;
- committing meaning of the words, the text, the formulae to memory;
- understanding the meaning of the words, the text, the formulae; and
- understanding the phenomenon that the words, the text, the formulae relate to and the meaning concerns.

To study with an intention to achieve only the first and/or the second, without the third and/or the fourth of these four ways would constitute a surface approach to learning.

The relational nature of approaches to learning

The second area of expressed disquiet about the student learning perspective has origins in the differences between the thinking behind this perspective, and that derived from cognitive psychology. The chief difference is the relational nature of the student learning perspective. From this perspective, students are not described as having an approach to learning. They adopt an approach to learning which is evoked by their conception of the task and of learning, their prior experiences (Chapter 3) and their perception of their situation (Chapter 4).

This concept was first identified and illustrated by Laurillard (1979) in her study of the problem-solving approaches of engineering students. While there is variation in approaches to learning, those approaches can and do change with the context as perceived by the student. Indeed, the physics Student B, in describing his approach to learning in the interview extracts in Chapter 4, describes characteristics of a deep approach to studying throughout the teaching period of the subject, then, as examinations approach, he describes adopting more of a surface approach to his preparation. Similarly, Gibbs (1993: 9) reports the following quotes from the same student talking about learning in two different subjects:

In geography: I read it, I read it very slowly, trying to concentrate on what it means, what the actual passage means. Obviously I've read the quotations a few times and I've got it in my mind, what they mean. I really try to read it slowly. There is a lot of meaning behind it. You have to really try to get into it and take every passage, every sentence, and try to really think, 'Well what does this mean?' You mustn't regurgitate what David is saying because that's not the idea of the exercise, so I suppose its really original ideas in this one, kind of getting it all together.

And then in computing:

I: When you use the word learning in relation to this course, what do you mean?
S: Getting enough facts so that you can write something relevant in the exam. You've got enough information so you can write an essay on it. What I normally do is learn certain headings. I'll write a question down, about four or five different headings, which in an exam I can go: 'Introduction' and I'll look at the next heading and I know what I've got to write about without really thinking about it really. I know the facts about it. I go to the next heading and regurgitate.

Eley (1992: 250) investigated the phenomenon quantitatively. He had observed that evidence of the sort described above was either from interviews (subject to what he describes as interpretational constraints; see Fleming, 1986) or was the result of between-group correlation studies. In commenting on his results, he concluded:

The more a course unit was perceived as supportive of student learning, as having clearly defined goals and structure, as explicitly focusing on the mental processing in learning, as emphasising a capacity for independent learning, and as providing support for modes of learning and study typical of higher education, the more likely that deeper approaches to study would be reported. This basic pattern of relationships was evidenced in the correlations amongst Study Process Questionnaire and Course Perception Questionnaire measures across the total student sample, and in the comparisons between sub-groups on those same measures. But importantly, it was also evidenced in the comparisons made by individual students between two recently completed concurrent course unit enrolments. This latter finding provided clear evidence that study approaches can vary within individual students sympathetically to those students' perceptions of variations in their teaching environment.

This relational nature of approaches to learning differentiates it from learning styles, which have their origins in cognitive psychology, and are considered to be (relatively) stable personal attributes (Ramburuth, 1997). There has clearly been some confusion resulting from this differentiation

(Biggs, 1993b). Studies (e.g. Christensen *et al.*, 1991) that report comparisons between research involving these relational approaches and research based on the more stable learning styles (see for example Schmeck, 1988; and Weinstein *et al.*, 1988), and as employed in inventories such as the Learning Styles Inventory (Dunn *et al.*, 1989), reflect that confusion.

Disintegrated perceptions and approaches to learning

Earlier we described the two qualitatively different approaches students take to learning. There is growing evidence that some students may be perceiving their learning situation as affording both deep and surface approaches to learning with dire academic consequences.

We saw in Chapter 4 an outline of the studies exploring the relations between students' perceptions of their situation and their approaches to learning. The results consistently show that deep approaches to learning are related to perceptions of good teaching, clear goals and standards and some choice in what students learn. Surface approaches are related to perceptions of inappropriate assessment and with perceptions of heavy workloads. As these studies become increasingly sophisticated, we are continuing to gain insight into the importance of this relationship. Recent results suggest that there may be a group of students who perceive the context to be supportive of both a surface and deep approach (disintegrated perceptions) and they adopt an approach that contains elements of both or neither approach (Chapter 4). Such approaches are associated with failure in university examinations (Meyer *et al.*, 1990; Entwistle *et al.*, 1991) or with learning outcomes that are significantly worse than those of their colleagues who adopt deep or surface approaches (Prosser *et al.*, 1996). In the case of the latter study, 20 of 131 students reported disintegrated perceptions, while another 55 students were in a cluster with relatively low deep and surface approach to learning means (Table 4.5, page 73).

These results suggest that while surface approaches to learning are undesirable, there are even more undesirable approaches to learning. While there remains little doubt that deep approaches to learning are most desirable, approaches associated with disintegrated perceptions, from which few students could be expected to enjoy or achieve anything of significance from their study, are even less desirable than surface approaches. We take up these relations in the next section.

Approaches to learning and learning outcomes

Throughout this book we have suggested that variation in approaches to learning has been considered to be a crucial element in understanding the teaching–learning process. If this is so, it is the association between approaches to learning and learning outcomes and the relevance of this association to teachers that makes it crucial. The earliest studies of approach to learning and learning outcomes (noted above) indicated that there were relations between a deep approach to learning and a more highly desired learning outcome (Marton and Säljö, 1997: 45). Numerous studies since have reported similar results, and many of them are noted in the next chapter. For the moment we will refer to two cases that we have reported so far in this book. The first is the example we used in the opening of the first chapter. Melissa had adopted a deep approach and had achieved a distinction. Antony had adopted a surface approach and had failed. The quantitative analysis of the results of the mathematics study were presented in Table 4.6, page 79. Antony is in Cluster 1, Melissa is in Cluster 2. The second case was also described in Chapter 4. The results of a quantitative study of learning in first year physics in two universities showed that students who adopted a deep approach had better results than students who adopted a surface approach, and both groups had better results than students who reported disintegrated perceptions of their learning situation (Table 4.5, page 73).

This empirical evidence is supported by teachers' perceptions and desires, as we will see in the next section.

Teachers' perceptions of approaches to learning

If one of the aims of a university education is a high-quality learning outcome, the research on student learning consistently confirms that to achieve that aim, surface approaches to learning should be discouraged and deep approaches to learning encouraged. Most university teachers are intuitively aware of this position (though they may not always be able to implement it). This is the main reason why, as a way of understanding aspects of learning and teaching, the student learning perspective is becoming so popular. In their own words, university teachers express their desire for students to seek meaning, to be able to relate what they are learning in one area to what they have learnt in another, and to avoid rote learning which is not aimed at understanding. Most teachers also acknowledge that the approaches students adopt are all too often more like surface approaches than deep approaches to learning.

These comments are consistently confirmed quantitatively in simple pen and paper exercises conducted with groups of university teachers about the nature of the learning of their students. Using a short version of the Study Process Questionnaire, university teachers are asked to respond according to how they suspect their students approach their studies in the subject they teach. When analysed, the results for the group always show a high score on the surface approach scale and a low score on the deep approach scale. At the same time, the university teachers are also asked to complete another copy of the same questionnaire, this time according to how they would prefer their students to approach their studies in the subject they teach.

The results are consistently the opposite, yielding low surface approach scale scores and high deep approach scale scores.

Teachers prefer students to be adopting deeper approaches than they perceive they are. Why is it then, that so many teachers tolerate the fact that most students adopt a surface approach to the learning of their subject? Two of the reasons are alluded to above. First, much of the literature on teaching suggests that there is not necessarily a best way for students to approach their learning. That literature argues that students have individual learning styles or orientations and that the role of a teacher is to offer to students a variety of experiences so that they each might, for some time at least, find a match between their learning style and the approach of the teacher. It is an aim of this book to challenge that literature. Many teachers are unaware of the fact that they can influence the approach students take to learning. While there is evidence that students do have a learning orientation (Entwistle and Ramsden, 1983) there is now also sufficient evidence that a student's orientation can be totally overridden by his or her perceptions of the demands of the learning task. As we saw above and in Chapter 4, the same student will adopt qualitatively different approaches in different contexts (Laurillard, 1979; Eley, 1992; Gibbs, 1993; Laurillard, 1997).

Second, as we also have argued above, some teachers equate surface approaches to learning with memorizing and rehearsal, and do not accept that these approaches are undesirable. As we noted, this is a problem more to do with the definitions of memorizing, rehearsal and of a surface approach, than with the conclusions of the research. When left to their own words, teachers prefer students to adopt 'deep approaches'.

The combination of evidence that, on the one hand, a deep approach to learning is desirable and a surface approach is less desirable and on the other hand the learning context (and in some cases students' perceptions) can be changed by university teachers and administrators to afford one or other approach, forms the basis of a powerful tool to improve the quality of student learning. Some principles of practice for teaching which follow from this analysis are outlined in the next section.

Principles of practice for learning and teaching resulting from variation in approaches to learning

The literature reviewed in the previous section suggests that students approach their studies through a focus on certain aspects of the teaching/learning context. That focus is evoked by their perceptions of their learning situation, and it may be associated with an intention to understand, and/or an intention to satisfice (meet the minimum external requirements) or both (disintegrated perception and approach). The principles of practice for learning and teaching which arise from this perspective are:

1. In the same learning context, there is qualitative variation in the way students approach their learning.
2. This variation in approach is related to students' perceptions of their learning situation and their prior experiences of learning.
3. Different teaching/learning contexts evoke different approaches to learning.
4. The way students approach their learning is fundamentally (not just empirically) related to their learning outcomes. For example, if they do not seek to understand, then they do not find understanding.

These principles help explain why, in the same class, some students engage with, and seek to understand, the material being studied, while others take a distant and mechanical approach. They help explain why some students value learning contexts (such as problem-based learning) in which they interact strongly with what is being learned and feel they have some choice in defining their own curriculum. They help explain why students tend to adopt a rote learning, reproducing approach to their preparation for multiple-choice tests, even when the tests might appear to the designer to be testing more than recall. And they help explain why some students have a qualitatively different learning outcome to others studying the same subject.

These four principles give some indication of the type of practices that might be adopted by university teachers and administrators to enhance the quality of learning and teaching. Together, the principles link context, students' perceptions of their situation, approach to learning, and quality of the learning outcome. They include students, teachers and the whole teaching–learning context, and yet within this vast 'educational system' they give clear pointers to action which could be taken. Based on relations with learning outcomes, deep approaches to learning are desirable, and surface approaches are undesirable. What are the approaches to learning adopted by students in your classes? Approaches to learning are relational, hence changes to the learning context may be sufficient to change students' approaches to learning. What factors in the learning context might be related to students' adopted approaches? Students' perceptions of their learning situation are related to their approaches to learning. What are their perceptions of their situation? How might those perceptions be related to the students' prior learning experiences?

Good teaching involves addressing some or all of these questions. It involves finding out how students in a particular subject or context approach their learning, and addressing it in the teaching of the subject matter. It involves finding out about students' perceptions of the learning task they have accepted or their description of their learning situation in which they are carrying out that task. It involves an exploration of the factors which may be related to the approaches adopted by students, and reflection on what can be done about any or all of those factors to encourage deeper approaches to learning. And finally, it involves monitoring the quality of the outcomes of learning resulting from the approaches students adopt.

Whatever else university teachers may do, and whatever ideas they use to underpin their practice, good teaching is not possible if it does not include, first, an awareness of these issues, and second, an attempt to address them.

Examples of the application of the principles of practice for learning and teaching, including classroom research

The principles derived from this analysis would suggest that as a minimum, the practice of teaching from this perspective should involve determining and addressing students' approaches to learning of the subject matter. This section contains three cases of teachers who have engaged in classroom development and research based on variations in students' approaches to learning. The first case focuses only on the first principle. In the second case, the lecturer uses the first three principles to improve the quality of student learning, and in the final case, all four principles are used in a classroom research project.

An awareness of the variation in approaches to learning

This case illustrates several ways in which a focus on a student's deep approach to learning can be encouraged and monitored. Using the Model of the Teaching–Learning Process developed by Entwistle (1987) as a heuristic, John Buchner (1991) integrated a suite of activities aimed at fostering a deep approach to learning into a second year subject, mass communication audiences. Several of the activities (a discussion group and informal interviews) also included formative evaluative elements designed to collect information on the approaches to learning being adopted by students.

In the first lecture he outlined the characteristics of the two qualitatively different approaches to learning, gave students material and references on approaches to learning, and informed them that he would be teaching 'according to the imperatives of deep [approaches to] learning' (p. 2).

Acknowledging the importance of perceived assessment demands in determining approaches to learning, he introduced two assessment items on approaches to learning into two formal assessment components. Eight weeks into the subject, students were asked a question in a mid-term test designed to elicit their approaches to learning, including asking them to provide evidence of the application of a deep approach to learning in one of five topics studied. The author notes that it was obvious from responses to the part of the question on deep approaches to learning that very few were adopting such approaches. The second item was one of four compulsory questions in the two-hour final examination paper. It required students to give 'an account of your learning effectiveness since the mid-term test

(in what way has there been any significant change or improvement?)'
(Buchner, 1991: Appendix B).

Seven weeks before the examination, students were given notice that a
question such as this (and the other three compulsory questions) would be
on the paper. Again the author notes, somewhat forlornly, that:

> With few exceptions, students enthusiastically reported improvement
> in their learning, in some cases as though this might earn them higher
> marks. Several merely described different approaches to learning that
> they had memorised, and grafted themselves into their description. It
> appears that most were able to discuss features of 'deep' [approaches
> to] learning and appropriated the desirable qualities, but did not actu-
> ally demonstrate 'deep' [approaches to] learning in their answer to
> this question or to others (p. 6).

Formal monitoring of students' approaches to learning was conducted using the Study Process Questionnaire with the whole class (30 students) and
interviews with 6 students who were also asked to indicate their position on
a learning approach scale. On the whole the results are more positive than
those obtained through the processes of fostering deep approaches to learning. Most students believe that they ought to be adopting deeper approaches
to learning, and were in fact doing so in comparison with earlier studies,
and credit was given by students to this subject for raising the salience of
this learning approach (pages 8–9).

This case illustrates two points. First, that while it may be difficult for
university teachers to establish a context that evokes a deep approach, it is
possible, and in this case students' awareness of their approaches to learning was enhanced. Second, that monitoring approaches to learning may be
done using qualitative and quantitative methods.

Using interviews about approaches to learning on a small scale to reveal factors which could lead to improved teaching and student learning

One of the more successful exercises developed to improve learning and
teaching first appeared in the Certificate in Teaching in Higher Education
from Oxford Brookes University (Oxford Centre for Staff Development,
1989). Participants in this and similar programmes (usually university
teachers) are asked to interview three of the students they are currently
teaching to assess the approaches the students are taking to learning and to
identify what they perceive to be the factors which could be related to that
approach. Based on this evidence, the participants write an analysis of the
changes they will make to their subject. It is the interview and how the
results might be used to improve learning and teaching that form the focus
of this case.

The exercise is based on the idea that learning approaches vary with tasks. Unlike more stable orientations to learning, learning approaches can be significantly influenced. That influence can come unwittingly, or be a deliberate intervention by teachers. This exercise was partly about finding out what could be done in teaching by exploring the approaches some students took and the factors they identified as being associated with those approaches.

In a study of student learning in a postgraduate law subject the lecturer interviewed three students. Each interview lasted about 20 minutes, and included questions such as, 'Can you tell me how you prepared for the exam?' and, 'You mentioned a bit about this concept of cramming the night before or soon before an exam, why does that occur do you think, and what are the factors that cause that?' The teacher analysed the transcripts, and in her report, she wrote:

> Victor and Janet appear to use a deep approach to learning and both of them understood learning to be a process of making sense or abstraction of meaning. Victor and Janet's conceptions of learning are advanced . . . and involves conceiving of learning as understanding reality.

> At the other end of the spectrum Ray appeared to use the surface approach to learning and his conception of learning was qualitatively different from Janet and Victor's conception. To Ray, learning was seen as acquiring facts, skills and methods that can be retained and used as necessary. His conception is very more a 'reproducing of information' approach. In this category, the information that is retrieved is exactly the same as what was put in and there is no transformation of the information by the learner.

With respect to the factors found to influence these approaches she listed open book exams; unrealistic workloads; time pressure; over-assessment; assessment in the form of only one exam; inappropriate feedback; lack of interest; and compulsory subjects as factors associated with a surface approach. Deep approaches were related to the converse of these, and with fear of failure. In the conclusion to her report she wrote:

> It is important to consider what can . . . I as a teacher in higher education learn from the case studies.

> The nature of a subject or a course, the extent and variety and method of assessment and workload are all matters outside the control of students and yet as we have seen these factors have a direct bearing on students' approaches to learning and conceptions of learning. As a teacher I see the importance of encouraging and fostering a deep approach to learning by my students. Teachers, myself included, face great challenges where they teach a subject where the content, timetable, workload and assessment are predetermined by people other

than the teachers involved in the subject or course. I consider that the current program at College encourages a surface approach to learning and I base this not only on the case studies I have carried out but on what many many students have said to me over the past two years there. This is a source of enormous disappointment, however at the time of writing this paper I am aware that a new program is being developed. I can only hope that the new program is one that will foster and encourage a deep approach to learning and is one that addresses quality of teaching and quality of learning.

The sheer volume of cases, rules, procedures, legislation that dominates law, tend to foster a surface approach to learning in law subjects. I believe that any law subject can address this problem and be structured in such a way so as to encourage a deep approach. For example, in the Graduate Diploma of Legal Practice in which I teach, one of the assessment methods used is the Real Estate and Commercial Practice Conferences. Students always speak favourably of the Partners' Conferences and work hard in their preparation for these assessment tasks. The Partners' Conference involves teams of three students researching (individually and together) complex problems . . . that might be found in legal practice. The students then present possible arguments and solutions on the problems to a visiting legal practitioner. Generally all participants discuss issues in an informal 'round table' manner.

It strikes me that this Partners' Conference task is in fact a 'process of problem solving'. Ramsden (1992) refers to recent studies showing that in professional subjects which usually involve a large amount of problem solving activity, in an important sense the approaches used are also the outcomes of learning: in other words students are learning a process which will be an essential part of their work as professionals. I believe we can learn from this. Further assessment of this nature should be encouraged particularly in law and practical legal training programs.

As a teacher in higher education I propose to examine my methods of teaching so that I can encourage a deep approach to learning. Notwithstanding the subject presently imposed upon me at College I believe that in my small group presentations and discussions in some way I can attempt to foster a deep approach to learning in my students.

The lecturer left university teaching two years after she completed this study, but thanks to her efforts and those of her colleagues, the new programme affords a deeper approach to learning.

Similar studies have been conducted by many university teachers. The interviews invariably reveal aspects of the students' learning that were previously unknown to most teachers. One said, 'I was amazed by what I learnt from the students even though I have been teaching for many years and thought I knew most of it.' Another realized that students were not able to understand at the level at which she had been teaching for years. A third was surprised by the maturity of the students' approach.

Many university teachers discovered that more of their students were adopting surface approaches than they had expected or desired. They also discovered that their students were adopting surface approaches for reasons that they had previously thought were 'the fault' of the student, but they now realized were functions of the subject or their own teaching.

As in the first example, university teachers involved with this project became aware of the difficulty of changing students' approaches from surface to deep. This case illustrates the value of in-depth interviewing in investigations of this sort to obtain some information on what can be addressed. The law lecturer deduced from her small sample that assessment and workload were major factors encouraging surface approaches in her subject.

Relations between learning approach and learning outcomes

As a result of what she describes as adjustments to the assessment system of her physiotherapy subject, Tang (1998) observed that some students spontaneously formed collaborative learning groups as a coping mechanism. A smaller group of students who continued to work alone appeared to be learning in ways that were very different to the collaborative learning group. When she explored the nature of that learning in interviews with 39 students after they had submitted their assignments, she found that the characteristics of the learning approach of the collaborating group (the majority) were very similar to the characteristics of a deep approach to learning, while the small group who did not collaborate in their learning described characteristics which were typical of a surface approach (Table 5.2).

As the two groups displayed considerable variation in their approach, she decided to investigate the effects of this variation on the quality of their learning. Using both the quantitative mark for the assignment (Assignment Score) and a score based on an analysis of the assignments using the Structure of the Observed Learning Outcome (SOLO) taxonomy (SOLO Score) (see Chapter 6 for more details on this approach) she found that the differences in Assignment Scores were not significant, but that the students who collaborated produced assignments that had higher SOLO Scores (Table 5.3).

Tang notes, as have others (Slavin, 1987, 1991; Topping, 1992; Nichols and Miller, 1994) that as the outcomes of collaborative learning are positive when compared with individualistic and competitive learning contexts, good teaching will involve establishing optimal conditions for spontaneous collaborative learning. From our perspective this is one way to establish a context that affords a deep approach to learning. In Tang's case, this involved structuring the teaching context so that group discussion was encouraged, and also developing appropriate collaborative learning skills while retaining as much student control as possible.

Table 5.2 Study strategies used by students in preparing assignments

Strategies	Collaborating students (%)	Self-studying students (%)
Organize information	32	80
Analyse question requirements	24	20
Copy from reference materials	18	40
Focus on basic concepts	9	20
Compare information	18	0
Supplement each other's missing points	18	0
Relate information	15	0
Criticize each other's ideas	12	0
Share and exchange ideas	12	0
Analyse information	6	0
Apply	6	0
Argue	3	0

Source: Tang, 1998.

Table 5.3 Mean (and standard deviation (sd)) on two assessment results by group

Group	Assignment score (mean)	SOLO score (mean)
Collaborating students (n = 34)	65.1 (sd = 10.2)	3.0 (sd = 1.2)
Self-studying students (n = 5)	57.8 (sd = 9.9)	1.8 (sd = 0.8)

Source: Tang, 1998.

The studies reported in this section also illustrate some of the ways teachers have conducted research into variation in approaches to learning. We hope this offers some stimulation for university teachers to conduct their own investigations into aspects of their own teaching context. Some of the research methods, and some of the available tools (questionnaires and interview methods) are mentioned above. From these examples and the research used to support the arguments in this chapter, it will be apparent that there is essentially one source of data on the variation in student approaches to learning (students) and three main ways of collecting it (interviewing students, asking students to write short responses to open questions and asking students to complete a learning approaches inventory).

Two learning inventories which accommodate the relational nature of approaches to learning have been described in the literature: the Study Process Questionnaire (Biggs, 1987b) and the Approaches to Learning Inventory (Entwistle and Ramsden, 1983; Richardson, 1990). We introduced these inventories in Chapter 3. A shortened version (18 items) of the Approaches to Learning Inventory as used by university teachers involved in the Improving Student Learning Project is described, along with a scoring outline, by Gibbs (1992). However, the author points out two problems with this version. First, that it may be too short for classroom research purposes – the 30 item version described by Richardson (1990) may be more appropriate. Second, that it is important to instruct students to bear in mind the specific topic being studied when they complete the questionnaire. From the perspective of approaches to learning used in this book, and from our own experience, instructing students on this second point may not be sufficient. Inventories of this sort require modification to focus the student's awareness on the task, topic or subject, rather than on their prior orientation as determined by other contexts. An example from the mathematics study is given in Figure 4.3, page 78.

Similarly, short response questions and interviews used to determine approaches to learning need to direct students to a specific task or topic. Extracts from an interview of this sort are included in Chapter 4, pages 59–63. Advice given to the university teachers who interviewed their students as part of their teaching practice (pages 101–3) is to prompt the student into talking about a relevant learning task, but in a non-leading way that asks them to expand on each of their explanations (Oxford Centre for Staff Development, 1989). University teachers who attempt this approach note that it is difficult but productive.

As we indicate above, the results of these interviews were often a surprise to university teachers. Many had no idea that the students they interviewed would have been adopting a surface approach to that topic. In terms of action research, this is a useful result, but it is of limited research use in its own right. Of more interest is an exploration of factors and outcomes related to approaches to learning. Some of the techniques and instruments (for example, the Course Experience Questionnaire; Ramsden, 1991) which can be used in these studies have been referred to in earlier chapters. Relations between the variables being studied can be carried out using methods such as the correlation, factor and cluster analyses described in Chapters 3 and 4.

Summary of Chapter 5

In this chapter we have taken the variation in students' approaches to learning as the focus. We have shown that there are two qualitatively different approaches to learning (deep and surface) and that students who adopt deep approaches are likely to be the students with the higher quality learning outcomes. However, the presence of students with disintegrated perceptions and approaches suggests first, that there are strong relations between perceptions and approaches, and second, that students' approaches to learning are invariably more complex than simply either surface or deep. As we noted earlier, the surface and deep approaches to learning metaphor picks up on the key aspects of variation – it does not fully describe students' approaches to learning. Methods of finding out how students are approaching their learning were introduced via the examples used throughout the chapter, and included interviews with students, open-ended written responses from students and the use of approaches to learning inventories.

We presented research evidence to support a model showing that variation in approaches to learning is related to the variation in students' prior experience and between students' perceptions of their learning situation. In Chapter 4 we described the relations between the learning context and students' perceptions of their learning situation, and built on this and the relational nature of learning approaches to show that by changing the learning context, it may be possible to evoke different approaches to learning. Establishing contexts which afford a deep approach is an important element of good teaching, but as we suggest in Chapter 4, it may not be sufficient as students' perceptions of that context and of their learning situation are also related to their approaches to learning.

We also presented research evidence linking a deep approach to learning with high-quality learning outcomes, and a surface approach to learning with low-quality learning outcomes – variation in approach to learning is associated with variation in learning outcome. From these relations, and the perspective of this chapter, good teaching involves finding out how students in a particular subject or context approach their learning, and addressing it in the teaching of the subject matter. It involves finding out about students' perceptions of the learning task they have accepted or their description of their learning situation in which they are carrying out that task. It involves an exploration of the factors which may be related to the approaches adopted by students, and reflection on what can be done about any or all of those factors to encourage deeper approaches to learning. And finally, it involves monitoring the quality of the outcomes of learning resulting from the approaches students adopt. In summary, good teaching is not possible if it does not include an awareness of these issues, and an attempt to address them.

6

Students' Learning Outcomes

Student's prior experience		Student's approaches to learning
	Student's perceptions of his/her situation	
Student's situation		**Student's learning outcomes**

Introduction

To have students achieve high-quality learning outcomes is one of the aims of most university teachers. It is the type of learning that is sought because it is the learning that remains after lesser quality outcomes have been forgotten. And it is the learning that involves an understanding that can be drawn upon in other and new contexts. But most university teachers also know that there is considerable variation in the outcomes actually achieved, with many students not reaching this desired level.

In Chapter 1 we saw why Melissa and Antony, two first year students, had received quite different grades for their mathematics subject. We outlined an explanation for this result, and in Chapter 2 presented the model (reproduced above) from which we drew the explanation. Chapters 3, 4 and 5 have each focused on one element in the model of a student's learning situation, while seeking to maintain an awareness of the other elements. We have presented the research consistent with our view that these elements are internally related, and we have given examples of how university teachers and researchers have used these relations in attempts to improve learning.

In this chapter, we focus on the variation in what students learn. We will also illustrate, as we have in previous chapters, how learning outcome is associated with the way students approach their study, their perceptions of their learning situation and their prior learning experiences. But in this chapter the variation in learning outcome is seen as being in the fore-ground, with the other elements being treated as a part of the background. Again we will address questions that university teachers trying to improve student learning may have, such as:

- What do students learn? How do university teachers find out what they learn?
- Do they learn a greater or less amount about something, or do they understand about something in different ways?
- What can students do with what they learn? What aspects of what they learn do they take beyond the subject?
- What can university teachers do to improve the quality of student learning?

Our argument in Chapter 6 is that students who are able to see relations between elements of their understanding in a subject and are aware of how that understanding and those relationships can be applied in new and abstract contexts have a higher quality learning outcome than students who cannot. We argue that a learning outcome, or a way of understanding, which includes the more complete ways of conceiving of something, is of a higher quality than an outcome involving limited conceptions.

Take, for example, the following variation where the students' object of study is learning to play music. Students studying at a conservatorium of music were asked what learning and teaching instrumental music meant to them (Reid, 1997). In their responses, the group also gave an indication of the variation in ways of understanding music in relation to the playing of music. Reid describes the focus of this understanding as the Music Object, and suggests that it has three components, as follows:

The Music Object may be divided into three related components: the technical (either physical or notational) which is an extrinsic aspect; as sound and communication which emphasises extrinsic meanings; and as personal meaning which is intrinsic and related to a view of the world and personal meaning.

The Music Object as technique relates to the physical aspects of playing the *instrument* as well as notational elements such as phrasing, accents or articulation.

[The Music Object as] sound and communication [is] related to the belief that each piece of music has an inherent meaning that is consti-tuted by such things as style, period, harmony and composer's intent. It is the [inherent meaning of the *music*] that is communicated to an audience.

Music as personal meaning ... involve[s] aspects of [technique and sound and communication], but these aspects were reinterpreted by the participants through the notion that music is a way of expressing personal meaning and understanding of the world through music performance. It is the *musicians* ideas that are expressed through the music's inherent meaning.

(Reid, 1997: 204, our emphasis)

Music as personal meaning is a far more complete view of music than a view limited to a focus on technique, if for no other reason than that the former also includes the latter (but not vice versa) and is therefore broader and more inclusive. But, as we saw in Chapter 3, it is also a qualitatively different view. No amount of work on technique by a student with a focus on the instrument, or demonstration of technique by the teacher, will result in the adoption of the more complete ways of understanding by the student. In this chapter we also argue (as we did in Chapter 5) that these more complete understandings are more likely when students adopt a deep approach to their learning than they are with students who adopt a surface approach.

This perspective on learning outcomes is in contrast to views that a successful learning outcome is one in which a student can accurately reproduce 50 per cent or more of what he or she is being taught. It is also in contrast to related views that the product of learning is *more* knowledge: adding an extra amount to what is there. Our view is that a teacher with a focus on the product of learning as experiencing something in a qualitatively different way is likely to engage in teaching that explores variation in ways of understanding, illustrates variation in ways of understanding and encourages deep approaches to learning (Chapter 7).

From the perspective of this book, as illustrated in the model above, the outcome of the learning of any student in a particular context is related to that context. The outcome is also a function of the student's perception of his/her situation and a similar understanding may not be evoked in different situations. In this chapter we will discuss the implications of this relationship. Such a relationship helps university teachers explain why students who have demonstrated that they understand something in one context cannot apply that understanding in a different context. It also gives university teachers an insight into ways of improving learning.

As in previous chapters, we present next an experience of variation (in this case of learning outcomes). Research describing the extent of the variation in student learning outcomes is presented on pages 115–27. Those studies focus on both the variation in the structure of the students' description of their learning and on its meaning. They also enable us to describe what it means to know something, and in doing so they make links back to variations in conceptions of learning and conceptions of the subject introduced in Chapter 3.

The later sections concentrate on the practical implications of variations in learning outcomes for learning and teaching and for classroom-based research. These sections contain principles of teaching derived from an awareness of variation in learning outcomes, they give examples of the application of those principles and describe some of the classroom-based research being conducted by university teachers into aspects of ways of understanding.

Experiencing the variation in students' learning outcomes

It would be unusual for any teacher, whether or not they be in higher education, not to have experienced variation in students' learning outcomes. Anyone who marks a collection of essays or students' attempts at solving a problem will be struck by the different ways in which students respond to the same question or task. Given that you have probably experienced that variation, how have you characterized it? As a quantitative difference (one student knowing more than another)? As one student knowing it differently to another? If there is a qualitative difference, how would you describe it? To what do you attribute the variation you have experienced?

Some of the variations (in the form of prior conceptions of the subject matter) and the reasons for this variation have been discussed in earlier chapters, and will be addressed again in detail later. In the next part of this section we present some examples of the forms of variation in learning outcomes in different disciplines and at different levels (concept, topic or subject) and use them to illustrate some of the ways that variation can be characterized. In all the cases below, the responses are from or about pairs of students (A and B) who have been studying in the same context, and are responding to the same question.

Biology – written response to the following question on photosynthesis (Hazel et al., 1996)

'A river has been infected with a rapidly growing green alga. In terms of photosynthetic reactions, describe what happens when light falls on the algae, what happens at night, and any differences between these two situations?'

Student A
Energy from the sun is stored via photosynthesis during the day. It is used at night by [plants] in the absence of light energy.

Student B
[In photosynthesis] chloroplasts in the algae utilise light energy and convert it to chemical energy to produce glucose (food). Photosynthesis happens in two stages: light and Calvin cycle. During the night, the light stage of photosynthesis does not occur, but the products from the

light stage are used in the Calvin Cycle. If these products are not present, the Calvin Cycle will not occur.

Nursing – written response to the following request (Trigwell and Prosser, 1991a)

'Describe what you think this communication subject is about or what the lecturer was trying to teach you.'

Student A
[The lecturer tried to teach us] to be able to communicate in an effective way; to pick up non-verbal behaviour when communicating (verbal behaviour is very important in trying to communicate, that is sound of voice); learning communication skills in order to understand and help others when working as a professional nurse; the difference between sympathy and empathy when communicating with clients; to be a good listener (p. 270).

Student B
[The subject] was about learning to effectively communicate and practice [sic] the skills of empathy and active listening. It was about relating communication techniques to nursing situations. The course was designed to improve your own interpersonal communication skills and to understand the communication of others (p. 269).

Chemistry – interview asking students about the arrangement of electrons in atoms (Keogh, 1991)

Student A
The nucleus is surrounded by orbiting electrons which are very, very much smaller than the particles making up the nucleus, almost infinitely small . . . You'd see the electrons at varying radii, depending on whether or not the atom was in an excited state . . . and yeah, the electrons would be moving in set orbits, there would be spaces between the orbits where the electrons couldn't orbit at that radius (p. 17).

Student B
You've got a positively charged nucleus, and you've got electrons going around it, I wouldn't localise electrons by saying it has a set orbit. It's got a probability of it being in like a shell . . . so it's more like an area, I imagine it to be this charge sort of smeared out, you know, a rough sort of spherical area . . . An electron isn't definitely here, it's different to like a hard sphere, where you say the electron is always at this radius, and it's always following such a path, that's not the case, it's uhm, a certain region of space that has a certain probability (p. 18).

History – essay on the causes of the Eureka Stockade (Biggs, 1988)

Biggs (1988), in an article on approaches to learning and essay writing, presents the following brief analysis of two essays (by Geoff and Syd) on the Eureka Stockade (which are produced in full in the Appendix of that article). The Eureka Stockade was a minor uprising in Australia in the mid-nineteenth century. Students were asked to 'Identify the basic causes of the Eureka Stockade, and try to establish which were the most important. Explain whether you think this revolt was inevitable. (About 1500 words.)' The analysis captures the essential features of the variation in outcome of the full essays.

Student A (Geoff)
[In his essay, Geoff] . . . does not present a unified point of view supported by evidence . . . He takes a series of events and lists them as possible causes and then selects the most likely, in his view. The events are not integrated into a causal sequence, each implicating the other . . . Something of this is indicated in [his] comments 'I like to present the facts . . . I more or less cover the thing from beginning to end.' This is straight forward knowledge-telling, and as the marker comments, his essay reads more like narrative than historical analysis . . .

He draws on his not inconsiderable knowledge to list the causes and then says what he knows about each cause, independently of the other. His conclusion is to settle for the one cause that seems most salient (government actions). Knowledge-telling traps him into giving far too much irrelevant detail, such as depth of mining shafts, the exact dates of various events, even repetition of bibliographic details in the text as well as the reference list (p. 215).

Student B (Syd)
[In Syd's essay] . . . the structure is highly appropriate . . . the particular event, the Eureka Stockade, is hypothesised as an example of a wider phenomenon, the rise of the middle class in Europe at that time. The details and events surrounding the rebellion – the personal backgrounds of the miners, their 'small business' rather than working-class value systems, the roles and values of the police officers and of the government officials – are all highly relevant to that structure and illustrate the thesis well. The marker commented: '. . . you are perhaps the only student who is capable of fitting both into a broad political/ historical framework'. All the other students used a structure . . . in which the details and the surrounding events were discussed only with respect to the rebellion itself (p. 213).

Education – interviews with students who have read a text on learning (Säljö, 1997)

A much-reported study by Roger Säljö of the Gothenburg education research group illustrates the students' variation in the construction of meaning from a text. Following their reading of a text on forms of learning, Suzi and Dave were asked to describe what it was about. The text they were describing began with an example of classical conditioning (in a Greek prison) followed by notes on classical conditioning, Skinner and instrumental conditioning, and the work of the Gothenburg group (Marton and Booth, 1997: 24). The following are extracts (Säljö, 1997) from their responses to the first part of the text:

Student A (Suzi)

There was a lot said about Skinner and, for instance Ivan Pavlov and the psychologist Ebbinghaus and research results. That's always fun to read about. And then all this, there were some statistics about Chile, for instance, and that's interesting and I've always been interested in South America . . . and Spain too. And then there was something about the torture methods of the Greek junta and you sort of got bad feelings when you read about that kind of thing, even if it's interesting (p. 95).

Student B (Dave)

A Greek was being tortured by the Greek junta and this was used as an example of classical conditioning, that is of conditioned responses. The person who was being tortured also got to see the electrodes, which gave electrical shocks and gradually he sort of felt the electricity in his body just by seeing the electrodes. This I suppose is an example of classical conditioning which was investigated and discovered by Pavlov . . . (p. 95).

In all five pairs of responses or comments illustrated above, those involving Student B are substantially different to those involving Student A. In some cases, the differences are such that in relation to the learning objectives of the subject or discipline, Student A's response is equivalent to a fail or maybe a bare pass, while Student B's response is equivalent to a pass with credit or distinction. The differences within each pair cannot be characterized quantitatively, that is in terms of Student B knowing more, or writing more than Student A. The differences between the outcomes amount to there being a qualitative difference in understanding between them. For example, in the last extract, Dave's interpretation of the reading is that the scene in the Greek prison is an example of, and therefore a component of, the sub-theme of classical conditioning. He sees a relationship between the example and the sub-theme. Suzi describes no such relation. Her response is an unconnected list of topics included in the reading, and interestingly, some which were not. (Her irrelevant references to Chile, South America and Spain have their origins in another article she had recently read.) In terms of learning quality, the response from Dave is far superior. Similarly, in the third extract, the understanding of atomic structure that Student B expresses is more complete because it has moved beyond the classical mechanical description of the atom expressed by Student A. As was illustrated in Chapter 3, the more complete understandings often accommodate most or all of the less complete understandings, but go beyond it in qualitatively different ways, as we saw above for the music object. In the second extract, nursing Student B gives a response which seems to be seeing different areas in the subject as part of the whole subject rather than as separate parts, whereas Student A lists the areas without linking them in any way.

The qualitative differences between these outcomes is such that quantitative approaches (such as working harder or doing more examples) will not change limited understandings to the more complete or inclusive understanding. So, for example, in a group of students learning to play music instruments, some may see the music object as the technical use of the instrument and some others as involving personal meaning. Both groups may be taught to the same level of technical competence, but the way they think about the learning of their music may be quite different. No amount of focus on the techniques of music will bridge the qualitative differences in these understandings. This is an illustration of how different people in the same context have quite different understandings.

Research on the variation in students' learning outcomes

All the examples given in the previous section are from research investigating qualitative differences in student learning outcomes. Learning outcomes can be, and often are, described in terms of how much students know, with variation being that student B knows more than student A. This is in contrast to the examples above where student B knows of it differently to student A. Research focusing on the differences between these ways of describing outcomes is the first topic of this section. The second topic is the research focused only on the qualitative variation in outcomes, and we conclude this section by returning to look at more studies relating approaches to learning and learning outcomes.

Qualitative and quantitative variations in learning outcomes

During investigations in the 1970s of the different ways in which science students conceptualize a phenomenon, science educators described what appeared to be a serious problem with respect to the quality of the understanding of these students. Their studies showed that physical science students' understanding of concepts and relations between concepts is less than might be expected from their assessment results. Put another way, the learning demonstrated by students in one context (in examinations) was not demonstrably drawn upon in a different context (in responses to interview questions). For example, in three of ten tests on a student group who scored highly in a senior secondary school physics examination, less than 55 per cent were able to explain correctly basic (non-formula-based) physics phenomena (Gunstone and White, 1981).

Other studies (Johansson *et al.*, 1985; Prosser and Millar, 1989) show that many students studying first year university Newtonian physics still work with limited conceptions that are not detected by traditional examinations. Prosser and Millar (1989, and Chapter 3) found that none of 14 students who had achieved well in secondary school were able to provide the acceptable Newtonian explanation for a basic physics phenomenon at the beginning of their university programme. Science graduates studying an Australian Diploma of Education and about to become secondary school science teachers were discovered to be working with conceptions from which they produced statements which were 'outrageously incorrect' scientifically (West, 1988: 53).

The differences between the results from a traditional examination and a qualitative analysis of learning outcomes is illustrated in a study by Dahlgren (1988) which focused on the longevity of learning. The research team asked economics students to respond to an open-ended question on the meaning of equilibrium in an economic system. Analysis of the responses yielded four qualitatively different meanings:

A. Equilibrium means that there is a balance between income and expenditure
B. Equilibrium means that there is a balance between export and import
C. Equilibrium means that there is a balance between supply and demand
D. Equilibrium means that resources are allocated in such a way that no one can profit from a reallocation except at the expense of someone else.

With respect to this subject, meaning D is the most complete, with meanings C and D being acceptable to university teachers. Meanings A and B are less complete and less acceptable. D takes equilibrium beyond a balance to include a systems-oriented or interdependence-based meaning, with an added qualification of efficiency. The 33 students who answered this question also completed a traditional examination on this topic, and the results for that test are given as the mean original test score in column 3 of Table 6.1.

In view of what we have described, the first striking thing about these results is that the mean original test score for the students grouped according to their Meaning Category A–D is negatively correlated with the levels of understanding expressed in their responses. This suggests that the examination is not testing the same understanding. The second striking thing is that only eight students have demonstrated the desired understanding. But what is even more interesting is the information in the final column. In collaboration with the Department of Economics, the authors gauged the

Table 6.1 Relations between understanding, test score and retention for economics students

Number of students	Meaning category	Original test score (mean)	Percentage retention (mean)
1	D	10.00	60
7	C	11.83	40
13	B	12.00	26
12	A	12.63	20

Source: Dahlgren, 1988.

extent of original test result retention two years later, and found that students who had demonstrated higher levels of understanding (Meaning Categories C and D) had considerably higher levels of retention. In this case retention was also negatively correlated with test score.

With the hindsight of research in a wider range of disciplines, Ramsden (1992: 30) summarized this overall position as follows:

In recent years, it has become clear from numerous investigations that:

- Many students are accomplished at complex routine skills in science, mathematics, and humanities, including problem solving algorithms.
- Many have appropriated enormous amounts of detailed knowledge, including knowledge of subject specific terminology.
- Many are able to reproduce large quantities of factual information on demand.
- Many are able to pass examinations.
- But many are unable to show that they understand what they have learned, when asked simple yet searching questions that test their grasp of the content. They continue to profess misconceptions of important concepts; their ideas of how experts in their subjects proceed and report their work are often confused; their application of their knowledge to new problems is often weak; their skills in working jointly to solve problems are frequently inadequate. Conceptual changes are 'relatively rare, fragile and context-dependent occurrences' (Dahlgren, 1984: 33).

(Ramsden, 1992: 30)

As Ramsden went on to show, the first four bullet points have explanations in the way university teachers establish the learning context, and the way students go about learning in that context. These factors contribute to the scenario described in the final bullet point. From the perspective of this book, aspects of this scenario also have their explanation in the relational nature of learning outcomes. As we saw for prior experiences in Chapter 3, when students learn in a certain teaching/learning context, their placement within that context constitutes a unique learning situation. Their perception of that situation evokes, or brings to awareness, a certain understanding. Given a changed context, the same understanding may not be evoked.

In this section we have tried to show that in many cases, to look for the variation in the quality of learning outcomes, we may have to go to sources beyond the easily accessible assessment results. We describe some of these in the next section. This is not to say that assessment data are not a useful resource. On the contrary, as we will see later, where the assessment tests understanding (Biggs, 1996a) appropriate analysis of the data can produce qualitative differentiation (Biggs, 1992).

Research describing the qualitative differences in learning outcomes

We will consider this research into qualitative differences in learning outcomes in three groups: research into the structure of learning outcomes; research into the meaning and structure of learning outcomes; and research into forms of understanding.

Research into variation in the structure of learning outcomes

Research into variation in the structure of learning outcomes has been greatly assisted by the idea of the SOLO (Structure of the Observed Learning Outcome) taxonomy. In 1982, Biggs and Collis described five structural levels of learning outcomes which ranged from incompetence to expertise (Figure 6.1). The first level (incompetence) was labelled pre-structural and is applicable to an outcome containing nothing of relevance to the knowledge in question. The second level is uni-structural, and includes outcomes where there is a reference to only one relevant item. Multi-structural outcomes are those where more than one relevant item is included, but those items are listed independently. Outcomes of a relational (level four) nature do not necessarily include a greater amount of knowledge than in the case of multi-structural outcomes. In outcomes of this sort, the understanding is integrated and related, and the separate elements are described as part of an overall structure. The final, and most complete level (extended abstract) includes those outcomes that demonstrate the generalizability of the understanding to new contexts. Students with this understanding are able to draw upon it in (some) new contexts.

We have used the SOLO taxonomy to gauge students' prior and post understanding of photosynthesis. Examples of how students' responses at the end of the topic can be classified according to differences in structure are given below. The quotes are from responses to the following question which we introduced in Chapter 3 and above (page 111): 'A river has been infected with a rapidly growing green alga. In terms of photosynthetic reactions, describe what happens when light falls on the algae, what happens at night, and any differences between these two situations?' (Hazel *et al.*, 1996).

Figure 6.1 Five structural levels of learning outcomes

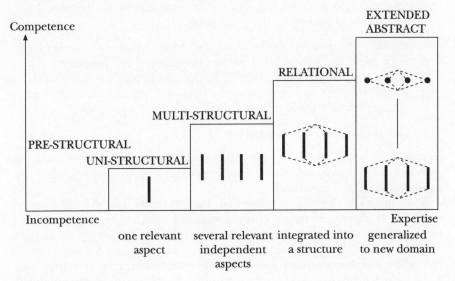

Source: Biggs, 1991, p. 13.

The key to the answer to this question is that in photosynthesis there are two reactions, Light and 'Dark' (Calvin Cycle) which are related (i.e. the dark reaction depends on the products of the light reaction). The responses below, classified according to the SOLO taxonomy, show, in order: no mention of any reaction (pre-structural), mention of only one reaction (uni-structural), mention of two unrelated reactions (multi-structural), and mention of two related reactions (relational).

Pre-structural – When light falls on the algae it blocks the sun from getting to plants below the algae and thus they cannot obtain light to photosynthesize. At night, as the plants under the algae release oxygen, the algae then absorb this oxygen and there is no oxygen left for marine life. The differences between these two situations is that one affects plants and the other affects marine animals.

Uni-structural – When the light hits the algae, they produce food and breathe. The process of photosynthesis can be described as the reaction between carbon dioxide and water, with energy to produce glucose and oxygen. This in turn will produce more algae as they reproduce themselves more rapidly. At night time not all of the photosynthesis process stops, because depending if there is light from other sources, the process will continue, therefore producing more algae.

Multi-structural – Light falls, the solar energy is converted to chemical energy (in chlorophyll). In the light stage, carbon dioxide and water are broken down into carbon, oxygen and hydrogen. There is also a dark stage. Photosynthesis gives the plant energy in the stored form of glucose. At night the dark stage, or Calvin cycle may occur, but not the light as the light stage requires energy.

Relational – When light falls on algae the photosynthetic reactions take place because the light energy excites the chlorophyll producing the energy needed in the dark reaction. Light also breaks down the water producing hydrogen ions. Without the light, none of this takes place so the dark reaction cannot proceed, hence no food is produced.

Extended Abstract – none observed

In this study, only 5 per cent of students gave responses that were classified as relational, yet only relational responses demonstrate an acceptable understanding of photosynthesis.

Boulton-Lewis (1998) has reviewed the literature on the analysis of variation in higher education student learning outcomes using the SOLO taxonomy. In that report she describes how she has picked up on Biggs's (1992) use of SOLO to analyse assessment data, and how 74 per cent of her adult learning students described their understanding of learning in a multi-structural way, with the remaining 26 per cent using relational descriptions (Boulton-Lewis and Dart, 1994). Trigwell and Prosser (1991a) and Tang and Biggs (1995) have used the idea of asking students to describe to a friend what the subject/topic was about, and then analysing those responses using the SOLO taxonomy. Tang and Biggs used this approach at the beginning and end of a subject as a means of monitoring conceptual change.

These reports give an indication of the proportions of students who describe their understanding in structural terms in a complete or partially complete way.

Research into variation in the structure and meaning of the
learning outcomes
While the SOLO taxonomy can be used to describe differences in structure generically, it does not describe differences in meaning at all. In this section we look at two other ways of describing qualitative differences – phenomenography, where the differences in structure and meaning are non-generic; and concept maps, which describe meaning non-generically and structure generically.

The music study described on pages 109–10, four of the five examples (excluding the essays) on pages 111–14, and the conceptions of equilibrium in economics on pages 116–17 are all taken from research studies into qualitative differences in variation in the structure and meaning of the learning outcome.

One set of results from the study on learning instrumental music (Reid, 1997) contains three ways of conceiving of the Music Object (an outcome of the learning of a musical instrument). The three ways are qualitatively different in meaning, with the focus being on the instrument; the music; or the musician (page 109). But there is also a structural differentiation present in the form of logically related hierarchies. Seeing the playing of music as a way of expressing personal meaning (focus on the musician) is still seen to be done through the development of technique and the communication of sound. And communicating the meaning of the music (focus on the music) is still accomplished through the playing technique and an awareness of phrasing, accents and articulation. The category which focuses on the musician is structurally related to the other two and would therefore appear to be the most inclusive and complete.

In 1994 Davey explored the understanding her second year nursing students had of aseptic technique. She asked, 'What principles and ideas do you think underlie the use of aseptic technique, and what do you think were the main things your tutor wanted you to learn from studying aseptic technique?' She found three qualitatively different levels of understanding in a group of 11 students. At the first level (U1) students focus on the principles of aseptic technique (all objects in a sterile field must be sterile; fluids flow in the direction of gravity; the skin cannot be sterilized and is unsterile, etc.). At the second level (U2) students focus on the procedural skills (such as non-touch technique; multiple handwashing; discarding contaminated waste, etc.) which derive from the principles of aseptic technique. At the third level of understanding (U3) students focus on the global idea of asepsis, that is, understanding aseptic technique as being about preventing the spread of micro-organisms (Davey, 1995). She found that while there was quantitative variation in understanding within a level (students expressing an awareness of greater or fewer principles or procedures) there was a qualitative variation in understanding across the three levels.

These two examples and many of the others used in this book to illustrate variation in outcomes and prior conceptions have been obtained using a phenomenographic approach. Marton describes phenomenography as

> the empirical study of the limited number of qualitatively different ways in which we experience, conceptualise, understand, perceive, apprehend etc., various phenomena in and aspects of the world around us. These differing experiences, understandings etc. are characterised in terms of categories of description, logically related to each other, and forming hierarchies in relation to given criteria. Such an ordered set of categories of description is called the outcome space of the phenomenon, concepts in question.
>
> (Marton, 1992)

The range of ways the mathematics students conceived of mathematics (Chapter 3) is an outcome space constituted using a phenomenographic approach.

The number of studies which report that there is qualitative variation in the way the object of study is understood is growing rapidly. In most of the fields studied, the majority of those categories of description or

Table 6.2 Some studies of variation in understanding by higher education field

Field		Reference
Biology	Photosynthesis	Hazel *et al.*, 1996
Chemistry	States of matter	Renström *et al.*, 1990
	Mole concept	Lybeck *et al.*, 1988
	Atomic structure	Keogh, 1991
Computing sciences	Programming	Booth, 1992
Economics		Dahlgren, 1997
Geology	Mapping	McCracken and Laurillard, 1994
Health science	Physiotherapy	Abrandt, 1997
	Aseptic technique	Davey, 1995
Mathematics		Crawford *et al.*, 1994
Music	Instrumental	Reid, 1997
Politics	Political power	Theman, 1983
Physics	Electricity and magnetism	Millar *et al.*, 1989; Prosser, 1994
	Sound	Linder and Erickson, 1989
	Mechanics	Johansson *et al.*, 1985; Prosser and Millar, 1989; Bowden *et al.*, 1992

understandings described by students are classified as incomplete. While this is not an indication of the proportions of students working with limited conceptions, it does show that there are a number of variants on limited ways of conceiving of the phenomenon. An indication of some of the higher education fields studied using phenomenographic methods is shown in Table 6.2.

The photosynthesis study listed first among the phenomenographic studies in Table 6.2 was part of a more extensive study of student learning. Table 6.3 shows a cluster analysis of the results of investigations of the relations between three indicators of learning outcome and students' approaches to learning and perceptions of their learning situation. One of the outcome indicators is the phenomenographic categories of description. (The same categories were used to determine prior understanding, as described in Chapter 3, Figure 3.3, page 52.) A second is the SOLO categories as described above. The third outcome indicator results from an analysis of the photosynthesis concepts maps drawn by students.[1] Table 6.3 shows the two clusters of students and the variation between them on the eight variables in the study. The phenomenographic and SOLO indicators for prior understanding and for learning outcomes were strongly correlated and the results have been combined in the table.

The outcome indicators for the concept maps are very similar to those for the phenomenographic methods and SOLO analysis. Students (n = 210) in Cluster 1 show moderately low mean scores on both outcome measures, as well as moderately low scores on deep approach and perceptions of the

Table 6.3 Cluster means for a two cluster solution for the outcome measures on photosynthesis, approaches to study, and perceptions of the learning situation

Variable	Cluster 1 (n = 210)	Cluster 2 (n = 62)
Prior understanding (phenomenography and SOLO)	−0.25	0.84
Prior understanding (concept maps)	−0.08	0.26
Deep approach	−0.10	0.34
Surface approach	0.23	−0.77
Perceptions affording a deep approach	−0.15	0.50
Perceptions affording a surface approach	0.19	−0.64
Outcome (phenomenography and SOLO)	−0.29	0.96
Outcome (concept maps)	−0.27	0.90

Source: Hazel *et al.*, 1996.

situation affording a deep approach. They are also moderately high on surface approach scores and perceptions affording a surface approach scores. Students (n = 62) in Cluster 2 tend to have high outcome scores, very low surface approach and perceptions affording a surface approach scores, and moderately high deep approach and perceptions affording a deep approach scores. In this study, the concept map scores are as expected for an indicator of student understanding.

In this photosynthesis study, students were asked to construct a concept map using 13 concepts of photosynthesis. The maps were analysed quantitatively using a modification of grading methods described by Boulton-Lewis and Dart (1994). Higher points scores are an indication that the map represents a more complete or integrated understanding of photosynthesis. The scores for each map were entered as data for the analysis producing the results in Table 6.3. This example shows how concept maps can be used in studies of the variation in the quality of learning outcomes.

Forms of understanding and knowledge objects
In the previous sections we have presented studies reporting the variation in the structure and meaning of students' learning outcomes. We have described these outcomes as involving more or less complete understandings of the material being learned. For example, a relational understanding of photosynthesis is more complete than a multi-structural understanding, and a high concept map score suggests a more integrated structure and more complete understanding of meaning. Students studying to understand something have, in describing understanding, 'gone beyond' structure and meaning (Entwistle and Entwistle, 1992). They talk about a *feeling* of coherence, connectedness and provisional wholeness, as expressed in the following quotation:

Understanding? To me that's the interconnection of lots of disparate things – the way it all hangs together, the feeling that you understand

Figure 6.2 Contrasting forms of understanding in revising for finals

---

Breadth of understanding – variation in the amount of material, information, ideas, integrated into the understanding
Depth of understanding – variation between reproducing the teacher's meaning and developing one's own understanding
Structure of understanding – variation in the structure used to organise the material:
  a Little or no structure being imposed on the facts learned;
  b Relying exclusively on the lecturer's structure;
  c Producing prepared answers to previous years, questions;
  d Adapting own understanding to expected question types; and
  e Relying on an individual conception of the topic.

Source: Adapted from Entwistle, 1998.

how the whole thing is connected up – you make sense of it internally. You're making lots of connections which then make sense and it's logical . . . It is as though one's mind has finally 'locked in' to the pattern. Concepts seem to fit together in a meaningful way, when before the connections did not seem clear or appropriate or complete . . . If you really understand something, why it works, and what the idea is behind it, you can't not understand it afterwards – you can't 'de-understand' it! And you know you understand [when you can] construct an argument from scratch . . . by yourself – can explain it so that you feel satisfied with the explanation.

(Entwistle and Entwistle, 1992: 148)

From this study, the authors constituted contrasting forms of understanding of students revising for final examinations, based around the differences in the breadth, depth and structure of that understanding (Figure 6.2).

From these studies of understanding a new way of conceiving of qualitative differences in learning outcomes is emerging. At this stage the work is still new and relatively undeveloped. However, as we believe that it has the potential to contribute substantially to the understanding of student learning, we have included a brief description in this chapter.

In the interview transcripts of student reports of their study for final examinations, Entwistle and Marton (1994) noted that some students talked about their understanding as something the authors describe as a knowledge object. Students 'were describing a feeling that the material being revised had become so tightly integrated, that it was experienced as an entity with form and structure . . . Additional associated knowledge was readily "available" when needed' (Entwistle and Marton, 1994: 168). The experienced entity of a tightly integrated body of knowledge and the availability of associated knowledge are both elements of what we have described in this chapter as high-quality learning outcomes. These students are aware of the relations between aspects of the topic, and they have an awareness of unfocused aspects of knowledge. Students with this awareness of understanding are more likely to be able to apply what they have learned in new situations, for reasons outlined by the authors:

> A knowledge object has an experienced and 'sensed' structure which can provide a generic form to explanations. Students rehearse explanations during revision and those explanations help to structure the knowledge object. In turn, the knowledge object seems, in some way, to control the evolving form of the answer. When faced with a particular question, a satisfactory explanation has to take into account the audience, the social context, and the specific wording and implicit requirements of the question. Comments made by some students implied that the logical structure needed for the answer had been guided by a knowledge object, the structure of which had sufficient flexibility to be adapted, as required, to the specific question. As the answer structure emerged, it 'pulled in' the evidence and detail necessary to support the developing answer. If the explanation were to be given on a different occasion, although the answer would have a similar generic form reflecting the structure of the knowledge object, the fine detail of the argument, together with the specific examples and detail provided, would almost certainly differ. The explanation would evolve in a slightly different way and 'trigger' rather different supportive material. This description of this relationship between knowledge objects and explanations must, however, be seen as being necessarily speculative as it is based on rather few instances.
>
> (Entwistle and Marton, 1994: 176)

From these descriptions, students who have experienced this form of understanding would have a qualitatively different learning outcome to students who have not reached the point of an integrated understanding and a broadened awareness of relevant and related aspects of that understanding.

Relations between learning outcomes and approaches to learning

As we saw in Chapter 5 it is our contention that the variation in student learning outcomes as described above is strongly related to the approaches to learning adopted by those students, and to a lesser extent to their perceptions of their learning situation, and the students' prior experience. These relations are supported by a substantial body of research. We introduced the study by Tang in Chapter 5 (page 104). She reported that students who have higher quality learning outcomes (as determined using the SOLO taxonomy) were the students who had adopted collaborative and deep approaches to learning (Tang, 1998). We have included brief descriptions of a further four studies below.

Table 6.4 Correlations between approach to learning and learning outcome
variables for a class of first year nursing students (n = 122)

Variable	Variable			
	1	2	3	4
1 Deep approach	–	−.09	−.09	.21
2 Surface approach		–	.03	−.06
3 Quantitative differences in outcome			–	.06
4 Qualitative differences in outcome				–

Source: Trigwell and Prosser, 1991a.

By now you will be familiar with the studies of the learning experiences of
the mathematics students (Crawford *et al.*, 1994) and with the quantitative
data showing strong correlations between students' approaches to learning
and their assessment results (Crawford *et al.*, 1998a). This was exemplified
in Chapter 1 where we noted how Antony had described a surface approach
to learning and had failed the subject, while Melissa had described a deep
approach and had received a distinction. The relations between the mathematics students' learning approach and learning outcomes are illustrated
in Table 4.6 (page 79). The cluster of 127 students who have high mean
scores on deep approaches are also the students who have high mean
scores on achievement (final mark) and who have an understanding based
on cohesive conceptions of the subject. This is the group that includes
Melissa. Antony is in the group where students adopt surface approaches
and have fragmented conceptions and low achievement.

In three of the five studies used on pages 111–14 to illustrate the variation in the outcomes of learning, correlations between these outcomes and
learning approach were included. The results are all of the form and in the
direction described above.

The Nursing Students A and B on page 112 are describing what they
thought their first year nursing communication subject was about or what
the lecturer was trying to teach them. As we have seen, the variation between these responses is considerable, with B being more in line with the
subject objectives than A. These quotes are taken from a study involving 122
first year nursing communication students (Trigwell and Prosser, 1991a)
and in addition to asking them for information about their subject, we
asked them to complete an approaches to study questionnaire. The results
we obtained showed that, at the subject level, students like Student B, whose
response can be classified as relational (SOLO Level 4), were more likely to
be students who described adopting a deep approach to learning.

Table 6.4 shows the correlations between the approaches to learning
variables (deep and surface approach) and the outcome variables (qualitative differences (from descriptions of the subject analysed using SOLO)
and quantitative differences (from assessment results)).

Table 6.4 shows that there is a positive relation between a deep approach to learning and the qualitative differences in learning outcome, but this approach is not related to the quantitative differences in outcome. Surface approaches are not related to either outcome indicator. Meyer *et al.* (1990) found similar results for engineering students, as did Watkins (1983) for students from faculties of arts, science and economics.

Results such as these have consistently been produced in studies at the task level. For example, in what was probably the first study to reveal the relations between learning approach and outcome, Marton and Säljö (1976) reported the variation in descriptions of their learning in the reading task carried out by Suzi and Dave (page 114). Suzi, with a poor learning outcome, had adopted a surface approach, while Dave was using a deep approach. Similar relations were obtained in a study of learning on chemical equilibrium tasks using concept maps to determine learning outcomes (Trigwell and Sleet, 1990) and for psychology students, where the SOLO taxonomy was used to determine learning outcomes (van Rossum and Schenk, 1984).

Table 6.3 (page 123) shows the results of a study of the associations between students' perceptions of their learning situation, approaches to learning and learning outcome in the topic of photosynthesis (Hazel *et al.*, 1996). Students' learning outcomes were analysed using the SOLO taxonomy (pages 119–20), phenomenography, and with concept maps. Again the higher quality outcomes were associated with a deep approach to learning. Prosser and Millar (1989) found similar results when they looked at physics learning at the topic level.

In summary, in this section we have looked at three types of research on the quality of outcomes of student learning. Our argument in Chapter 6 is that there is variation in the quality of student learning and that students who achieve higher quality outcomes are students who adopt a deep approach. They are more aware of relations between elements of their understanding of a subject and are aware of how that understanding and those relations can be applied in new and abstract contexts. Second, we argue that a learning outcome, or a way of understanding, which includes the more complete or inclusive ways of conceiving of something are of a higher quality than those involving limited conceptions, and that ways of understanding which include relations between elements in that understanding are of a higher quality than those which lack those relations. And third, we argue that the way students approach their learning is fundamentally related to their learning outcomes. These three arguments form the basis of the principles of practice for learning and teaching described in the next section.

Principles of practice for learning and teaching resulting from the variation in outcomes

From the model we are using to explain individual learning, and the research on the variation in outcomes described in this and previous chapters, four principles of practice for learning and teaching emerge.

1. In the same learning context, there is qualitative variation in the outcomes of students' learning.
2. This variation in outcomes is related to students' perceptions of their learning situation, their prior experiences of learning and their approach to their learning.
3. Different teaching/learning situations evoke different understandings.
4. The quality of students' learning is fundamentally related to their ability to draw on their understanding in new and abstract situations.

In the remainder of this section, we look at the implications of these principles for good teaching, and in the next section give some examples of practices that illustrate the points in this discussion.

There are two implications for teaching in the first principle. The first is that variation from higher to lower quality learning will be an outcome of the range of individual learning situations experienced by the students, and the teacher will need to determine the nature of that variation. The second is that many conventional assessment methods used as an indicator of the variation may conceal the qualitative variation.

In the earlier sections of this chapter we have demonstrated why the (lack of) learning currently being concealed by the predominant assessment methods in higher education should be of concern to university teachers. Qualitative approaches to monitoring the variation in learning outcomes indicate that students who are currently deemed to be successful may have difficulty in drawing upon what they have learned in new contexts. Good teaching requires the use of assessment methods that reveal students' understanding, and ways of analysing the data that differentiate on qualitative and quantitative grounds. Assessment or similar practices should enable university teachers to determine the variation in understanding and give students a guide as to what is a quality outcome (this includes the nature of understanding in that area, such as 'What is mathematics? What is music?').

If the assessment is geared to testing understanding, student responses can be used to determine qualitative differences. Approaches to assessment that focus on ways of encouraging high-quality learning have been summarized by Ramsden (1992) in a chapter that discusses aims, models and examples of good assessment practice, and concludes with 14 rules for better assessment (pp. 210–12). Biggs (1996a) also presents an analysis of the importance of assessment in determining the quality of learning outcomes, and argues (1996b) for an alignment between objectives, teaching methods and assessment that, from a constructivist perspective, parallels our arguments in this book.

Good teaching also requires an awareness of the different ways of understanding the phenomenon being taught. Experienced university teachers have usually built up an extensive experiential database of the areas in which students express alternative or less complete conceptions and the nature of those conceptions. This information comes from discussions with students, from the responses students give to formal and informal questions, from areas expressed by students as causing difficulty, and from discussions with colleagues. While this information is valuable, it may still not be sufficient for the reason that it may not differentiate qualitatively. No amount of teaching effort focused on working with limited or less complete conceptions will increase students' chances of adopting more complete conceptions. High-quality learning is more likely to be achieved if the teacher has an awareness of the variation in the ways students understand the phenomenon being learned.

Finally, good teaching would involve preparing a curriculum or part of a curriculum using an understanding about the qualitatively different ways students understand.

The implications for teaching of the second and third principles have been discussed in detail in Chapters 3, 4 and 5. From the research described in this chapter, being able to draw upon understanding in different contexts is more likely in students with a high-quality learning outcome. We have shown how a high-quality learning outcome is likely to be related to a deep approach to learning, so good teaching involves encouraging deep approaches to learning and discouraging surface approaches. And because students' approaches to learning relate to their perceptions of their learning situation and their prior experience, good teaching involves an awareness of students' prior experiences and their perceptions of their learning situation. This information may enable university teachers to create a context which may be perceived by students to afford a deep approach to learning.

Examples of the application of the principles of practice for learning and teaching, including classroom research

The cases presented in this section illustrate the ways some university teachers have gone about finding out about the variation in the quality of learning of their students. As we noted above, this is the first step in improving the quality of learning. Once this is known, the second and third principles described above give some guidance as to the ways of affecting the quality of the outcome. Examples of how university teachers can influence students' approaches to learning were described in Chapter 5, and issues related to perceptions of their learning situation and prior experiences were addressed in Chapters 4 and 3 respectively.

The first case describes a phenomenographic approach to the investigation of learning outcomes in physics. The second example focuses on collecting information about student understanding during the subject. Example 3 describes the use of concept mapping and the SOLO taxonomy in looking at the structure and meaning of learning outcomes, and the fourth case demonstrates a method of using the understanding of learning outcomes which experienced university teachers have accumulated.

Identifying the variation in meaning of the learning outcome at the end of the subject

At the end of a first year physics (mechanics) subject, three of the lecturers investigated their students' conceptions of mechanics using a phenomenographic method (Millar *et al.*, 1989). They used as data student responses to a typical question on constant velocity: 'A car is driven at a high constant speed along a straight line on a highway. What forces act on the car to let it travel like this?' In their analysis they constituted three qualitatively different responses to the question.

A. The object had a constant velocity because the external frictional force between the tyre and the road in the direction of motion was equal to the external frictional force due to air resistance in the opposite direction.
B. The object had a constant velocity because the internal force due to the engine in the direction of motion was equal to the external frictional force between the tyre and the road.
C. The object had a constant velocity because the internal force due to the engine in the direction of motion was greater than the external frictional force between the tyre and the road in the opposite direction.

These categories of description, or conceptions of velocity, form a logical hierarchy. Conception A is correct in terms of a Newtonian conception. Conception B is partially correct, and Conception C is incorrect in Newtonian terms. When the responses from the 14 students in the study were distributed according to the highest conception in their response, there were four students associated with Conception A, four with B and six with C.

While this information was not necessarily generalizable to the whole class, it was sufficient to suggest that changes to the programme were needed to encourage more students to develop Conception A. The lecturers were aware of the principle relating students' perceptions of their situation and learning approach to learning outcomes. They began to focus more on real world friction examples, the amount of content was reduced, and students were encouraged to be active in lectures by, for example, engaging in 'buzz groups' designed to stimulate reflection on their varying conceptions of the subject matter. In this process, students became aware that there were a number of different conceptions being used by colleagues in the class, and individual students found that many other students disagreed with their conceptions. This was often a surprise for students. Laboratory classes were changed to engage students more in hypotheses and predictions in conducting experiments. In voluntary assignments, students were encouraged to write qualitative explanations to accompany their quantitative answers.

In drafting their report on this intervention, the authors argue that their interventions were contextualized to particular learning contexts and are unlikely to be found in general theories of learning. The results of the phenomenographic approach to studying learning in a particular context are readily interpretable to university teachers engaged in the curriculum deliberations in that context.

Identifying the variation in the meaning of the learning outcome during the subject

Angelo and Cross (1993) present an array of what they call class assessment techniques, which are aimed at assessing students' understanding of subject matter in the classroom. One of those methods (direct paraphrasing) aims to assess whether students understand a particular lecture or reading by seeking feedback from students in their own words on what the lesson was about. Angelo and Cross describe the process as follows:

Step by step procedure

- Select an important theory, concept, or argument that students have studied in some depth. This should be a topic with some implications outside the classroom.
- Determine who would be a realistic yet challenging audience for a paraphrase of this topic, what the purpose of such a paraphrase should be, and how long – in number of written words or amount of speaking time – the Directed Paraphrase should be. If your students are well prepared in the material and/or experienced in the field, direct them to paraphrase the same topic for two very different audiences.
- Try responding to the Directed Paraphrase yourself, to see how realistic the assignment is. Can you write an effective paraphrase within the limits given?
- Direct the students to prepare a paraphrase of the chosen topic. Tell them who the intended audience is, what the purpose is, and what the limits are on speaking time or on number of words or sentences. Let students know how much time they will have to respond to the assessment. (Unless you plan to review video – or audiotapes, have the students write out their Directed Paraphrases, even though in real life many of them would be spoken.)

Turning the data you collect into useful information

If you have collected written feedback, you can begin by separating the responses into four piles, which might be labelled 'confused,' 'minimal,' 'adequate,' and 'excellent.' Then assess the responses by comparing them within and across categories. Pay particular attention to the three characteristics of the response: the accuracy of the

---

paraphrase, its suitability for the intended audience, and its effectiveness in fulfilling the assigned purpose. Another approach is simply to circle the clearest and muddiest points in each paraphrase, using different-colored pens or pencils, and then to look for common patterns of clarity and confusion.

Pros

- Directed Paraphrasing builds on and builds up the students' skills in actively and purposefully comprehending and communicating information learned on a course.
- This technique allows the teacher to find out quickly and in some detail how well students have understood a given lesson, lecture, or segment of the course. This information can provide direction for instruction, as well as for syllabus revision.
- It forces teachers and students to consider the wider relevance of the subject being studied and the importance of considering the needs and interests of the audience being addressed.

Cons

- Unless strict length limits are enforced, Directed Paraphrases can take considerable time and effort to assess adequately.
- It is difficult to establish qualitative criteria for a good paraphrase and also to make those criteria explicit to students.
- The paraphrasing skills of some students will not improve appreciably unless the instructor provides some focused, individualised feedback. Once again, this is a rather time-intensive technique.

Caveats

- If a Directed Paraphrasing exercise is to be a meaningful assessment and learning task, it must be well structured and planned. The choices of audience(s) and purpose are particularly important.
- Students' first efforts are likely not to look much like their own words; after all, most students have had many years of practice in not writing in their own words.
- This CAT must be used more than once during the course if students, as well as the instructor, are to learn from the process.

Angelo and Cross, 1993: 234–5

This is a good example of an approach to obtaining information about the student's own awareness of the subject matter. Based on the work described in this book, an alternative method of analysing the data is to identify the qualitatively different ways students describe their understanding, and classify them using a phenomenographic analysis of the form described in the example above or the SOLO taxonomy as described below.

Table 6.5 SOLO levels at the beginning and end of term

SOLO level	Statement (beginning)	Assignment (end)
Unistructural	2 (9%)	0 (0%)
Multi-structural	19 (74%)	19 (74%)
Relational	4 (17%)	6 (26%)

Source: Boulton-Lewis and Dart (1994).

Identification of the variation in the structure and meaning of the learning outcome

The third case is a study by Boulton-Lewis and Dart (1994) in the field of education. They investigated their students' understanding of learning at the beginning and end of term using a SOLO analysis of written statements and assignments respectively. They also monitored understanding on the same topic using concept mapping exercises at the beginning and end of term. The distribution of students by SOLO level at the beginning and end of term is shown in Table 6.5.

During the term, concept map scores increased substantially but with little or no change in the range within the group, indicating that concept mapping can be used quantitatively to map qualitative changes in student understanding.

They describe the value of the exercises as providing them with an idea of the aspects of understanding that the students possessed individually and as a group. The study provided them with information about the level of structural organization of that understanding, which they used to guide their teaching.

The study was also designed to compare the results between the two outcomes (for 23 students). It showed that 18 of the 23 students received identical scores on concept mapping and the conventional assessments, confirming the appropriateness of concept mapping as a means of assessing understanding, and giving them a better indication of students who are more likely to be able to draw upon their understanding in different contexts.

Identifying the variation in the content of the learning outcome using university teachers' experiences

The final case does not require a direct approach to students for their response. Instead, the practice encouraged by Bowden (1988) utilizes the understanding that most university teachers have of the variety of ways students conceive of the key concepts in the discipline they teach. This understanding, accrued over a period of contact with student questions; test, tutorial and examination answers; debates and discussions; and interactions with other university teachers is, on reflection, a crude, but valuable database of the form established in the cases above. Bowden conducted a series of workshops aimed at helping university teachers change their conception of teaching. They contained an activity which asked participants, in groups, to represent different conceptions of a key understanding they want students to develop in their subject. Individuals were to record several alternative conceptions of that particular phenomenon commonly held by students, and to discuss them with their colleagues. He consistently found that university teachers were able to do this task, thus demonstrating that they have an awareness of qualitative differences in students' understanding. Bowden concluded that:

> Many teachers, previously unfamiliar with phenomenography itself or the view of learning on which it is based, are able within a few hours to grasp the basic ideas and apply them to their own teaching and the learning of their own students. This is related to their teaching experience. Over the years they have interacted with students and, in a sense, collected data about student conceptions. They will be less accurate, perhaps less comprehensive, than those obtained through research, but if teachers are given the opportunity to develop an understanding of how to convert the data they have collected over time into a rough representation of likely student conceptions of a particular phenomenon, they will be able to use that as a basis for teaching. They will probably be catering for the majority of students if they assume that the range of conceptions, such as those developed in the workshops ... represent the ways their students are likely to understand the phenomenon. Provided they develop strategies to test students' understanding, they will be able to modify their model in the light of experience.
>
> (Bowden, 1988: 263)

Two of the four examples used here to illustrate teaching practices associated with the principles developed in the chapter involve data collected by university teachers as part of action research programmes to improve learning and teaching or as a contribution to the research literature to improve student learning. In both cases the results have been published.

Summary of Chapter 6

Much of this chapter has been aimed at addressing the issue of the qualitative variation in understanding expressed by students in the same class. We have seen that some of the usual assessment methods, and the way the results are collected and analysed (marks and grades), offer little by way of information on qualitative variation. And yet the structure and meaning in the assessment items produced by students, in most cases, is an extremely valuable and under-utilized source of data on qualitative variation in understanding. We have indicated that one of the most appropriate approaches to the determination of qualitative variation is the use of phenomenography. Other ways of finding out include use of the SOLO taxonomy and concept mapping.

The results of studies using these approaches suggest that students with high-quality learning outcomes understand things in a different way to students with lower quality outcomes. They are able to bring more aspects of relevance to the foreground of their awareness. They are able to link their understanding to more and different sorts of related understandings. And in the case of knowledge objects, they have the feeling that the material being studied has become so tightly integrated that it was experienced as an entity with form and structure, and that they could draw on their understanding when needed.

Students with this form of understanding will most likely be well prepared for their next related learning situation. Because they are able to draw on their understanding when needed the new situation is likely to evoke a deep approach and a high-quality learning experience.

From the perspective of this chapter, good teaching involves becoming aware of the different ways students understand the phenomenon being taught. Experienced university teachers have usually built up an extensive experiential database of the areas in which students express limited conceptions and the nature of those conceptions. It also involves the use of assessment methods that reveal students' understanding, and ways of analysing the data that differentiates on qualitative and quantitative grounds. Assessment or similar practices should enable university teachers to determine the variation in understanding and give students a guide as to what is a quality outcome. Finally, good teaching involves preparing a curriculum or part of a curriculum using an understanding about the qualitatively different ways students understand.

This leads to an important research question for all university teachers: 'What are the qualitatively different ways that students use to express their understanding of the concepts they are learning?'

Note

1. Concept maps were developed and used extensively within the science education research paradigm to gain some insight into the way individuals conceptualize a phenomenon, by asking them to describe the relations between its concepts (Novak and Gowin, 1984). Typically, students are asked to arrange concepts on a page in a way which illustrates the structural relations (such as hierarchies and links) between the concepts. They are also asked to describe the nature of the connections or links they establish which gives some idea of the meaning they

ascribe to a concept. McKeachie *et al.* (1990) describe a range of procedures for assessing the structure of a student's knowledge, including concept mapping.

From the perspective of this book, we adopt a relational view of concept mapping. Students' maps are a response to the particular task and context and are therefore an indication of the relation between the student, the task and the context. The same type of map may not be produced by the same student on the same topic in a different context or on a different task.

7

Experiences of Teaching in Higher Education

```
┌─────────────────────────────────────────────────────────┐
│  Teacher's                                               │
│  prior                          Teacher's                │
│  experience              ·    ·  approaches              │
│                                  to teaching             │
│                    Teacher's                             │
│                    ·perceptions of                       │
│                    his/her situation                     │
│                                                          │
│  Teacher's                              Teaching         │
│  situation                              outcomes         │
└─────────────────────────────────────────────────────────┘
```

Introduction

In Chapters 3, 4, 5 and 6 we have looked at teaching and learning in higher education from the students' perspectives. We have shown how students' prior experiences of teaching and learning relate to their present experiences and how those present experiences relate to their learning outcomes. We have shown how different students can experience the same teaching and learning context in different ways – the teaching and learning situation for each student is to some extent unique. Students' perceptions of their situation are fundamental to how they approach their studies and to the quality of the outcomes resulting from those studies.

But if this is the situation from the students' perspective, what does it look like from the teacher's perspective, and how does the way the teacher sees the situation relate to the way students see the situation? Is each student's experience so unique that there can be little or no relation between what the teacher does and sees and what the students do and see? Can university teachers in large first year classes affect the way their students approach their studies, and if so, how?

These are questions which have only recently begun to be explored from the student learning perspective adopted in this book. In this chapter, we will look at the results of much of this research, with a view to showing how university teachers perceive their teaching situation, how they approach their teaching in that situation, and the outcomes of that teaching in terms of the quality of student learning resulting from their teaching. In particular, we will address the following questions:

• How do university teachers in higher education approach and conceive of their teaching and their students' learning?
• How does what they focus on in their teaching situation relate to the way they approach their teaching?
• How does the way they approach their teaching relate to their students' learning?
• What can they do to improve their students' learning?

These four questions are designed to complement the sorts of questions asked in the previous four chapters about student learning. This chapter is written from the student learning perspective discussed so far in this book. It will be argued that university teachers approach their teaching in qualitatively different ways, with qualitatively different conceptions of what constitutes teaching and learning underlying these approaches. It will also be argued that they focus on different aspects of their teaching context, and that what they focus on is fundamentally related to how they approach their teaching. Finally, it will be argued that the relation between the way university teachers approach their teaching and their students approach their learning is such that for university teachers there are better and worse ways of approaching teaching.

Experiencing the variation in teachers' experiences of teaching

We begin this chapter by asking you to read extracts from interviews with two teachers of first year university subjects talking about how they approach their teaching. In reading through the two extracts we ask you to think about how you would characterize the differences in the way these two teachers:

• approach their teaching;
• conceive of teaching and learning; and
• perceive the context in which they are teaching, and their situation within that context.

First, an extract from Lecturer A, a male teacher of first year chemistry:

Lecturer A

Q: Just as a general lead-in question, what do you think, generally that the course is about?

A: What are the objectives of it? Well I, many years ago prepared a list of specific objectives for the course and they were very useful for helping me in planning the course. Planning the assessment, planning the lectures and so on, and in the past I have given that list to the students, but now I make them aware of them in the way I lecture rather than giving them a whole list. I find preparing a list of specific objectives relating to the chemistry content, I mean, for example, one specific objective might be that a student should be able to develop the ability to classify molecules as polar or non polar. And a whole list of very specific objectives like that. As I say, I find that very helpful planning my own lectures and just planning the whole course. At the start of each lecture, or during the lecture or at times which I think appropriate I make the student aware just exactly the sort of skill I hope they are going to develop as a result of the learning experience that we're currently involved in and it's very very important.

Q: How do you go about, what do you do in preparing for lectures?

A: I think it's very important to have it clear in your own mind and let the students be very clear too about what you expect them to do as a result of any learning experience, what you expect them to be able to achieve. So in preparing for an hour lecture I decide what I want the students to get out of this lecture, specifically what I want them to be able to do as a result of this lecture. So that is one of the first parts of planning my list if you like, planning my lecture. I also plan them in a way so that I know the notes that I want the students to get. I'll write my notes in such a way so that the students don't have to decide when to take notes, I tell them to. I'll dictate to them, I have handouts prepared, I have gaps in them that they fill in and I take that decision away from the students about when and how to take notes because I feel it's very important that the lecture, tutorial or whatever the session, is a learning experience at least and not just a note taking exercise. And indeed in the very first lecture of any class I have, not just first year students, I explain to the students about my lecturing style, so they know where they stand. I explain to them the sort of things I'm just telling you, that is, they don't have to worry about when to take down lecture notes, I'll tell them, now it's time to take down some notes. And normally what I like to do is to get them thinking with me, for say five or ten minutes or so about various concepts, skills, and then we'll take some notes.

Q: Can I ask about your decision when to suggest they take notes and when they should just listen. For each of those could I ask why, when you decide it's a good time for them to take notes, why do you do that?

A: Why do I do it, rather than let them decide?

Q: No, why do you think it's, in the periods that you think it's a good time for them to take notes, why do you do so?

A: Well as I say the lecture, tutorial, whatever is tightly structured before I go in there. In other words I like things carefully planned, so that you know, I've made the judgement about when it's time to take down some notes. I make that judgement. I think it's important the students do get a good set of lecture notes, particularly when we're talking specifically now about first year, I think it's very very important. At all undergraduate levels, I think it's important they come away with a good set of notes. After all there are exams we expect these students to pass, and you know, we could debate the merits and demerits of examinations but the point is they have to pass formal examinations. There are certain skills which they are expected to be able to achieve so they can pass these examinations, and I think having a good set of notes can help them.

Now, an extract from Lecturer E, a male teacher of first year physics:

Lecturer E

Q: Mm. Yeah, . . . It's probably better to move on. You've kind of answered it . . . but . . . I'm asking now, 'What do you do in lectures?'

A: What do I do in lectures? Well, talk mostly. But . . . taken up, eh, I do some . . . things . . . use a reasonable number of what we call buzz sessions. We ask the students some questions, to get them to discuss it, [mumbles] take answers back. I've been doing that for the last few years, um.

Q: Mm. All right . . .

A: And . . . we discuss the answers.

Q: So you've already told me some other things that you're doing, so we might go through the list and ask what you hope to achieve by doing those things. So, let's just, the buzz session. What do you hope to achieve by doing them?

A: Well, getting the students to eh, to think, to be actively involved in what's going on, to think about it themselves. And I think the buzz-session technique eh, is, is easier than asking individual people to respond to direct questions. People come back and say . . . things without necessarily having to represent only their own point of view. I use it just to get people involved eh, getting them to think about . . .

Q: Why do you want them to do that?

A: 'Cause I think that's how learning happens. And I think the tradition of lectures is a pretty passive sort of thing, just spraying out information. What I read about research on the subject indicates it's not a terribly good method of transmitting information . . .

Q: Mm. Mm.

A: [pause] I think, more explicitly what I want to achieve with, eh, buzz sessions and the questions, and stuff is confronting students with their pre-conceived ideas about the subject which quite often conflict with what we're talking about, the official dogmas as it were. Um, so you've got to bring out that conflict and make the people aware that what they already know may not be what is the official line, as it were.

Q: Mm.

A: And I think the buzz sessions and quizzes attempt to do that. I mean, I select questions for those things, which are designed to bring up those conflicts.

Q: Right, eh, great, um. Demonstrations? What do you hope to achieve by giving demonstrations?

A: Same sort of thing quite often, create a bit of interest, break it up, eh, . . . put a bit of variety into the thing first up. But I think that demonstrations are fairly memorable, if they're good ones, you can remember seeing something, they provide some pegs to hang things on quite often, even if they're quite silly demonstrations. I do some silly things sometimes, like throw lumps of jelly around, which is, um, nothing in itself, but I guess it's just a bit of showmanship.

Q: So . . .

A: You, you hang the ideas on something. That gives people something to remember.

Q: Right, so memory, and interest and any . . . any other specific reasons or . . . ?

A: Well, there's the traditional one, that this is, you know, we're showing you what really happens, and this is . . . what . . . the principles of the subject, in operation . . . um, and I guess if they're short ones, so that's that's not . . . eh, I tend to keep away from demonstrations that are fairly long taking lots of readings and writing them down, saying look at all those total numbers and that proves this thing or not that works.

Yeah, it's illustrating, illustrating examples, applications . . . principles that we're talking about. But also sometimes the puzzle, the quiz . . . here you get a demonstration, do something, and quite often something unexpected, and get people to say, 'Look I'm gonna do this, what's gonna happen?' And do it, and what happens is different from what most people are going to guess, and then you get them thinking about that. And quite often they would answer the question wrong, then, say, 'Hey that's homework, go and think about that for next time.'

Q: Great. All right . . . and one final topic is the questions that you prepare to ask the students. What do you, when you prepare questions . . . hope to achieve?

A: Same sorts of things, getting 'em involved, confronting their conceptions with . . . eh, well, confronting them with the conflict between conceptions they already have . . . and eh . . . the new knowledge we want them to acquire . . . and in general, keep encouraging people to think about it and get involved.

These extracts clearly show that these two university teachers approached their teaching in fundamentally different ways, with fundamentally different conceptions of what constituted teaching and learning within the context in which they are teaching.

Lecturer A seems to have adopted an approach to teaching based upon what he does. The focus is on the lecturer, and then what students do in relation to the lecturer. Lecturer E, on the other hand, seems to have a focus on what the students do and think and then what he should do in relation to that. This lecturer's focus seems to be on the students. Here we are not talking about how well each of the lecturers did what they set out to do, but on the variation in what they are trying to do and how they are trying to do it. From another perspective, it seems that Lecturer A is trying to transfer his knowledge to the students. The intention seems to be to transfer knowledge and information. On the other hand, Lecturer E seems to be trying to develop and change the way the students think about and understand the concepts and ideas constituting the subject matter. His intention seems to be to engage students in the process of conceptual change and development.

If these different approaches represent fundamentally different ways of approaching teaching – which is what we will argue in this chapter – do such fundamentally different ways relate to different ways in which these lecturers conceive of learning and teaching? Do they see the teaching and learning context differently? And in any event, and most importantly, does it have any relation to how and what students learn?

Research describing the variation in university teachers' experiences of teaching

When university teachers enter a teaching and learning context, they enter it with certain prior conceptions of what constitutes good learning and teaching in their discipline. They form certain perceptions of their teaching and learning situation and adopt certain approaches to teaching in that situation. In this section we will review some of the research which has looked at the experience of teaching in higher education in terms of these conceptions, perceptions and approaches. We hope to show that, like students, the situation university teachers find themselves in evokes certain prior experiences of teaching and learning, that they adopt certain approaches in relation to these evoked prior experiences and perceptions of their situation, and that these approaches relate to the way their students approach their learning.

In this section we show that university teachers who focus on their students and their students' learning tend to have students who focus on meaning and understanding in their studies, while university teachers who focus on themselves and what they are doing tend to have students who focus on reproduction.

In the next section we review some of the research into the way university teachers in higher education conceive of their teaching and their students' learning.

Conceptions of teaching and learning

How do teachers in higher education conceive of their teaching and their students' learning? In one of the earliest studies of university teachers' conceptions of teaching from the student learning perspective, Dall'Alba (1991) interviewed 20 teachers from the fields of economics, English, medicine and physics in Australian universities. She identified seven different ways in which those teachers conceived of or understood their teaching in their particular teaching and learning situations. They are:

A. Teaching as presenting information
B. Teaching as transmitting information (from teacher to students)
C. Teaching as illustrating the application of theory to practice
D. Teaching as developing concepts/principles and their relations
E. Teaching as developing the capacity to be expert
F. Teaching as exploring ways of understanding from different perspectives
G. Teaching as bringing about conceptual change.

In discussing these conceptions, Dall'Alba argues for a logical ordering:

> The categories described above are ordered from less to more complete understandings of teaching. At the lowest level, teaching is seen in terms of the teacher alone and, more particularly, in terms of what the teacher does. From there, the focus shifts to incorporate the content and, at higher levels, students' understanding of the content becomes prominent. Finally the most complete conception focussed on the relationship between teacher, students and content.
>
> (Dall'Alba, 1991)

In this quote Dall'Alba highlights the idea that there are conceptions of teaching which are more or less complete in that the later conceptions go beyond and/or include aspects of the former conceptions but not vice versa. Similar conceptions and their relationships have been identified in other studies (Figure 7.1).

In the less complete conception, the lecturer's awareness is only of him/herself and what he/she is doing. In the more complete conceptions, in the words of Martin and Ramsden, the lecturer's awareness has been expanded to include him/herself, the content and students' understanding of the content (Martin and Ramsden, 1993). From these studies it can be assumed that lecturers in higher education enter teaching and learning contexts with a range of conceptions of teaching. But do these conceptions relate in any systematic way to their students' learning? We will answer this in detail in two parts. First, how do these conceptions of teaching relate to the

Figure 7.1 Summary of research on conceptions of teaching from a relational perspective.

	Dall'Alba (1991)	Martin and Balla (1991)	Samuelowicz and Bain (1992)	Prosser et al. (1994b)
Complete conceptions			Supporting student learning (postgraduate)	
	Bringing about conceptual change	Relating teaching to learning	An activity aimed at changing students' conceptions or understanding of the world	Helping students change conceptions
	Exploring ways of understanding from particular perspectives	Encouraging active learning: experiential focus vocational variation	Facilitating understanding	Helping students develop conceptions
	Developing the capacity to be expert			
Intermediate conceptions	Developing concepts and their interrelations	Encouraging active learning: discussion focus	Transmission of knowledge and attitudes to knowledge within an academic discipline	Helping students acquire: D: teacher's knowledge C: concepts of the syllabus
	Illustrating the application of theory to practice	Encouraging active learning: motivational focus		
	Transmitting information	Presenting information: content organisation focus		
Limited conceptions	Imparting information	Presenting information: delivery focus	Imparting information	Transmitting: B: teacher's knowledge A: concepts of the syllabus

Source: McKenzie, 1995.

teacher's understanding or conception of learning, and second, do these conceptions have any relationship to how university teachers approach their teaching and how students approach their learning?

In a series of studies looking at 24 university teachers' conceptions of teaching and learning, approaches to teaching and relationship between approaches to teaching and approaches to learning, again in particular teaching and learning contexts, we identified six conceptions of teaching and five conceptions of learning (Prosser *et al.*, 1994b). Details of the categories with illustrative quotes are given below. It should be noted that the quotes may represent only a fragment of the category of description.

Teaching Conception A: Teaching as transmitting concepts of the syllabus
Teachers holding this conception focus on the concepts detailed in the syllabus or textbook, but see their role as transmitting information based upon those concepts to their students. The focus is not on how the components of the information are related to each other, or on students' prior knowledge.

> Well I suppose teaching is showing the way, underlining the key ideas which show the way from one idea to the next and show how to apply these ideas . . . So you know, in a way all that's there, present there in the textbook, you're just underlining key ideas that are there in the textbook.

Teaching Conception B: Teaching as transmitting the teachers' knowledge
With this conception of teaching, teachers focus on their own structure of knowledge, but again see their role as transmitting information based upon those conceptions to their students. Similarly the focus is not on how the components of information are related or on students' prior knowledge.

> Presenting is probably too bland, but guiding, I don't try to present things as, you know, this is a fait accompli sort of thing, it's just a series of . . . important ideas. It amounts to presentation, but presentation doesn't describe the detail . . . Guiding you're giving them something that you're totally involved with yourself.

Teaching Conception C: Teaching as helping students acquire concepts of the syllabus
With this conception of teaching, as in Conception A, teachers focus on the concepts as detailed in the textbook or the syllabus, but rather than being transmitters, they see themselves as helping their students acquire those concepts and relations between them. Unlike Conceptions A and B, students' prior knowledge is seen as being important.

> I'm committed to the syllabus – the reason we have the syllabus is to give that student the foundation he or she needs, to go on to the rest

of the course. I am committed to that syllabus. I believe that's very important for the student. What I've got to do is to conduct classes in such a way that the students understand the basic physics concept of what's going on in the topic that I'm teaching . . . I'm viewing it (knowledge) as hierarchical. I put the topics in a logical way, and then it's students actually building up the concepts.

Teaching Conception D: Teaching as helping students acquire teacher's knowledge

Teachers holding this conception, as with Conception B, focus on their own understanding of concepts. But like Conception C and unlike Conception B, they see themselves as helping their students acquire those concepts and relations between them. Unlike Conceptions A and B, students' prior knowledge is seen as being important.

When I sat down to write the course I thought two things: what do they need to know, and what are they likely to want to know. And the two things are quite different . . . in terms of how I develop my course is I try to relate the need to know to the wants to know. If I can do that then there's a chance that as a teacher I can get the interest of the students . . . So I guess that's really where I see teaching, as relating what I think they need to know with what they already know . . .

Teaching Conception E: Teaching as helping students develop conceptions

Teachers holding this conception of teaching focus on their students' world views or conceptions of the subject matter rather than their own conceptions or the concepts in the text. They see their role as helping their students develop their conceptions in terms of further elaboration and extension.

I suspect that the function of teaching as distinct from what is in the text is perhaps to provide a review or an overview of the information – to explore some critical parts of it more deeply, to actually explore those in a different mode than you normally would have available in your reading a text on your own. To explore those things in conversation. Like I make a distinction between having something as a presence and something somewhat removed from that as a concept . . . but the lectures provide a presence that some book doesn't, and you can utilise that a lot in the lecture by directly engaging in question . . . in a more interactive situation (than a book) the lecturer or teacher can actually engage you in that question and doesn't necessarily guarantee to have available anything else until you've engaged in that. So that's part of it, it brings things into the present, much more interactive mode.

In this course and every other course, an overall aim, which is to spark a spirit of inquiry, to engender that creative or inventive spirit in the students.

Teaching Conception F: Teaching as helping students change conceptions
Teachers holding this conception of teaching again focus on their students' world views or conceptions of the subject matter rather than their own conceptions or the texts' concepts. They differ from those holding Conception E in seeing teaching as helping students change their conceptions or world views.

> ... [Conceptual understanding is developed] by arguing about things, and trying to apply ideas, and being again confronted by differences between what you think and what actually happens ... to get people to make predictions about what's going to happen, and then when it doesn't happen, maybe they might backtrack and revise their ideas about things ... what's going on in their heads ... What we're trying to achieve in learning physics, is for people to shift their view from the layperson's view, to what we would call a scientific/physicist's view ... view of the world. I think that's what I'm on about.

Again, the more complete understandings do focus on students as well as the teacher and the context, while the less complete understandings focus on the teacher or the context only. The teachers' conceptions of the learning of their students are as follows:

*Learning Conception A: Learning as accumulating more information to
satisfy external demands*
Teachers with this conception focus on the learning of their students as involving an accumulation of facts, principles, laws, definitions, strategies, formulas and skills which are added to or replace existing knowledge through processes such as rote learning. The focus is on the information rather than on how the new information is related to the students' existing knowledge. This does not mean that teachers do not see and use links to the real world. Nearly all of them do. It is that the links to the world are the teachers', not the students', which may mean the links are not relevant to the students. There is some recognition that components of the information are related, but little focus on *how* the components are related. The new knowledge is seen as discipline or objective knowledge. There is a correct way to see that knowledge and lecturers and textbooks are sources of that knowledge. Most teachers classified as holding this conception focus on learning as being the ability of students to use information to help them solve exercises of the type introduced in the course, and hold the view that students would know they had learned something if they could successfully complete those exercises.

> Learning chemistry is like learning a language, you have to learn the vocabulary, which is rote learning, right? You have to learn to be able to speak chemistry which is writing chemical names and writing chemical formulae, etc. so there is a certain amount, degree of rote learning. Then there is using that material to solve problems. And it's just simply that.

Q: How would students know if they had learned something?

A: By how well they do in the exam. By what mark they get in the exam.

Learning Conception B: Learning as acquiring concepts to satisfy external demands

The difference between this and the previous conception (Conception A) is in the way lecturers see the acquisition of knowledge. Learning is seen to involve a process of developing meaning by acquiring the concepts of the discipline and knowledge of how those concepts are related. (Here the term 'concept' refers to the generally accepted public knowledge, and not people's understanding of that knowledge.) There is a recognition that prior knowledge and experience are important in learning and that 'correct' understanding of concepts can be acquired by attempting to link new information with prior knowledge or attempting to illustrate meaning through relating new information to students' experiences, though relevance is still seen from the teachers' perspective. Concept acquisition involves an adding on to, an extension of, or an elaboration of that prior knowledge in the direction of the knowledge of the discipline. Like Conception A, the outcome of learning is something that students determine extrinsically. Most of the teachers with this conception see the outcome of learning as the ability of the students to use their knowledge to help them solve exercises they have seen before and to transfer problems which cannot be solved by routine algorithmic processes.

> If they've been taught properly before [coming to university], they'll be thinking and reasoning, they won't just have been taught to rote learn, although I suspect that a great number of them are. When you say learning I suppose really there's rote learning or there's the deeper kind of learning, which is building on your previous ideas and knowledge, modifying them according to the new information and all that kind of stuff. And the ability to take all the information and decide on its importance or relevance to the particular area you're studying.

Learning Conception C: Learning as acquiring concepts to satisfy internal demands

The process of learning is seen here as acquiring the concepts of the discipline as described in Conception B. The difference is that the outcome of learning is seen, in this conception, as not only the need to satisfy external requirements, but more importantly as something internal to the students. The students will know when they have learned something because it will have personal meaning for them.

Q: How do students know if they've learnt something?

A: Well it depends on how they study. The student who wants to know, wants to learn, will generally work by themselves, do prac reports, this sort of thing, without making use of something that somebody else has done, because they will realise that the exercise of doing that is a way of them working out whether they know or not. If they make mistakes then those mistakes become apparent, because they're corrected and they can discuss their mistakes with their demonstrator or lecturer. So those students will always know if they are understanding or not, because they're given lots of opportunities to test their knowledge for themselves. The group of students who is oriented to passing the subject rather than to understanding the work may never find out they don't understand until they do the quiz.

Learning Conception D: Learning as conceptual development to satisfy internal demands
Teachers with this conception see learning as involving a process of developing meaning through the construction of a fuller, more elaborate and systematic knowledge of phenomena within a particular world view. Learners come to see things in their own way through development of their own meaning rather than according to the discipline knowledge. It is the recognition that the students' structure of knowledge may not be the same as that held by the teacher or the knowledge of the discipline that differentiates this conception from the earlier conceptions. However, like Conception C, learning here is also seen as a personal process and students themselves use their own criteria of understanding to determine whether they have learned something.

The process of learning is a process of invention ... It means that if you're really going to learn something, then you have to invent it for yourself ... If you look at the explanations that people provide for various things when you question them in tutorials, people have got idiosyncrasies, you know, very individual ways of explaining things, and ways of understanding things and really it's a matter of refining or keep reinventing them.

Learning Conception E: Learning as conceptual change to satisfy internal demands
Teachers with this conception see learning as the development of personal meaning through a paradigm shift in the students' world view of phenomena in the discipline. Students change the way they think about the discipline by restructuring their current world view to produce a new world view. Conceptual change therefore differs from conceptual development in involving the adoption of a new world view rather than the development of meaning within a world view, but it is still a process in which students are aware that they have learnt something.

I think you can have different conceptions of the world. People do have and I think even physicists have different conceptions and interpretations of what it's all about ... What we're trying to achieve in

Table 7.1 Relation between conceptions of teaching and conceptions of learning

Conception of teaching	Conception of learning					Total
	A	A/B & B	B/C & C	D	E	
A	5	1				6
A/B & A/C	2		2			4
B & C	1	3	1			5
B/D & C/D	1	1	1			3
D		1	2	1		4
E				1		1
F					1	1
Total	9	6	6	2	1	24

Spearman rho = .68, p < .001
Source: Trigwell and Prosser, 1996b: 279.

learning physics, is for people to shift their view from the layperson's view, to what we would call a scientific/physicist's view.

(Prosser *et al.*, 1994b)

The hierarchical relationship between these conceptions of teaching is summarized in the following quote from another paper based upon that study:

The purposes of teaching are to increase knowledge through the transmission of information to help students acquire the concepts of the discipline, develop their conceptions and change their conceptions.

(Trigwell and Prosser, 1996b: 278)

Similarly the hierarchical relationship between the conceptions of learning is shown in the following quote:

Knowledge is increased through accumulation of information such that students will acquire the concepts of the discipline, develop their conceptions and change their conceptions.

(Trigwell and Prosser, 1996b: 278)

These two quotes exemplify the hierarchical relationship between conceptions described by Dall'Alba in terms of being less to more complete conceptions.

In that study we also found a strong empirical relation between conceptions of teaching and conceptions of learning. These relations are shown in Table 7.1.

We see from Table 7.1 that university teachers who hold conceptions of teaching as being about their transmission of information, with little or no focus on the students or their understanding (A–D), also hold conceptions of learning as being about students accumulating more information rather than developing and changing their conceptions and understandings (A–C). Similarly, the teachers who hold the more complete conceptions of teaching – with an expanded awareness of what teaching is about – also hold more complete understandings of learning. Thus it seems that in any teaching and learning situation, university teachers have coherent conceptions of teaching and learning in that situation, and that for teachers to focus on their students developing understanding in their teaching may require a change in what they conceive teaching and learning to be.

If these are the teachers' prior conceptions of teaching and learning, how do they perceive the teaching and learning situation, and how do these perceptions relate to the way they approach their teaching?

University teachers' perceptions of their teaching situation

Like students, university teachers form certain perceptions of their teaching situation. On entering each teaching and learning context, teachers focus on, or are aware of, certain aspects of their resulting situation as it affects the way they approach their teaching in that situation. While a teaching context may be designed to afford a particular approach to teaching, individual university teachers will form certain perceptions of their situation in that context, which relate to the way they approach their teaching. We identified five aspects which, from interviews with university teachers, were seen to affect the way they approached their teaching (Prosser and Trigwell, 1997a). They are that:

- teachers have some control over what and how they teach: they focus on the amount of material included in the first year curriculum and the very little room for variation and diversity in what is taught and how it is taught;
- their class sizes are not too large to prevent engagement in interaction with their students: they focus on the extent to which appropriate class size influences the nature and amount of interaction between student and lecturer;
- their students are able to cope with the subject matter: they focus on the increasing variation in the ability of the students, the language background and gender;
- teaching is valued in their departments: they focus on the lack of balance between the valuing of teaching and research at the departmental level;
- their academic workload is appropriate: they focus on the amount of time spent on teaching and/or assessment and its interference with time for research.

Thus, in the teachers' experiences, when they enter teaching and learning contexts, certain aspects of their situation in the context are in the

Table 7.2 Perceptions of Teaching Environment Inventory sub-scales, defining items and scoring

Sub-scale	Comment	Defining item
Control of teaching	Focus on the amount of material included in the first year curriculum and the very little room for variation and diversity in what is taught and how it is taught	The department allows me considerable flexibility in the way I teach in this topic (scored positively)
Appropriate class size	Focus on the extent to which appropriate class size influences the nature and amount of interaction between student and lecturer	I stick closely to my notes when teaching large classes (scored negatively)
Enabling student characteristics	Focus on the increasing variation in the ability of the students, the language background and gender	Students have such variable skills that I find it hard to know what they know and what they don't know (scored negatively)
Departmental support for teaching	Focus on the lack of balance between the valuing of teaching and research at the departmental level	This department's view of teaching makes it less rewarding to focus much attention on teaching (scored negatively)
Appropriate academic workload	Focus on the amount of time spent on teaching and/or assessment and its interference with time for research	Increasing workload makes it difficult for me to maintain my enthusiasm for teaching this topic (scored negatively)

Source: Prosser and Trigwell, 1997a.

foreground of their awareness. Their feelings of freedom and control over how and what they teach; their perceptions of the size of their classes; their views on how well they think their students can cope with the subject matter that they are teaching; how well they think their department values teaching; and their perceptions of their own workloads are among the aspects of the context which they say relates to the way they approach their teaching. As a result of this qualitative study we developed a Teaching Environment Inventory which was designed to provide indicators of teachers' perceptions of their teaching and learning situation which this study suggested would relate to the variation in the way they approached their teaching. The sub-scales, comment on the sub-scales and a defining item for each sub-scale are shown in Table 7.2.

In the next section we will show how these perceptions of teaching situations relate to the way university teachers approach their teaching.

Approaches to teaching

Given that there is substantial variation in the way university teachers *conceive* of teaching and learning, what is the variation in the way they *approach* their teaching in higher education? And how does this variation relate to their perceptions of their teaching situation? Does any of this have any relation to the outcomes of teaching – students' learning?

In the study of 24 university teachers referred to earlier in this chapter, Trigwell *et al.* (1994) identified five different approaches to teaching. Like the students' approaches to learning, these approaches were constituted in terms of the teachers' intentions and strategies in the teaching of one of their first year subjects. The approaches are briefly described below. They are:

Approach A: A teacher-focused strategy with the intention of transmitting information to students
This approach is one in which the teachers adopt a teacher-focused strategy, with the intention of transmitting to the students information about the discipline. In this transmission, the focus is on facts and skills, but not on the relationships between them. The prior knowledge of students is not considered to be important and it is assumed that students do not need to be active in the teaching–learning process.

Approach B: A teacher-focused strategy with the intention that students acquire the concepts of the discipline
This approach is one in which the teachers adopt a teacher-focused strategy, with the intention of helping their students acquire the concepts of the discipline and the relationships between them. They assume, however, that their students can gain these concepts by being told about the concepts and their relationships. Like Approach A they do not seem to assume that their students need to be active for the teaching–learning process to be successful.

Approach C: A teacher/student interaction strategy with the intention that students acquire the concepts of the discipline
This approach is one in which the teachers adopt a student–teacher interaction strategy to help their students acquire the discipline-based concepts and the relationships between them. Like Approaches A and B, students are not seen to construct their own knowledge, but unlike Approaches A and B they are seen to gain this disciplinary knowledge through actively engaging in the teaching–learning process.

Approach D: A student-focused strategy aimed at students developing their conceptions
This approach is one in which the teachers adopt a student-focused strategy to help students further develop the world view or conception they already hold. A student-focused strategy is assumed to be necessary

because it is the students who have to construct their knowledge in order to change their conceptions.

Approach E: A student-focused strategy aimed at students changing their conceptions

This approach is one in which teachers adopt a student-focused strategy to help their students change their world views or conceptions of the phenomena they are studying. Like Approach D, students are seen to have to construct their own knowledge, and so the teacher has to focus on what the students are doing in the teaching–learning situation. A student-focused strategy is assumed to be necessary because it is the students who have to reconstruct their knowledge to produce a new world view or conception. The teacher understands that he/she cannot transmit a new world view or conception to the students.

(Trigwell *et al.*, 1994)

The descriptions of approaches to teaching described here have elements similar to those identified in students' approaches to learning. For example, university teachers with a teacher-focused strategy seem to have characteristics in common with students' surface approaches to learning. University teachers with a student-focused strategy seem to have characteristics in common with a deep approach to learning. How do these approaches relate to the way university teachers conceive of their teaching and learning? As might be expected, Table 7.3 shows a reasonably close relation between the way the 24 university teachers approached their teaching of a particular topic and their conceptions of teaching and learning of that topic (Trigwell and Prosser, 1996b).

Table 7.3 shows that university teachers who adopted a student-focused approach to their teaching of a topic conceived of their teaching and learning of the topic in more complete ways. University teachers who approached their teaching from a teacher-focused perspective conceived of their teaching and their students' learning in that topic in less complete ways. It is clear that teachers who approach their teaching from a student-focused conceptual development/conceptual change perspective also conceive of teaching and learning of the topic in the context in more complete ways. University teachers who are interested in adopting more complete approaches to teaching need to consider carefully how they conceive of teaching and learning.

So if university teachers do adopt these more complete approaches to teaching, having carefully examined their own conceptions, is this likely to bear any relation to the way their students approach their studies? In order to examine this question, which will be addressed in the following section, we developed an Approaches to Teaching Inventory (Trigwell and Prosser, 1996a). That inventory is composed of two scales with four sub-scales. One scale is the conceptual change/student-focused approach scale and the other is the information transmission/teacher-focused approach scale. Both scales have intention and strategy sub-scales. An example of an item

Table 7.3 Relations between conceptions of teaching and learning, and approaches to teaching

	Approach to teaching					*Total*
	A	A/B & B	C	D	E	
Conception of teaching						
A	6					6
A/B & A/C	2	1				3
B & C	5	1				6
B/D & C/D	1	1	1			3
D		2	2			4
E				1		1
F					1	1
Total	14	5	3	1	1	24

Spearman rho = .79, p < .001

Conception of learning						
A	7	1	1			9
A/B & B	3	2	1			6
B/C & C	4	1	1			6
D		1		1		2
E					1	1
Total	14	5	3	1	1	24

Spearman rho = .45, p < .05
Source: Trigwell and Prosser, 1996b.

from each sub-scale is shown below. The full inventory is included in the Appendix.

Conceptual change/student-focused (CCSF) approach
   Intention item: I feel a lot of teaching time in this subject should be used to question students' ideas
   Strategy item: In my class/tutorial for this subject I try to develop a conversation with students about the topics we are studying

Information transmission/teacher-focused (ITTF) approach
   Intention item: I feel it is important to present a lot of facts in classes so that students know what they have to learn for this subject
   Strategy item: I design my teaching in this subject with the assumption that most of the students have very little useful knowledge of the topics to be covered

In the first administration of the inventory with 58 first year university science teachers, substantial relationships were found between the cognate

Table 7.4 Correlation matrix of Approaches to Teaching sub-scale scores

Sub-scale	Sub-scale			
	IT	CC	TF	SF
Intention				
Information transmission (IT)	–	–.17	.61	–.19
Conceptual change (CC)		–	–.22	.45
Strategy				
Teacher-focused (TF)			–	–.23
Student-focused (SF)				–

n = 58

sub-scales, as shown in Table 7.4. That is, an information transmission intention is associated with a teacher-focused strategy and a conceptual change intention is associated with a student-focused strategy. The table shows large positive correlations between the cognate intention and strategy sub-scales, while all other correlations are small and negative. This analysis confirms the close relationship between intention and strategy found in the studies of student learning using similar inventories.

This inventory was administered along with the Perception of Teaching Environment Inventory to confirm the relations between teachers' perceptions of their teaching environment and their approaches to teaching (Prosser and Trigwell, 1997a). The results have since been replicated in a study by Ramsden *et al.* (1997). That study included over 400 teachers from 55 classes in 11 universities across four fields of study. The results of a factor analysis of the Approaches to Teaching and Perceptions of the Teaching Environment Inventories for the latter study are shown in Table 7.5.

Table 7.5 shows that a conceptual change/student-focused approach to teaching is associated with perceptions that the workload is not too high, the class sizes are not too large, that the teacher has some control over what and how he/she teaches and that the variation in student characteristics is not too large. It also shows that an information transmission/teacher-focused approach to teaching is associated with perceptions that the teacher has little control over how and what he/she teaches and that there is little commitment to student learning in the department.

So far we have been able to describe university teachers' experiences of teaching in a structurally similar way to how we described university students' experiences of learning. University teachers enter their teaching situations with a range of conceptions of teaching and learning. They adopt a range of approaches to teaching, consistent with their perceptions of their teaching situation. There is substantial coherence between their conceptions, perceptions and approaches. Remember, we are not talking here of general orientations, but specific responses to perceived specific situations. The same teachers may well have different conceptions, perceive their

Table 7.5 Teacher approaches to teaching and perceptions of the teaching environment

Scale	Factors	
	1	2
Perceptions of the teaching environment		
Teacher workload	70	
Class size	83	
Teacher control	46	−66
Student characteristics	80	
Commitment to student learning		−72
Approaches to teaching		
Information transmission/teacher-focused		80
Conceptual change/student-focused	43	−37

Source: Ramsden *et al.*, 1997.

teaching situation in different ways and adopt different approaches to teaching in different teaching contexts. But if we get teachers to focus on their teaching for a specific teaching situation, they exhibit substantial coherence in their experience of that situation. But the next, and possibly the most vital, question is how these experiences of teaching relate to the learning experience of students.

Relating university teachers' experiences of teaching to their students' experiences of learning

Everything in this chapter would be for naught if we were not able to find a link between the way university teachers teach and the way their students learn. As Biggs (1989) argued, the outcomes of teaching need to be seen in terms of the quality of student learning. There have been innumerable studies in higher education of the relation between the way students evaluate their teaching and the quantity of their learning outcome (Marsh, 1987), though the outcomes have not always been described in the qualitative way expressed in Chapter 6. They show that student achievement is related to student evaluation of teaching (high-achieving students rate their teachers highly). These studies, however, do not address the issue of the relation between the way university teachers experience teaching (in terms of their conceptions, perceptions and approaches) and the way their students experience their learning (in terms of conceptions, perceptions, and approaches).

In one of the first studies of the relation between teaching and learning from the perspective adopted for this book, Kember and Gow (1994) used Biggs's Study Process Questionnaire administered to students, and their

Table 7.6 Factor analysis of student approaches to learning and teacher approaches to teaching

Scale	First study factor	Second study factor	
	1	1	2
Student approaches			
Surface approach	−66	−35	73
Deep approach	80	87	
Teacher approaches			
ITTF	−31		85
CCSF	69	73	−39

own Teaching Orientation Questionnaire administered to university teachers. The Study Process Questionnaire was described in Chapters 3 and 5. Its scales are: surface approach, deep approach and achieving approach. The Teaching Orientation Questionnaire, developed by Kember and Gow on the basis of semi-structured interviews with university teachers, had two scales: learning facilitation and knowledge transmission. These two scales have a number of characteristics in common with our Approaches to Teaching Inventory. Using the academic department as the unit of analysis, they detected substantial and consistent relationships between the teachers' orientations to teaching and the students' approaches to learning. That study focused on general orientations to teaching and learning, and looked at the relationship at the academic organizational unit level. It did not study the relationship in particular teaching and learning situations.

In a more recent study, we used a topic-specific version of Biggs's Study Process Questionnaire and our own topic-specific version of the Approaches to Teaching Inventory (Trigwell *et al.*, 1999) to study the relationship at the individual classroom level. This study, the results of which have recently been confirmed by Trigwell *et al.* (1998), showed the expected, and very important, relationship between the way university teachers approach their teaching of a particular topic in higher education and the way their students approach their learning in that topic. Table 7.6 shows the factor analyses from both of these studies.

The first study shows clearly that for students a deep approach to study is associated with a non-surface approach. And for university teachers, a conceptual change/student-focused approach to teaching is associated with a non-information transmission/teacher-focused approach. But more importantly, it shows that the deep and non-surface approach to study is associated with the conceptual change/student-focused and non-information transmission/teacher-focused approach to teaching. The second study confirmed the results of the first, showing that a deep approach to study is associated with a conceptual change/student-focused approach to teaching, and a surface approach to study is associated with an information transmission/teacher-focused approach to teaching.

These results are vital to our argument and show that the way university teachers approach their teaching in a range of large first year classes in higher education is associated with the way their students approach their learning in those classes. It confirms much of the previous research, and completes the link between students' high-quality learning outcomes on the one hand and the way teachers approach their teaching on the other.

In summary then, we have seen that teachers in higher education, like students, enter teaching and learning contexts with a range of prior experiences of teaching and learning and ways of conceiving teaching and learning. The context itself evokes certain kinds of prior experiences, which then situate the university teachers in those contexts. The experienced contexts are the teaching and learning situation the teachers find themselves in. The teacher then adopts certain approaches to teaching relating to the situation. The teacher focuses on or is aware of certain aspects of the context. Finally, *and most importantly*, the approach the teachers adopt to their teaching is related to the approach their students adopt to their study.

We do not wish to contend that there is a causal relation between the way university teachers approach their teaching and the way their students approach their learning. Rather, the situation the teacher finds him/herself in is constituted in terms of the physical setting, the departmental and institutional context and, very importantly, the students. If we are correct when we say that the situation evokes approaches to study, then an important part of that situation is the students. From this perspective then, it would be surprising if there was not a relation between the way teachers approach their teaching and the way students approach their learning. The teachers and the students are both internally related to the context, and the situation as perceived by the teacher includes the students and the situation as perceived by the students includes the teacher.

In changing the learning and teaching context there is necessarily a change in the students' and teachers' situations. The key issue for the university teacher, wishing to improve the quality of his/her students' learning, is to try to see and understand the student's situation, and change and adapt his/her teaching in relation to the way he/she perceives the student's situation. This is what we mean by a student-focused perspective.

Principles of practice related to the variation in university teachers' experiences of teaching

Having focused on and reviewed mainly our own work on the teacher's experience of teaching in higher education, we will now identify some of the key principles of practice for teaching and learning to emerge from the review. We have argued that university teachers need to adopt a student-focused view of teaching in terms of which they try to see the teaching and learning situation from the student's perspective. The way students approach their studies is fundamentally related to the way they perceive the teaching and learning situation. If university teachers wish to enhance the quality of their students' learning they need to think carefully about how they themselves conceive of teaching and learning, think about the impact of their situation upon how they approach their teaching, try to see the teaching and learning situation from the students' perspective, and adjust their teaching accordingly.

Thus the key principles of practice underlying good teaching and learning to emerge from this chapter are:

1. Teachers need to become aware of the way they conceive of teaching and learning within the subjects they are teaching.
2. Teachers need to examine carefully the context in which they are teaching and become aware of how that context relates to or affects the way they teach.
3. Teachers need to be aware of and seek to understand the way their students perceive the teaching and learning situation.
4. Teachers need to be continually revising, adjusting and developing their teaching in the light of this developing awareness.

But how can these principles be put into practice? An example will be presented in the next section. Here it is important to note that university teachers and students see and experience something in the world in relation to other things. We see things as they vary from, and are similar to, other things. If we are not aware of the variation in the way that teaching and learning can be conceived, then we cannot become aware of our own way of conceiving it. Becoming aware of the variation in the way our colleagues and others conceive of teaching and learning and approach teaching and learning is a key step in developing our own awareness of our own way of conceiving and approaching teaching and learning.

Examples of practice and research related to teaching and learning principles

Examples of the ways university teachers can use the ideas presented in this chapter have been outlined in earlier chapters. In this section we wish to describe one additional example which exemplifies the issues discussed in this chapter. That example is student evaluation of teaching in the context of quality assurance of teaching. From the perspective of high-quality teaching and learning adopted for this book, how should teachers in higher education approach, interpret and act upon the results of student evaluations of teaching?

There are various ways in which teachers in higher education can understand and act upon the results of their student evaluation of teaching. At one extreme university teachers can conceive of the evaluations as a way of obtaining students' judgements on various aspects of their teaching to be used for management purposes. At the other extreme, there are two ways to use the results of the questionnaires developmentally. The first way involves the common practice of identifying those items on which the teacher did poorly, and implementing strategies to improve the scores on those items. The second way is a process in which the results of the student evaluation are interpreted in terms of the way the students experienced the teaching. The issue in the second developmental case is not whether the students' ratings were right or wrong on particular items. It is what the students' responses say to the university teacher about the way the students experienced the teaching; was that the way the university teachers planned or meant the students to experience the teaching and what can the teachers do to bring these aspects into closer alignment?

As an example of the second developmental approach – one which we believe is consistent with the perspective adopted in this book – we will describe the approach to students' evaluation of teaching adopted at an Australian university (Martens and Prosser, 1998). The student evaluation of teaching system is one in which university teachers wishing to have their teaching evaluated contact the local academic development unit. They receive a package of information about the system, including an item bank. The item bank is composed of several sets of items, including a set of items based upon the Course Experience Questionnaire (CEQ) (Ramsden, 1991). As has been discussed previously, the CEQ has been specifically designed to obtain information about the students' experience of teaching and the course. The teacher makes a selection of items, based upon guidelines included in the package and further consultation with a member of staff in the academic development unit. The results are collated by the academic development unit and returned to the university teachers with suggestions about how to interpret the analysis.

In interpreting the analysis it is suggested to the teacher that he/she not look for the items that students have judged to be inadequate, but engage in a process of:

- self-evaluation, by completing the questionnaire him/herself;
- checking the distribution of results, identifying items with high and low means and, very importantly, wide distributions;
- pattern searching of high- and low-scoring items;
- reflection on the patterns and distributions to try to understand how the students have experienced the teaching;
- comparing the perceived student experience with the teacher's experience; and
- deciding on some action to take to improve the students' experience in subsequent years.

The important points to note about this process are that:

- the questionnaire is not designed to provide student judgements on the quality of the teacher's teaching, but to provide information to help the teacher understand the students' experience;

- the suggested process for the interpretation of the results focuses the teacher's attention on the student experience, how that compares with the teacher's planned experience, and on changes to be made to revise the planned experience and to help bring the student experience in line with the planned experience.

The focus of the process is not on students providing judgements, but on the teacher trying to understand the students' experience.

Summary of Chapter 7

In previous chapters we have focused on the research from the student learning perspective into students' experiences in higher education. We have shown that students enter higher education courses with certain prior understanding and experience, and that when situated in our subjects and courses, certain aspects of this prior understanding and experience are brought to the foreground of their awareness while other aspects are in the background – the situation evokes certain aspects of the prior understanding and experience. If we wish to have other experiences brought to the foreground, then these will need to be carefully planned for. Given that the situation evokes certain aspects of their prior experience, these aspects interact with the students' perceptions of the present situation, resulting in their adopting certain approaches to their study. The approaches adopted can vary from task to task, depending on the evoked prior understanding and experience and perceptions of the particular task. These perceptions and approaches relate to the quality of the learning outcomes.

In this chapter we have shown that there is a similar structure to the pattern of university teachers' experiences. Teachers enter teaching and learning contexts with certain prior conceptions of teaching and learning and prior experiences of teaching and learning. The teaching and learning situations they find themselves in evoke certain aspects of these prior experiences. This interacts with the context to result in certain perceptions of the teaching situation. They adopt certain approaches to teaching related to their perceptions of the situation and their prior experiences which are associated with certain outcomes in terms of the students' experience. The teacher's experience is related to the students' experience.

The relation between teachers' experiences and their students' experiences is such that university teachers who adopt a conceptual change/student-focused approach to teaching are more likely to teach students who adopt a deep approach to their learning, while teachers who adopt an information transmission/teacher-focused approach to teaching are more likely to teach students who adopt surface approaches to their study.

Finally, we will return to the questions posed at the beginning of this chapter. In response to the first question we have shown that teachers show substantial qualitative variation in how they approach their teaching and conceive of their teaching and their students' learning. In terms of the second and third question we have shown that different university teachers focus on different aspects of their teaching situation and that what they focus on relates to how they approach their teaching. We have shown that the way teachers in higher education approach their teaching is related to the way their students approach their learning. Finally, in response to the fourth question, we have described an example of teaching practices consistent with the findings of the chapter.

In the next and last chapter, we summarize the argument we have been putting throughout the whole book, identify a number of issues for classroom teaching and research which have not been dealt with so far, and make some concluding comments about our own experiences as university teachers.

8

Understanding Learning and Teaching

In the preceding chapters in this book we have argued for a particular perspective on learning and teaching, and have outlined some of the research and its interpretation consistent with this perspective. In this final chapter we wish to summarize the view of learning and teaching espoused in this book and the principles for the improvement of students' learning drawn from each chapter. We will then examine some of the implications that this particular view and the associated principles have for classroom learning and teaching, for classroom research and for academic development. We will conclude with a personal reflection on our own developing awareness of teaching, learning and academic development.

Summary of the view of learning and teaching espoused in this book

In the first chapter of this book we described the experiences of two students studying first year university mathematics. We showed how each approached his/her studies in mathematics, how each perceived his/her learning and teaching situation and the quality of their learning outcomes. We explained the variation in their experiences of studying mathematics in terms of their prior experience of studying mathematics, their awareness of their learning environment, and the approaches to study they adopted in their environment.

We have argued that both students and teachers form certain perceptions of their situation. In forming those perceptions, certain aspects of the context are in the foreground of their awareness, and certain aspects are in the background. For example in the case of students attending physics lectures we showed that while some students focused on some aspects of the context – e.g. on the blackboard presentations – others focused on other aspects – e.g. small group discussions. We showed how the variation in what they focused on – their variation in perception – was systematically related to their previous experiences of studying in similar topics, the way they approached their learning and the quality of their learning outcomes.

We argued for a change in the way teachers conceive of their students' prior experience. We argued that prior experience is better thought of in terms of those aspects of prior experience which are brought to the foreground of awareness by the situation in which students and teachers presently find themselves. Prior experience need not be conceived of as stable entities that students and teachers bring to learning and teaching situations, but as dynamic entities related to their present situation.

It is learners' and teachers' perceptions of their present learning and teaching situations which are fundamental to:

- the prior experiences that are evoked by the situation;
- the approaches to learning or teaching adopted in their situations; and
- the outcomes resulting from activities within those situations.

It is the situation as perceived which is central to the quality of learning and teaching. This is in contrast to other views such as behavioural responses to stimuli in the environment or the processing of information within cognitive structure. The view of learning espoused here puts the students or the teachers and their experiences at the centre of efforts to improve learning and teaching.

In Chapter 1 we asked the question, 'How might university teachers teach to help students learn?', and we said this question would be answered by addressing a series of related sub-questions:

- What is the nature of students' prior orientations to learning and how does this vary?
- What is the nature of students' varying views on what is meant by learning and understanding and the subject matter when they begin their courses?
- What sorts of things do students focus on, or are aware of, when engaged in studying their courses?
- How does what they focus on, or are aware of, relate to how university teachers have designed and constructed courses?
- What effect does this variation in perception have on the quality of the students' learning?
- How do students go about their study? How do university teachers find out how they go about their study? What can university teachers do to affect the way they go about studying?
- What do students learn? How do university teachers find out what they learn?
- Do they learn a greater or smaller amount about something, or do they understand about something in different ways?
- What can students do with what they learn? What aspects of what they learn do they take beyond the subject?

We believe we have addressed these questions in the previous chapters of this book, and from the answers to them, we have identified a number of principles of practice which might be used to guide classroom learning and teaching, and classroom research.

Principles of practice arising from the view of learning underlying this book

In this section we list the principles of practice for good learning and teaching described in Chapters 3–6. These principles have been identified from the research reviewed in each of these chapters. They provide a concise summary of the ideas presented in each chapter and a basis for practical development of learning and teaching contexts. They are also a set of principles against which existing practice can be examined and point to issues which need careful consideration in the development of new practices. They are not meant to be guidelines for, or provide templates or recipes for, good practice, but to highlight those aspects which teachers need to maintain in the foreground of their awareness when designing or redesigning learning and teaching contexts in higher education.

The principles are shown in Figure 8.1. There is a structure across the sets of principles. The first principle in each set focuses on the variation in the aspect of awareness which is the focus of the chapter from which it is derived, the second principle focusing on relations with other aspects of awareness discussed in the other chapters, the third principle focusing on how that aspect of awareness is evoked by the specific learning and teaching situations learners and teachers find themselves in, and the final principle focusing on the relation between the particular aspect of awareness and the students' learning outcomes.

Implications from the principles of practice for good classroom learning and teaching

Having reviewed the questions asked in Chapter 1 and the principles of practice identified in Chapters 3–6, we now wish to refer to a number of topical issues associated with these principles. We argue that good teaching in higher education involves a continuous awareness:

- of students' present learning situations;
- of the contextually dependent nature of teaching;
- of students' perceptions of teaching technologies (including information technology) used in teaching;
- of the student diversity (including cultural diversity) in classrooms; and
- of the need to continually evaluate and improve teaching.

In the remainder of this section we focus a little more on each of these five issues and indicate where further information consistent with our principles and the student learning perspective may be obtained.

Figure 8.1 Analysis of principles of practice for Chapters 3–6

Aspect	Variation in aspect	Relationship between aspects	Situation evocation	Learning outcomes
Student's prior experience	3.1 Students enter our learning and teaching situation with substantial qualitative variation in their prior experiences of learning and teaching	3.2 These prior experiences of learning and teaching are related to specific prior situations in which those experiences occurred	3.3 A new learning and teaching situation they find themselves in evokes certain aspects of these prior experiences, the aspects evoked being related to the congruence between the previous situation and the new situation	3.4 The aspects evoked have a subsequent substantial impact on what and how students learn in the new situation
Student's perception of learning situation	4.1 Students have substantial qualitative variation in the way they perceive their learning and teaching situation	4.2 This variation in perceptions is related to their prior experiences of study and present approaches to study	4.3 In a new learning and teaching context, different students focus on or perceive different aspects of their situation in that context	4.4 The aspects focused on or perceived are related to their approach to study in integrated or disintegrated ways, the nature of this relationship being fundamentally related to their post conceptual understandings and achievement
Student's approach to study	5.1 In the same learning context, there is qualitative variation in the way students approach their learning	5.2 This variation in approach is related to students' perceptions of the learning situation and their prior experiences of learning	5.3 Different teaching/learning situations evoke different approaches to learning	5.4 The way students approach their learning is fundamentally (not just empirically) related to their learning outcomes. For example, if they do not seek to understand, then they do not find understanding
Student's learning outcome	6.1 In the same learning context, there is qualitative variation in the outcome of students' learning	6.2 This variation in outcome is related to students' perceptions of the learning situation, their prior experiences of learning and their approach to their learning	6.3 Different teaching/learning situations evoke different learning outcomes	6.4 The quality of students' learning is fundamentally related to their ability to draw on their understanding in new and abstract situations

Good teaching involves a continuous awareness of students' learning situations

From the perspective of this book, good teaching is not about applying predetermined recipes, techniques or templates to learning and teaching situations. Each learning and teaching situation is unique. What is required is an understanding of some general principles for good learning and teaching, careful monitoring of what students are experiencing in their learning situations and how they are doing so, and the awareness of a range of responses that can be made to emerging situations. Suggestions for possible responses can be found in series such as the Gibbs, Habeshaw and Habeshaw *53 Interesting Things . . . Series* (1984–8) which includes a large number of useful and practical suggestions for teachers. As well Paul Ramsden's *Learning to Teach in Higher Education* (Ramsden, 1992) provides a powerful discussion of many of the issues raised in this book. For example, Ramsden lists six principles for good teaching in higher education. The final one is 'Learning from Students', and in discussing this principle Ramsden says:

> None of the forgoing principles is sufficient for good teaching. Effective teaching refuses to take its effect on students for granted. It sees the relation between learning and teaching as problematic, uncertain, and relative. Good teaching is open to change: it involves constantly trying to find out what the effects of instruction are on learning, and modifying that instruction in the light of the evidence collected.
>
> (Ramsden, 1992: 102)

This perspective is consistent with ours, and indicates that good teaching is about a continuous process of looking at the learning and teaching situations from the perspective of the student and adjusting the teaching in the light of this continuous monitoring.

Good teaching involves an awareness of contextual dependency of learning and teaching

The second issue relates to the first in that good learning and teaching are contextually dependent. That is, what works in one learning and teaching context may or may not work in another context. What works in one discipline or field of study may or may not work in another. What works with the learning and teaching of subject matter A may or may not work with subject matter B. What works with one cohort of students may or may not work with another cohort etc.

We take current developments in flexible learning as an example of the importance of the awareness of this contextual dependence. In designing for flexible learning, university teachers often take a teacher-focused approach. The message in this book is that they need to take a student-focused approach and to design the learning context from a student perspective. Diane Laurillard's book *Rethinking University Teaching: A Framework for the Effective Use of Information Technology* (Laurillard, 1993) addresses the detail of approaches to the design of some flexible learning contexts from the same perspective as this book. Preparing distance and open learning contexts has been addressed by Race (1992).

Good teaching involves an awareness of students' perceptions of teaching technologies (including information technology) used in teaching

Following from the previous sub-section, one way of introducing more flexible learning is through the use of information technology. In this book we have not addressed specific teaching techniques or teaching technologies. We acknowledge that the use of technology in learning and teaching is assuming increasing importance in higher education, but we assert that the principles and ideas for which we have argued underlie all good teaching practice including using information technology in learning and teaching. All of our principles apply to such learning and teaching environments.

One of the key issues in the use of information technology is the way students perceive the role of information technology in learning and teaching. Their perceptions of learning and teaching situations incorporating the use of such technologies are not given the attention that is necessary for good practice and that they deserve. Again, Laurillard's book (1993), like Ramsden's (1992), provides a powerful introduction and analysis for the use of information technology in learning and teaching from a perspective on learning and teaching similar to ours. An evaluation from this perspective of the use of information technology in teaching is provided by Alexander and McKenzie (1998).

Good teaching involves an awareness of the student diversity (including cultural diversity) in classrooms

Another major issue of substantial concern in learning and teaching in higher education is that of the diversity in the student population. While we have discussed the variation in aspects of the students' experience in this book we have not addressed any of the diversity issues specifically. In Chapter 5 we touched on perceptions of the learning of Confucian-heritage students, and we summarize those comments here as a way of illustrating how the general principles we have espoused apply to the learning and teaching situations involving student diversity. It is often argued that students from non-European background cultures adopt more rote learning approaches to learning. In Chapter 5 we concluded that while some students may give the impression that they are rote learning or using surface approaches to learning, they may be rehearsing with the intention to understand or engaging in meaningful memorizing, rather than rote or mechanical memorizing. It is the intention and not the strategy in students' approach that is the key to understanding this apparent paradox. This very complex area is addressed more thoroughly, and from the student learning perspective, by Watkins and Biggs (1996).

As we have indicated throughout this book, good teaching involves attempts to ascertain individual students' perceptions of their learning situation, and trying to change the learning context to evoke a deep approach to learning. Good teachers will be monitoring the approaches and perceptions of all students. The process of accommodating the variation in students' experiences also accommodates diversity, including cultural diversity. From our perspective, teaching with an awareness of cultural diversity is simply good teaching.

Good teaching involves continuing efforts to evaluate our teaching for improved learning

We end this section with the issue of the evaluation of teaching because we see it as vital to the achievement of good teaching practice. We have argued that good teaching involves teachers maintaining an awareness of how their students are perceiving their learning situations. For us, the evaluation of teaching should focus more on using evaluative information to find out how the students are perceiving the learning and teaching situation, and focusing in particular on the variation in perceptions. As we showed in our quotes from students' experiences of physics teaching in the opening section of Chapter 3, and as we have argued throughout the book, the documentation of the variation of students' experiences is vital. Thus the use of open-ended evaluative questions (e.g. the best thing? the worst thing? what to improve?); the use of questionnaires designed to identify students' perceptions and experiences rather than judgements (e.g. Ramsden's Course Experience Questionnaire); a focus on the variation in response to questionnaires (e.g. the spread, distribution, standard deviation) rather than the mean; and informal discussions with students are all approaches well suited to a focus on students' perceptions rather than their judgements. Further information on gathering students' perceptions from this perspective are given in *Improving Teaching and Courses: A Guide to Evaluation* (Ramsden and Dodds, 1989).

These are just some of the specific issues on which the perspective from which we have been arguing can provide an interpretation and provide a direction for practice. In the next section we will identify and discuss some issues for classroom research arising from the perspective on learning and teaching underlying this book.

Implications for classroom research arising from the view of learning underlying this book

For those interested in classroom-based research into learning and teaching from the perspective in this book, we wish to highlight a number of issues for further consideration. These include the what and how of research, the complementarity of qualitative and quantitative research methodologies, the issue of contextual dependency of research results and finally the descriptive and analytical nature of the research results.

Object of study and research methodology

We have argued elsewhere in this book that in conducting classroom research into learning and teaching in higher education, two of the more important things to be considered are the object of study of the research and the methodology for the conduct of the research. Too often, the methodology and research instrumentation takes precedence over the object of study. Data are collected without careful consideration of the question or issue to be investigated. A classroom researcher discovers a new questionnaire which seems interesting, or an interview protocol which addresses interesting issues. The questionnaire is administered or interviews are conducted before the object of study is carefully delineated. This often results in a great deal of data being collected, with little direction about how the data will be analysed and interpreted. It is only when the analysis and interpretation begins that the issue of what the analysis and interpretation is directed towards is raised. At this stage it is often too late. Inappropriate data has been collected and cannot be analysed to address the issue the classroom researcher is really interested in.

We have come across many examples of this, such as:

- the use of general orientation to study questionnaires to provide information about how a student has approached his/her studies in a particular subject;
- the use of a quantitative questionnaire to identify the approach to study taken by students when such questionnaires cannot identify the approach but only provide comparative scores on a scale;
- trying to relate learning approach to learning outcome without identifying students in both sets of data.

These are just some of the examples of the traps for classroom researchers who do not carefully consider their object of study before adopting particular research methods and instruments. We will finish this sub-section by reiterating the key questions we posed for the planning of classroom research in Chapter 3. They were: 'What is it I want to find out about?' and 'How can I find out about it?', in that order.

Complementary qualitative and quantitative research methods

There is a great deal of discussion and argument in the research literature about the use of qualitative and quantitative research methods. Much of the discussion is about the merits of one approach over the other. We hope that we have been able to show in this book how qualitative and quantitative methods can be used in complementary ways to address research questions. A key issue to keep in mind in using both qualitative and quantitative methods is how the results can be interpreted in complementary ways. We have argued in this book for the central importance of awareness in the relationship between students and teachers and their particular learning and teaching situations. When using both qualitative and quantitative methods, how the results are to be interpreted in terms of the awareness of the participants in the study is of central concern.

Our approach has been to use questionnaires that have been designed to focus on students' and teachers' experiences of learning and teaching situations, including questionnaires on approaches and perceptions. The results of the questionnaires can then be interpreted not as indicators of stable constructs within cognitive structure but as indicators of students' and teachers' experiences. In completing questionnaires, students and teachers have always been asked to complete them in relation to a particular learning and teaching situation, either past or present. In this way we have tried to ensure that when completing the questionnaires the awareness of students and teachers has been directed towards a particular situation and, in this sense the results are relational.

Descriptive and analytic rather than causal and explanatory

In adopting the perspective espoused in this book for classroom-based research, an important consequence is that the results of research should be interpreted as descriptive and analytic, not as causal and explanatory. This is a clear consequence of the model of awareness that we have used to guide and structure the interpretation of research results in this book. Our model is meant to be interpreted in ways that help describe students' and teachers' experiences of particular learning and teaching situations. The models are not meant to describe relationships which are considered to be causal or explanatory. They are meant to help in the process of describing and analysing the experience of learners and teachers in learning and teaching situations, helping university teachers understand rather than explain their experiences.

Human awareness is holistic; it is not composed of independently constituted entities. But for analytic purposes we focus on various aspects of human awareness. We are not trying to say that approaches are constituted independently of perceptions or of outcomes. But in trying to describe people's experiences of learning and teaching in terms of their awareness we analytically focus on various aspects and attempt to describe the relationships between them.

As we hope to have shown throughout this book, descriptions and analyses of students' and teachers' experiences are central to trying to understand learning and teaching and subsequently to working towards the continued improvement and enhancement of learning and teaching.

Implications for academic development from the view of learning underlying this book

In trying to highlight some of the implications of this book for academic development, we return to some of the principles of practice relating to the teachers' experiences of teaching described in Chapter 7. These principles offer firm guidelines to those engaged in the processes of academic development. This may include heads of academic organizational units as well as members of academic development units.

In Chapter 7 we spelt out these principles as follows:

1. Teachers need to become aware of the way they conceive of learning and teaching within the subjects they are teaching.
2. Teachers need to examine carefully the context in which they are teaching and to become aware of how that context relates to or affects the way they teach.
3. Teachers need to be aware of and seek to understand the way their students perceive the learning and teaching situation.
4. Teachers need to be continually revising, adjusting and developing their teaching in the light of this developing awareness.

We believe that one of the primary roles of academic development is to work with university teachers in expanding their awareness of their learning and teaching situations (Prosser and Trigwell, 1997b). Just as we argue that good teaching is about taking a student's perspective, we believe good academic development is about supporting university teachers in taking a student's perspective. Academic development is less about the development of teaching skills, and more about the development of an enhanced awareness of students' perceptions of learning and teaching situations. For as Paul Ramsden has said so eloquently:

> There can be no single right answer to the problem of promoting the quality of teaching. That this perspective is by no means generally accepted is easily shown by reference to many policies of performance appraisal and staff development. The ideology of staff appraisal presents a one-dimensional model of better teaching which focuses narrowly on the quality of individual lecturers' performances and inter-lecturer competition for excellence. Staff development that is focussed on training lecturers to use teaching techniques is driven by an equally simplistic theory which says that if we add extra skills to each lecturer's repertoire, then we will get better teachers.
>
> (Ramsden, 1992: 253–4)

We support Ramsden's conclusions on both of these matters. From our perspective, it is only in relation to the teachers' awareness of their students' perceptions that development of teaching skills becomes important. Teachers need to understand their students' experiences as a part of the process of developing their teaching. Academic development is in part about working with university teachers to focus on and interpret their students' experiences.

The principles detailed above give an indication of what this means. Academic developers need to structure situations where they work with university teachers to focus on the teachers' conceptions of learning and teaching and approaches to teaching in particular learning and teaching situations. Academic development staff may also work with university teachers who are exploring how their past experiences and present learning and teaching contexts relate to the way they presently teach. They may also work with university teachers in looking at their subject and programme aims and objectives and their teaching and assessment methods from the students' perspective. And finally good academic development from this perspective is about working with university teachers to develop their teaching context in ways to help bring the students' perspectives more in line with their own.

Concluding remarks

We began this book by discussing the experiences of two students beginning their university studies. We conclude this book by commenting on our own experiences of learning, teaching and academic development. For both of us, our basic education has been in the physical sciences. We both began our teaching careers as tutors and lecturers of undergraduate students in the physical sciences. At the beginning of our teaching careers we both thought, like many science teachers, that good university teaching was about getting the subject matter correct and developing the skills of presenting that subject matter to students. We both believed that there were certain generic teaching skills, and that once we had developed those skills all we needed to do was to keep up to date in our subject matter. We hope that having read this book you can see that we do not believe any of this any more.

We could not understand why some things we did one year for one cohort of students did not work the next year. We could not understand why our students, having studied and passed examinations in certain subject matter before enrolling in our subjects seemed either unwilling or unable to draw upon that understanding in the subject we were teaching. We could not understand that having spent many hours on developing concise explanations of physical phenomena and intricate lecture theatre demonstrations our students still did not seem to understand what we had taught them. We hope that you are now able to see how we can now understand these problems.

We now understand that our students were entering our subjects with certain prior experience of learning and teaching. We structured and taught our subjects with little or no reference to, understanding of, or awareness of this prior experience. We made no attempt to help our students see how the subject they were entering related to their previous subjects. We made no attempt to bring to the foreground of their awareness the understanding which they had previously been aware of and which was needed for our present subjects. We made little or no attempt to help our students understand the aims of our subject. We assumed that by making them do things they would learn. We were more concerned about getting reliable measures of their learning than valid indicators of their understanding. We made little or no attempt to help them develop an understanding of our teaching and assessment methods. We assumed that students did not need to be aware of what we as teachers were trying to do and achieve: all they as students had to do was to do what we told them to do. All of this seems somewhat naive to us now, but from our experience of learning and teaching in higher education many of the same mistakes are still being made.

We are not trying to say that we are now excellent university teachers, but we are sure that we have improved our teaching. We now work in academic development units. Much of our 'teaching' is with university teachers. We hope that we are maintaining an awareness of how they experience their teaching, and that we are providing opportunities to help them develop more complete understandings of their students and of their own teaching. Learning and teaching in higher education needs to be seen as a scholarly activity, teachers need to be continually researching their students and their students' learning. Teachers need to be continually trying new ways of helping their students develop their understanding of the subject matter being taught. There is not one right way to teach, just as there is not one right way to learn. There are certain principles for good teaching and good learning, but the practice of learning and teaching needs to be continually invented. We, as teachers, need to develop a sense of wonder about the variation in our students and our students' learning. We need to help our students develop a sense of wonder about our subject matter. There can be no good learning or teaching without a sense of excitement, without an awareness that we are all, students, teachers and academic developers, on a path of continuous discovery.

Appendix

Approaches to Teaching Inventory

The Approaches to Teaching Inventory has been developed to measure the ways teachers approach their teaching in a particular situation. It is composed of 16 items. Eight items are part of a sub-scale describing an approach which is intended to change students' conceptions or ways of seeing things through a focus on the student (conceptual change/student-focused (CCSF) approach). Four items refer to the motive of the approach and four to the strategy. The other eight items form a sub-scale labelled information transmission/teacher-focused approach (ITTF) with four items referring to the intentions to transmit information and four to the use of a teacher-focused strategy to achieve that intention.

The items are grouped as follows

Sub-scale: Conceptual change/student-focused (CCSF) approach	
Intention items	Item no.
I feel that the assessment in this subject should be an opportunity for students to reveal their changed conceptual understanding of the subject	5
I encourage students to restructure their existing knowledge in terms of the new way of thinking about the subject that they will develop	8
I feel that it is better for students in this subject to generate their own notes rather than always copy mine	15
I feel a lot of teaching time in this subject should be used to question students' ideas	16

Strategy items	Item no.
In my class/tutorial for this subject I try to develop a conversation with students about the topics we are studying	3

We take time out in classes so that the students can discuss, among themselves, the difficulties that they encounter studying this subject — 6

In lectures for this subject, I use difficult or undefined examples to provoke debate — 9

Formal teaching time is made available in this subject for students to discuss their changing understanding of the subject — 14

Sub-scale: Information transmission/teacher-focused (ITTF) approach

Intention items	Item no.
I feel it is important that this subject should be completely described in terms of specific objectives relating to what students have to know for formal assessment items	2
I feel it is important to present a lot of facts in classes so that students know what they have to learn for this subject	4
I think an important reason for giving lectures in this subject is to give students a good set of notes	11
I feel that I should know the answers to any questions that students may put to me during this subject	13

Strategy items	Item no.
I design my teaching in this subject with the assumption that most of the students have very little useful knowledge of the topics to be covered	1
In this subject I concentrate on covering the information that might be available from a good textbook	7
I structure this subject to help students to pass the formal assessment items	10
When I give this subject, I only provide the students with the information they will need to pass the formal assessments	12

All items are scored positively

We have not published norms, nor will we, as we have gone to some lengths in writing on the research behind this inventory, to point out that responses to it are relational and are specific to the context in which they are collected. Teachers who adopt one approach in one context may not adopt the same one in a different context. Our main use of the inventory has been as a source of data for analysis of associations within a specific context, for example the associations between approach to teaching and perceptions of leadership in departments, or relations between approach to teaching and student approaches to learning.

Permission to use this inventory is given, provided:

1. that its source is acknowledged in all publications;
2. that users notify Keith Trigwell of their intention to use the inventory; and
3. that once data have been collected and used as intended, the raw results on the inventory items are available for the use of Michael Prosser and/or Keith Trigwell.

Approaches to Teaching Inventory

This inventory is designed to explore the way that academics go about teaching in a specific context or subject. This may mean that your responses to these items may be different to the responses you might make on your teaching in other contexts or subjects.

Please describe the context here: ....

For each item please circle one of the numbers (1–5). The numbers stand for the following responses:

1   –   this item was **only rarely** true for me in this subject.
2   –   this item was **sometimes** true for me in this subject.
3   –   this item was true for me **about half the time** in this subject.
4   –   this item was **frequently** true for me in this subject.
5   –   this item was almost **always** true for me in this subject.

Please answer each item. Do not spend a long time on each: your first reaction is probably the best one.

	only rarely	almost always
1 I design my teaching in this subject with the assumption that most of the students have very little useful knowledge of the topics to be covered.	1 2 3 4 5	
2 I feel it is important that this subject should be completely described in terms of specific objectives relating to what students have to know for formal assessment items.	1 2 3 4 5	
3 In my class/tutorial for this subject I try to develop a conversation with students about the topics we are studying.	1 2 3 4 5	
4 I feel it is important to present a lot of facts in classes so that students know what they have to learn for this subject.	1 2 3 4 5	
5 I feel that the assessment in this subject should be an opportunity for students to reveal their changed conceptual understanding of the subject.	1 2 3 4 5	

	only rarely	almost always

6 We take time out in classes so that the students can discuss, among themselves, the difficulties that they encounter studying this subject.

    1 2 3 4 5

7 In this subject I concentrate in covering the information that might be available from a good textbook.

    1 2 3 4 5

8 I encourage students to restructure their existing knowledge in terms of the new way of thinking about the subject that they will develop.

    1 2 3 4 5

9 In lectures for this subject, I use difficult or undefined examples to provoke debate.

    1 2 3 4 5

10 I structure this subject to help students to pass the formal assessment items.

    1 2 3 4 5

11 I think an important reason for giving lectures in this subject is to give students a good set of notes.

    1 2 3 4 5

12 When I give this subject, I only provide the students with the information they will need to pass the formal assessments.

    1 2 3 4 5

13 I feel that I should know the answers to any questions that students may put to me during this subject.

    1 2 3 4 5

14 Formal teaching time is made available in this subject for students to discuss their changing understanding of the subject.

    1 2 3 4 5

15 I feel that it is better for students in this subject to generate their own notes rather than always copy mine.

    1 2 3 4 5

16 I feel a lot of teaching time in this subject should be used to question students' ideas.

    1 2 3 4 5

Thank you

References

Abrandt, M. (1997) *Learning Physiotherapy: The Impact of Formal Education and Professional Experience.* Linköping University, Studies in Education and Psychology, No. 50.

Alexander, S. and McKenzie, J. (1998) *An Evaluation of Information Technology Projects for University Learning.* Canberra, Australian Government Publishing Service.

Angelo, T.A. and Cross, K.P. (1993) *Classroom Assessment Techniques: A Handbook for College Teachers,* 2nd edition. San Francisco, Jossey-Bass.

Ausubel, D.P., Novak, J.S. and Hanesian, H. (1978) *Educational Psychology: A Cognitive View.* New York, Holt, Rinehart and Winston.

Biggs, J.B. (1978) Individual and group differences in study processes, *British Journal of Educational Psychology,* 48, 266–79.

Biggs, J.B. (1979) Individual differences in study processes and the quality of learning outcomes, *Higher Education,* 8, 381–94.

Biggs, J.B. (1987a) *Student Approaches to Learning and Studying.* Hawthorne, Victoria, Australian Council for Educational Research.

Biggs, J.B. (1987b) *The Study Process Questionnaire (SPQ) Users' Manual.* Hawthorne, Victoria, Australian Council for Educational Research.

Biggs, J.B. (1988) Approaches to learning and to essay writing. In R.R. Schmeck (ed.) *Learning Strategies and Learning Styles.* New York, Plenum.

Biggs, J.B. (1989) Approaches to the enhancement of tertiary teaching, *Higher Education Research and Development,* 8, 7–25.

Biggs, J.B. (ed.) (1991) *Teaching for Learning: The View from Cognitive Psychology.* Hawthorne, Victoria, Australia.

Biggs, J.B. (1992) A qualitative approach to grading students, *HERDSA News,* 14, 3–6.

Biggs, J.B. (1993a) From theory to practice: a cognitive systems approach, *Higher Education Research and Development,* 12, 73–85.

Biggs, J.B. (1993b) What do inventories of student learning processes really measure? A theoretical review and clarification, *British Journal of Educational Psychology,* 63, 3–19.

Biggs, J.B. (1996a) Assessing learning quality: reconciling institutional, staff and educational demands, *Assessment and Evaluation in Higher Education,* 21, 5–15.

Biggs, J.B. (1996b) Enhancing teaching through constructive alignment, *Higher Education,* 32, 347–64.

Biggs, J.B. and Collis, K.F. (1982) *Evaluating the Quality of Learning: The SOLO Taxonomy.* New York, Academic Press.

Bligh, D.A. (1971) *What's the use of lectures?* Exeter, D.A. Bligh and B. Bligh.

Booth, S.A. (1992) *Learning to Program: A Phenomenographic Perspective.* Göteborg, Acta Universitatis Gothoburgensis.

Boulton-Lewis, G.M. (1998) Applying the SOLO Taxonomy to learning in higher education. In B.C. Dart and G.M. Boulton-Lewis (eds) *Teaching and Learning in Higher Education.* Melbourne, Australian Council for Educational Research.

Boulton-Lewis, G.M. and Dart, B.C. (1994) Assessing students' knowledge of learning: a comparison of data collection methods. In G. Gibbs (ed.) *Improving Student Learning: Theory and Practice.* Oxford, OCSD.

Bowden, J. (1988) Achieving changes in teaching practices. In P. Ramsden (ed.) *Improving Learning: New Perspectives.* London, Kogan Page.

Bowden, J.A. and Walsh, E. (eds) (1994) *Phenomenographic Research: Variations in Method.* Melbourne, Royal Melbourne Institute of Technology.

Bowden, J., Dall'Alba, G., Martin, E., Masters, G., Laurillard, D., Marton, F. *et al.* (1992) Displacement, velocity and frames of reference: phenomenographic studies of students' understanding and some implications for teaching and assessment, *American Journal of Physics,* 60, 262–8.

Buchner, J. (1991) *Report Prepared for Graduate Certificate in Higher Education.* University of New South Wales, Sydney, Australia.

Christensen, C.A., Massey, D. and Isaacs, P. (1991) Cognitive strategies and study habits: an analysis of the measurement of tertiary students' learning, *British Journal of Educational Psychology,* 61, 290–9.

Cope, C., Garner, M. and Prosser, M. (1996) Using phenomenographic perspectives in the classroom, *Research and Development in Higher Education,* 19, 125–9.

Crawford, K., Gordon, S., Nicholas, J. and Prosser, M. (1994) Conceptions of mathematics and how it is learned: the perspectives of students entering university, *Learning and Instruction,* 4, 331–45.

Crawford, K., Gordon, S., Nicholas, J. and Prosser, M. (1998a) Qualitatively different experiences of learning mathematics at university, *Learning and Instruction,* 8, 455–68.

Crawford, K., Gordon, S., Nicholas, J. and Prosser, M. (1998b) University mathematics students conception of mathematics, *Studies in Higher Education,* 23, 87–94.

Dahlgren, L.O. (1984) Outcomes of learning. In F. Marton, D. Hounsell and N.J. Entwistle (eds) *The Experience of Learning.* Edinburgh, Scottish Academic Press.

Dahlgren, L.O. (1988) 'Enduring and short term effects of higher education'. Paper presented at the 14th International Congress of Psychology, Sydney.

Dahlgren, L.O. (1997) Learning conceptions and outcomes. In F. Marton, D. Hounsell and N.J. Entwistle (eds) *The Experience of Learning: Implications for Teaching and Studying in Higher Education,* 2nd edition. Edinburgh, Scottish Academic Press.

Dahlgren, L.O. and Pramling, I. (1985) Conceptions of knowledge, professionalism and contemporary problems in some professional academic cultures, *Studies in Higher Education,* 10, 163–73.

Dall'Alba, G. (1991) Foreshadowing conceptions of teaching, *Research and Development in Higher Education,* 13, 293–7.

Davey, J. (1995) 'Aseptic technique: what and how students of nursing learn', unpublished Master of Nursing Thesis. University of Sydney.

Dunn, R., Dunn, K. and Price, G.E. (1989) *Learning Style Inventory (LSI).* Lawrence, Kansas, Price Systems Inc.

Eisenberg, N. (1988) Approaches to learning anatomy: developing a programme for preclinical medical students. In P. Ramsden (ed.) *Improving Learning: New Perspectives.* London, Kogan Page.

Eley, M.G. (1992) Differential adoption of study approaches within individual students, *Higher Education,* 23, 231–54.

Entwistle, N. (1987) A model of the teaching–learning process. In J. Richardson, M. Eysenck and D. Warren Piper (eds) *Student Learning: Research in Education and Cognitive Psychology.* Milton Keynes, SRHE and Open University Press.

Entwistle, N. (1988) Motivational factors in students' approaches to learning. In R.R. Schmeck (ed.) *Learning Strategies and Learning Styles.* New York, Plenum.

Entwistle, N. (1998) Approaches to learning and forms of understanding. In B.C. Dart and G.M. Boulton-Lewis (eds) *Teaching and Learning in Higher Education.* Melbourne, Australian Council for Educational Research.

Entwistle, A.C. and Entwistle, N.J. (1992) Experiences of understanding in revising for degree examinations, *Learning and Instruction,* 2, 1–22.

Entwistle, N.J. and Marton, F. (1994) Knowledge objects: understandings constituted through intensive academic study, *British Journal of Educational Psychology,* 64, 161–78.

Entwistle, N.J. and Ramsden, P. (1983) *Understanding Student Learning.* London, Croom Helm.

Entwistle, N.J., Meyer, J.H.F. and Tait, H. (1991) Student failure: disintegrated patterns of study strategies and perceptions of the learning environment, *Higher Education,* 21, 246–61.

Fleming, W.G. (1986) The interview: a neglected issue in research on student learning, *Higher Education,* 15, 547–63.

Fransson, A. (1977) On qualitative differences in learning. IV – Effects of motivation and test anxiety on process and outcome, *British Journal of Educational Psychology,* 47, 244–57.

Gardner, H. (1987) *The Mind's New Science.* New York, Basic Books.

Gibbs, G. (1992) *Improving the Quality of Student Learning.* Bristol, Technical and Educational Services.

Gibbs, G. (1993) The CNAA Improving Student Learning project, *Research and Development in Higher Education,* 14, 8–19.

Gibbs, G., Habeshaw, T. and Habeshaw, S. (1984–8) *53 Interesting Things . . . Series.* Bristol, Technical and Educational Services.

Gunstone, R.F. and White, R.T. (1981) Understanding gravity, *Science Education,* 65, 291–9.

Hazel, E., Prosser, M. and Trigwell, K. (1996) Student learning of biology concepts in different university contexts, *Research and Development in Higher Education,* 19, 323–6.

Jackson, M.J. and Prosser, M.T. (1985) De-lecturing, *Higher Education,* 14, 651–63.

Jackson, M.J. and Prosser, M. (1989) Less lecturing, more learning, *Studies in Higher Education,* 14, 55–68.

Johansson, B., Marton, F. and Svensson, L. (1985) An approach to describing learning as change between qualitatively different conceptions. In L.H.T. West and A.L. Pines (eds) *Cognitive Structure and Conceptual Change.* New York, Academic Press.

Kember, D. (1997) A reconceptualisation of the research into university academics' conceptions of teaching, *Learning and Instruction,* 7, 255–75.

Kember, D. and Gow, L. (1994) Orientations to teaching and their effect on the quality of student learning, *Journal of Higher Education*, 65, 59–74.

Keogh, L. (1991) 'Student conceptions of atomic structure: a phenomenographic study', unpublished BSc(Hons) dissertation. University of Western Australia.

Laurillard, D. (1979) The processes of student learning, *Higher Education*, 8, 395–409.

Laurillard, D. (1993) *Rethinking University Teaching: A Framework for the Effective Use of Educational Technology*. London, Routledge.

Laurillard, D. (1997) Styles and approaches in problem-solving. In F. Marton, D. Hounsell and N.J. Entwistle (eds) *The Experience of Learning: Implications for Teaching and Studying in Higher Education*, 2nd edition. Edinburgh, Scottish Academic Press.

Linder, C.J. and Erickson, G.L. (1989) A study of tertiary physics students' conceptualization of sound, *International Journal of Science Education*, 11, 491–501.

Lybeck, L., Marton, F., Strömdahl, H. and Tullberg, A. (1988) The phenomenography of the 'Mole Concept' in chemistry. In P. Ramsden (ed.) *Improving Learning: New Perspectives*. London, Kogan Page.

McCracken, J. and Laurillard, D. (1994) 'A study of conceptions in visual representations: a phenomenographic investigation of learning about geological maps'. Paper presented at the Ed-Media World Conference in Educational Multimedia and Hypermedia, June 1994, Vancouver, Canada.

McKeachie, W.J., Pintrich, P.R., Lin, Y.G. and Smith, D.A.F. (1990) *Teaching and Learning in College Classrooms*, 2nd edition. University of Michigan, National Center for Research to Improve Postsecondary Teaching and Learning.

McKenzie, J. (1995) 'Changing conceptions of university teaching', unpublished Doctoral Assessment paper. University of Technology, Sydney.

Marsh, H.W. (1987) Students' evaluation of university teaching: research findings, methodological issues, and directions for the future, *International Journal of Educational Research*, 11, 253–388.

Martens, E. and Prosser, M. (1998) What constitutes high quality teaching and learning and how to assure it, *Quality Assurance in Education*, 6, 28–36.

Martin, E. and Balla, M. (1991) Conceptions of teaching and implications for learning, *Research and Development in Higher Education*, 13, 298–304.

Martin, E. and Ramsden, P. (1993) An expanding awareness: how lecturers change their understanding of teaching, *Research and Development in Higher Education*, 15, 148–55.

Marton, F. (1981) Phenomenography – describing conceptions of the world around us, *Instructional Science*, 10, 177–200.

Marton, F. (1986) Phenomenography – a research approach to investigating different understandings of reality, *Journal of Thought*, 21, 28–49.

Marton, F. (1992) Phenomenography and 'the art of teaching all things to all men', *Qualitative Studies in Education*, 5, 253–67.

Marton, F. and Booth, S. (1997) *Learning and Awareness*. New Jersey, Lawrence Erlbaum Associates.

Marton, F. and Säljö, R. (1976) On qualitative differences in learning. I – Outcome and process, *British Journal of Educational Psychology*, 46, 4–11.

Marton, F. and Säljö, R. (1997) Approaches to learning. In F. Marton, D. Hounsell and N.J. Entwistle (eds) *The Experience of Learning: Implications for Teaching and Studying in Higher Education*, 2nd edition. Edinburgh, Scottish Academic Press.

Marton, F., Dall'Alba, G. and Beaty, E. (1993) Conceptions of learning, *International Journal of Educational Research*, 19, 277–300.

Marton, F., Watkins, D. and Tang, C. (1995) 'Discontinuities and continuities in the experience of learning: an interview study of high school students in Hong Kong'. Paper presented at the 6th European Conference for Research on Learning and Instruction, August 26–31, Nijmegen, The Netherlands.

Marton, F., Dall'Alba, G. and Tse, L.K. (1996) Memorizing and understanding: the keys to the paradox? In D. Watkins and J.B. Biggs (eds) *The Chinese Learner: Cultural, Psychological, and Contextual Influences.* Hong Kong, Comparative Education Research Centre and Melbourne, Australian Council for Educational Research.

Marton, F., Hounsell, D. and Entwistle, N.J. (eds) (1997) *The Experience of Learning: Implications for Teaching and Studying in Higher Education*, 2nd edition. Edinburgh, Scottish Academic Press.

May, J.D. and Bemesderfer, K.F. (1972) *Social and Political Inquiry.* Belmont, Duxberry.

Meyer, J.H.F., Parsons, P. and Dunne, T.T. (1990) Individual study orchestrations and their association with learning outcome, *Higher Education*, 20, 67–89.

Millar, R., Prosser, M. and Sefton, I. (1989) Relationship between approach and development in student learning, *Research and Development in Higher Education*, 11, 49–53.

Nichols, J.D. and Miller, R.B. (1994) Cooperative learning and student motivation, *Contemporary Educational Psychology*, 19, 167–78.

Novak, J. and Gowin, D. (1984) *Learning How to Learn.* New York, Cambridge University Press.

Oxford Centre for Staff Development (1989) *Certificate in Higher Education, Module 9.* Oxford, OCSD.

Perry, W.G. (1970) *Forms of Intellectual and Ethical Development in the College Years.* New York, Holt, Rinehart and Winston.

Prosser, M. (1993) Phenomenography and principles and practices of learning, *Higher Education Research and Development*, 12, 21–31.

Prosser, M. (1994) A phenomenographic study of students' intuitive and conceptual understanding of certain electrical phenomena, *Instructional Science*, 22, 189–205.

Prosser, M. and Millar, R. (1989) The 'how' and 'what' of learning physics, *European Journal of Psychology of Education*, 4, 513–28.

Prosser, M. and Trigwell, K. (1997a) Perceptions of the teaching environment and its relationship to approaches to teaching, *British Journal of Educational Psychology*, 67, 25–35.

Prosser, M. and Trigwell, K. (1997b) Using phenomenography in the design of programs for teachers in higher education, *Higher Education Research and Development*, 16, 41–54.

Prosser, M. and Webb, C. (1994) Relating the process of undergraduate essay writing to the finished product, *Studies in Higher Education*, 19, 125–38.

Prosser, M., Trigwell, K., Hazel, E. and Gallagher, P. (1994a) Students' experiences of teaching and learning at the topic level, *Research and Development in Higher Education*, 16, 305–10.

Prosser, M., Trigwell, K. and Taylor, P. (1994b) A phenomenographic study of academics' conceptions of science learning and teaching, *Learning and Instruction*, 4, 217–31.

Prosser, M., Walker, P. and Millar, R. (1995) Different student perceptions of learning physics, *Physics Education*, 31, 43–8.

Prosser, M., Hazel, E., Trigwell, K. and Lyons, F. (1996) Qualitative and quantitative indicators of students' understanding of physics concepts, *Research and Development in Higher Education*, 19, 670–5.

Prosser, M., Hazel, E., Trigwell, K. and Lyons, F. (1997) 'Students' experiences of studying physics concepts: the effects of disintegrated perceptions and approaches'. Paper presented at the 7th European Conference for Research on Learning and Instruction, August 1997, Athens.

Race, P. (1992) *53 Interesting Ways to Write Open Learning Materials.* Bristol, Technical and Educational Services.

Ramburuth, P. (1997) 'Learning style preferences and approaches to learning of international students studying in Australia', unpublished EdD dissertation. University of New South Wales, Australia.

Ramsden, P. (1979) Student learning and perceptions of the academic environment, *Higher Education*, 8, 411–28.

Ramsden, P. (1991) A performance indicator of teaching quality in higher education: the Course Experience Questionnaire, *Studies in Higher Education*, 16, 129–50.

Ramsden, P. (1992) *Learning to Teach in Higher Education*. London, Routledge.

Ramsden, P. and Dodds, A. (1989) *Improving Teaching and Courses: A Guide to Evaluation*. Melbourne, Centre for the Study of Higher Education, University of Melbourne.

Ramsden, P., Prosser, M., Trigwell, K. and Martin, E. (1997) 'Perceptions of academic leadership and the effectiveness of university teaching'. Paper presented at the Annual Conference of the Australian Association for Research in Education, December 1997, Brisbane, Australia.

Reid, A. (1997) The meaning of music and the understanding of teaching and learning in the instrumental lesson. In A. Gabrielsson (ed.) *Proceedings of the Third Triennial European Society for the Cognitive Sciences of Music Conference.* Uppsala, Uppsala University.

Renström, L., Andersson, B. and Marton, F. (1990) Students' conceptions of matter, *Journal of Educational Psychology*, 82, 555–69.

Richardson, J.T.E. (1990) Reliability and replicability of Approaches to Study Questionnaires, *Studies in Higher Education*, 15, 155–68.

Säljö, R. (1979) *Learning in the Learner's Perspective. 1. Some common-sense conceptions.* (Reports from the Department of Education, University of Gothenburg, No. 76). Gothenburg, Department of Education and Educational Research, University of Gothenburg.

Säljö, R. (1997) Reading and everyday conceptions of knowledge. In F. Marton, D. Hounsell and N.J. Entwistle (eds) *The Experience of Learning: Implications for Teaching and Studying in Higher Education*, 2nd edition. Edinburgh, Scottish Academic Press.

Samuelowicz, K. and Bain, J.D. (1992) Conceptions of teaching held by teachers, *Higher Education*, 24, 93–112.

Schmeck, R.R. (ed.) (1988) *Learning Strategies and Learning Styles.* New York, Plenum.

Scouller, K. and Prosser, M. (1994) Students' experiences in studying for multiple-choice question examinations, *Studies in Higher Education*, 19, 267–79.

Slavin, R.E. (1987) *Cooperative Learning: Student Teams.* Washington, DC, National Education Association.

Slavin, R.E. (1991) Synthesis of research in cooperative learning, *Educational Leadership*, 48, 71–82.

Tang, K.C.C. (1991) 'Effects of different assessment methods on tertiary students' approaches to study', unpublished PhD dissertation, University of Hong Kong.

Tang, C. (1998) Effects of collaborative learning on the quality of assignments. In B.C. Dart and G.M. Boulton-Lewis (eds) *Teaching and Learning in Higher Education.* Melbourne, Australian Council for Educational Research.

Tang, C. and Biggs, J.B. (1995) Letter to a friend: assessing conceptual change in professional development, *Research and Development in Higher Education*, 18, 698–703.

Theman, J. (1983) *Uppfattningar av polititisk makt* (Conceptions of political power). Göteborg, Acta Universitatis Gothoburgensis.

Tobias, S. (1994) Interest, prior knowledge, and learning, *Review of Educational Research*, 64, 37–54.

Topping, K. (1992) Cooperative learning and peer tutoring: an overview, *The Psychologist*, 5, 151–7.

Trigwell, K. (1997) Phenomenography: an approach to research. In J. Higgs (ed.) *Qualitative Research: Discourse on Methodologies*. Sydney, Hampton Press.

Trigwell, K. and Prosser, M. (1991a) Relating approaches to study and the quality of learning outcomes at the course level, *British Journal of Educational Psychology*, 61, 265–75.

Trigwell, K. and Prosser, M. (1991b) Relating learning approaches, perceptions of context and learning outcomes, *Higher Education*, 22, 251–66.

Trigwell, K. and Prosser, M. (1996a) Congruence between intention and strategy in science teachers' approach to teaching, *Higher Education*, 32, 77–87.

Trigwell, K. and Prosser, M. (1996b) Changing approaches to teaching: a relational perspective, *Studies in Higher Education*, 21, 275–84.

Trigwell, K. and Prosser, M. (1997) Towards an understanding of individual acts of teaching and learning, *Higher Education Research and Development*, 16, 241–52.

Trigwell, K.R. and Sleet, R.J. (1990) Improving the relationship between assessment results and student understanding, *Assessment and Evaluation in Higher Education*, 13, 290–7.

Trigwell, K., Prosser, M. and Taylor, P. (1994) Qualitative differences in approaches to teaching first year university science, *Higher Education*, 27, 75–84.

Trigwell, K., Prosser, M., Ramsden, P. and Martin, E. (1998) Improving student learning through a focus on the teaching context. In G. Gibbs, *Improving Student Learning*. Oxford, Oxford Centre for Staff Development.

Trigwell, K., Prosser, M. and Waterhouse, F. (1999) Relations between teachers' approaches to teaching and students' approach to learning, *Higher Education*, 37, 57–70.

van Rossum, E.J. and Schenk, S.M. (1984) The relationship between learning conception, study strategy and learning outcome, *British Journal of Educational Psychology*, 54, 73–83.

von Glasersfeld, E. (1995) *Radical Constructivism: A Way of Knowing and Learning*. London, Falmer Press.

Walberg, H.J. and Haertel, G.D. (1992) Educational psychology's first century, *Journal of Educational Psychology*, 84, 16–19.

Watkins, D. (1983) Depth of processing and the quality of learning outcomes, *Instructional Science*, 12, 49–58.

Watkins, D. and Biggs, J.B. (eds) (1996) *The Chinese Learner: Cultural, Psychological, and Contextual Influences*. Hong Kong, CERC and Melbourne, ACER.

Webb, G. (1997) Deconstructing deep and surface: towards a critique of phenomenography, *Higher Education*, 32, 195–212.

Weinstein, C.E., Goetz, E.T. and Alexander, P.A. (1988) *Learning and Study Strategies: Issues in Assessment, Instruction and Evaluation*. San Diego, Academic Press.

Wertsch, J.V. (1985) *Vygotsky and the Social Formation of Mind.* Cambridge, MA, Harvard University Press.

West, L.H.T. (1988) Implications of recent research for improving secondary school science learning. In P. Ramsden (ed.) *Improving Learning: New Perspectives.* London, Kogan Page.

West, L.H.T. and Pines, A.L. (eds) (1985) *Cognitive Structure and Conceptual Change.* New York, Academic Press.

Index

academic ability
  prior, 27
academic development, 173–5
  units, 161, 173–5
accommodation, 13
accumulating information, 147, 150
achievement
  student, 36–7, 41, 50, 71–5, 79–80,
    85, 126, 157
action research, 106, 134
affordance
  of deep approach to learning, *see*
    approaches to learning, surface
    and deep
  of surface approach to learning,
    see approaches to learning,
    surface and deep
aims of subject, 3–4, 43–5, 76, 174–5
analytic research results
  classroom based research, 172
  see also descriptive research results
Angelo, T.A., 131, 132
approaches to learning
  and approaches to teaching, 157–9
  and conceptions of learning, 2–5,
    20, 26
  prior, 43, 56
    see also learning outcomes and
      approaches to learning
  relational nature, 4, 94–6
    see also relational perspective
  surface and deep, 2–5, 14, 20, 33,
    36–7, 44, 64–5, 69, 71–4,
    79–80, 84–5, 90–7, 100, 123

  see also non-engagement;
    reproduction; rote learning
approaches to teaching, 144–55
  and approaches to learning, 157–9
  see also relational perspective
arts, 30, 127
assessment, 3, 4, 65–6, 93, 102–5, 128
  appropriate and inappropriate, 68,
    71, 96
  examinations, 124
  feedback, 89
  and learning outcomes, 3, 73, 79,
    105, 116–17, 126–8, 133
  methods, 131–2, 134–5
  multiple choice, 80
  perceptions of, 65, 74, 82, 100
  results, 23, 72, 78, 116, 124, 126
assimilation, 13
Ausubel, D.P., 31
awareness, 6, 13–14, 166
  foreground and background, 6, 14,
    17–18, 23–5, 81, 87, 164–5,
    175
  of simultaneity, 17–18, 24

Biggs, J.B., 11, 12, 13, 33, 34, 41,
    88–90, 113, 118, 128
biology, 51–2, 111, 118–23, 127, 174
Booth, S.A., 44
Boulton-Lewis, G.M., 120, 133
Buchner, J., 100, 101
business administration, 35
buzz groups, 45–6, 62–3, 76, 130,
    140–1

classroom research, 49–51, 53–6,
77–81, 100, 106, 130–4, 170–2
into differences in learning
outcomes, *see* learning
outcomes; research
see also research
cluster analysis, 69, 72, 73, 78–9, 122–3
cognitive psychology, 94, 95
cognitivist perspective of learning, 13
see also information, processing
collaborative learning, 104
computer programming, 43–5, 122
concept maps, 72, 120, 122–3, 127,
133, 135, 136
relational view, 136
conceptions
complete and limited, 4, 19–22, 43,
109, 116, 122, 127–9, 135, 143,
144, 150, 151
hierarchically inclusive, 38, 40, 53,
150
of learning, 4–5, 14–17, 20, 27,
37–8, 42–4, 102, 138, 142, 145,
149, 150, 156
prior, 20, 26, 35, 37, 42–3, 44, 46,
56, 121, 142
of learning and teaching
teachers', 20, 23, 146–7, 154,
156–7, 162, 174
of subjects, 21, 22, 28, 29, 40, 52, 77,
126, 130, 147
of teaching, 20, 21, 138, 142, 143–5,
150, 151, 156
prior, 22
multistructural, 35
relational, 20, 35, 41, 150, 154
Conceptions of Mathematics
Questionnaire, *see*
questionnaires and inventories
conceptual change, 142–4, 153–8,
162
Confucian-heritage culture, 93, 169
constitutionalist perspective, 13, 14,
17, 24
see also dualistic and non-dualistic
perspective
constructive alignment, 128
constructivist perspective, 13, 128
individual, 13
social, 13

context
and approach to learning, 19–20,
25, 33, 36–7, 64–5, 71–3, 79,
81, 84–5, 101, 104, 107, 129,
170
see also perceptions of learning
defined in relation to environment,
18
defined in relation to situation,
17–18, 25, 29, 107
see also situation
learning, 2–6, 8–9, 13–20, 23–5,
31–3, 36–7, 42, 58–82, 92,
94–6, 110
teaching, 7, 11–13, 21–3, 30–1, 39,
42, 71, 75, 137–63, 166, 168,
173–4
Cope, C., 43
correlation analysis, 66–8, 95, 126–7,
156
Course Experience Questionnaire, *see*
questionnaires and inventories
Course Perceptions Questionnaire, *see*
questionnaires and inventories
Crawford, K., 5, 8, 15, 16, 27, 28, 36,
40, 77–9
cultural diversity, 166, 169–70

Dall'Alba, G., 143, 150
Davey, J., 121–2
deep approach, *see* approaches to
learning, surface and deep
descriptive research results, 171, 172
see also analytic research results
direct paraphrasing
assessing understanding, 131–2
disintegrated perceptions and
approaches, 33, 71–4, 80, 96,
106
see also perceptions of learning, and
students'
dualistic and non-dualistic perspective,
10, 13, 14
see also constitutionalist perspective

economics, 32, 116–17, 122, 143
education, 133
Eley, M.G., 95
engineering, 35, 85, 94, 127
English, 143

Entwistle, N., 30, 32–3, 41, 66, 67,
    71–2, 88, 90, 94, 123–5
environment, 46–9
    learning, *see* context, learning
essay-writing, 34–5, 46–9, 113
    checklist for analysis, 46–9
    political science, 46–9
    sociology, 29, 34–5
evaluation of teaching, 170
    student, 157, 160, 161
examinations, *see* assessment
experiences
    descriptions and analyses, 173–5
    relationship between students' and
        teachers', 157, 160–1, 162
    students', 20, 24, 135, 137, 156, 161,
        162
        of learning, prior, 20, 24, 66, 137,
            148, 162, 165
        teachers', 133–4, 138–9, 142, 151,
            156–7, 159, 162
        of teaching, prior, 21, 23, 137,
            159, 162, 165

factor analysis, 68, 70
first year university students
    learning experiences, 1–8, 27–37,
        45–56, 59–63, 71–4, 77–9,
        126–7, 130
forms of understanding, *see*
    understanding, forms of
Fransson, A., 64

Gardner, H., 13
general study process, *see* orientations
    to learning, prior
geology, 122
Gibbs, G., 67–70, 94, 106, 168
good teaching, 11, 75, 99–100, 107,
    128–9, 160, 166–75
    and approaches to teaching, 153–4
    assessment methods, 128
    awareness of students' perceptions,
        107, 128–9, 135, 160, 166,
        168
    contextual dependency, 107, 160,
        166, 168–9
    continuous evaluation, 166, 168
    and deep approaches to learning,
        96, 104, 107, 129, 157–9

student diversity, 129, 169
    teaching and learning technologies,
        166, 169
Gothenburg University, 3, 15, 88
government, *see* political science
Gunstone, R.F., 116

Hazel, E., 51, 52, 111, 118, 123, 127
health sciences, 68, 104, 121–2
hierarchically inclusive conceptions,
    38, 40, 53, 150
history, 113

individual variation in learning, *see*
    variation, in students'
    approaches to learning
individual variation in teaching, *see*
    variation, in approach to
    teaching
information
    processing, 143
        see also cognitivist perspective of
        learning
    transfer, 11, 142
    transmission, 21, 143–5, 150, 153–8
information technology and teaching,
    169
intellectual development, 37
intention and motivation
    learning, 3, 14, 27, 40, 41, 91,
        93–4
    teaching, 22, 142, 144, 153–6
interest, 3, 30–1, 91
internal relationship, 12, 13
inventories, *see* questionnaires and
    inventories

Jackson, M.J., 46, 48, 49, 75, 76
Johansson, B., 32

Kember, D., 21, 157, 158
Keogh, L., 112
knowledge objects, 123, 124–5, 135
    see also understanding
knowledge and understanding, 35,
    37–8, 40, 123
knowledge structures, 13, 21

Lancaster University, 88
Laurillard, D., 39, 94, 169

law, 68, 102–4
learning approach, *see* approaches to
	learning
learning context, *see* context, learning
learning environment, *see* context,
	learning
learning outcomes, 108–36
	and approaches to learning, 15, 17,
		74–5, 96–7, 104–6, 108–13,
		125–7, 130, 171
	see also approaches to learning
	assessment, *see* assessment, and
		learning outcomes
	classroom research into differences
		in, 3, 4, 73, 96, 115, 118–25
	quality of, 15, 19–20, 57, 73–4,
		84–5, 115–25, 130–3
	quantity of, 3, 73, 79, 105, 115–17,
		126–8, 133, 157
	research, 14, 16, 115, 118–20, 122,
		133–4
	structure of, 118–23, 133
	student variations in, *see* variation,
		in students' learning
		outcomes
learning styles, 41, 95–6
Learning Styles Inventory, *see*
	questionnaires and inventories
lectures, 45, 60–4, 86, 139–40
logical inclusiveness, 44, 53

Marsh, H.W., 157
Martens, E., 161
Martin, E., 143, 144
Marton, F., 13, 14, 15, 38, 39, 44, 57,
	88, 89, 90, 93–4, 121, 127
mass communication, 100
mathematics, 1–6, 15–16, 27–9, 35–7,
	40, 126
	and classroom based research,
		77–80
medicine, 143
memorization, 4
	cultural effects, 93, 169
	meaningful and meaningless, 38–44,
		93, 169
	mechanistic, *see* memorization,
		meaningful and meaningless
	rote, *see* memorization, meaningful
		and meaningless

teachers' attitudes to, 98
	with understanding, *see*
		memorization, meaningful and
		meaningless
	see also rehearsal
Meyer, J.H.F., 33, 71–4, 85, 127
model
	of learning, 10–13, 16–19
	3P Presage Process Product,
		see Presage Process Product
		model
	and cognitivist perspective, 13
	and constitutionalist perspective,
		16–19
	and individual constructivist
		perspective, 13
	and social constructivist
		perspective, 13
	of teaching, 21–4
motivation, *see* intention and
	motivation
multiple choice examinations, *see*
	assessment
Multiple Choice Questions
	Questionnaire, *see*
	questionnaires and inventories
music, 109–10, 115, 120–1
	music object, 109, 120

Newcastle University, 88
non-engagement, 92
	see also approaches to learning,
		surface and deep
nursing, 80, 112, 121, 126

object of study, 12, 81, 109, 121,
	171
open-ended written questionnaire, *see*
	questionnaires and inventories,
	open-ended written
	questionnaires
orientations to learning
	contexualised within a discipline,
		40–1
	deep orientations, 40–1
	prior, 6, 28–9, 38–41, 44, 50,
		87
	surface orientations, 40–1
outcome space, 57
outcomes, *see* learning outcomes

perceptions of learning, 4, 12–13, 16,
    17, 58–9, 81–2
research, 27–8
    classroom based, 77–81
    quantitative, 66–7
    and students' perceptions of their
        learning situation, 5, 8, 9, 10,
        23, 25, 58–64, 66, 71–4, 75, 81,
        107, 127–30, 137
    see also disintegrated perceptions
        and approaches
    and students' perceptions of their
        subjects, 69, 70, 73, 77–9
    see also situation, student learning;
        variation, in students'
        perceptions of their learning
        situation
    teachers' and approaches to
        learning, 97–8, 99, 130
perceptions of teaching, 11
    students', 4, 59, 65–6, 68, 86
    teachers', 7, 22, 142
        perceptions of their teaching
            situation, 151–3, 156–7, 162–3
        see also situation
Perry, W.G., 37, 38
phenomenography, 10–14, 51, 53, 57,
    120–3, 129–32
    see also research
physics, 21–2, 31–3, 43, 45–6, 53–6,
    59–63, 72–3, 86, 116, 122, 130,
    140, 164, 170
physiotherapy, 104, 122
political science, 46–9, 75–6
Presage Process Product model
    learning and teaching, 42–3, 74–5,
        98–100, 127–9, 159–60, 166–7
    see also model
prior approaches to learning,
        see approaches to learning,
        prior
prior conceptions, *see* conceptions, of
    learning and teaching, prior
prior conceptual understanding, *see*
    understanding, prior
prior orientations, *see* orientations to
    learning, prior
prior understanding, *see*
    understanding, prior
problem-based learning, 75–6, 99

problem solving, 28, 40, 44, 77, 94,
    103, 111, 117
Prosser, M.T., 21, 22, 29, 31, 33, 34,
    45–6, 53–5, 59, 72, 73, 86, 96,
    116, 127, 145, 150, 151, 152, 156

qualitative studies, *see* research,
    methodology
quantitative studies, *see* research,
    methodology
questionnaires and inventories, 172
    Approaches to Learning Inventory,
        67, 105
    Approaches to Study Inventory, 41
    Approaches to Teaching Inventory,
        154, 158, 176–9
    Conceptions of Mathematics
        Questionnaire, 77–8
    Course Experience Questionnaire,
        33, 36, 66, 67, 68, 72, 77, 106,
        161, 170
    Course Perceptions Questionnaire,
        66, 67
    Learning Styles Inventory, 41, 85
    Multiple Choice Questions
        Questionnaire, 80
    open-ended written questionnaires,
        40, 53, 116
    Perceptions of the Teaching
        Environment Inventory, 151–2,
        156–7
    Study Process Questionnaire, 33, 36,
        41, 50, 68–70, 72, 78, 80, 89,
        95, 97, 101, 105, 157–8
    Subject Perceptions Questionnaire,
        68–9
    see also research

Ramsden, P., 4, 15, 33, 65, 66, 68, 69,
    70, 103, 117, 128, 157, 168, 169,
    170, 173
reading, 88–9, 114, 127, 131–2
rehearsal, 4, 5, 93, 98
    see also memorization
Reid, A., 109, 110, 120
relational perspective
    on learning, 5
        see also approaches to learning
    on teaching, 8, 21, 144
        see also approaches to teaching

reproduction, 3, 27, 54, 69, 74, 80, 84,
90–1, 142
see also approaches to learning,
surface and deep
research
analytic and descriptive, 172
see also phenomenography;
questionnaires and inventories
methodology, qualitative and
quantitative, 8, 25, 39, 41, 66,
106, 171
relational, 3–7, 14–16, 20, 144
object of study, 171
see also classroom research; variation,
classroom research on
Richardson, J.T.E., 106
rote learning, 3, 5, 91, 93–4, 97, 99,
147, 169
see also approaches to learning,
surface and deep

science, 39, 115, 116, 155
Scouller, K., 80
situation
defined in relation to context, 18, 107
defined in relation to environment,
18
student learning, 16, 18, 39
see also context; perceptions of
learning, and students'
perceptions of their learning
situation; perceptions of
teaching, teachers' perceptions
of their teaching situation
small group discussion, 45
sociology, 29, 34–5
SOLO, *see* Structure of Observed
Learning Outcome
strategies
learning, 3, 80, 88–93
teaching, 22, 153–7
structure of the learning outcome,
118–23, 133
Structure of Observed Learning
Outcome (SOLO), 118–23,
125–9
student evaluation of teaching, *see*
evaluation of teaching, student
Study Process Questionnaire, *see*
questionnaires and inventories

surface approach, *see* approaches to
learning, surface and deep

teachers' knowledge, and approach to
teaching and learning, 124, 141,
144–55
perceptions, *see* perceptions of
learning; perceptions of
teaching
teaching, conceptions of, *see*
conceptions, of teaching
teaching approach, *see* approaches to
teaching
teaching context, *see* context, teaching
Teaching Environment Inventory,
see questionnaires and
inventories
teaching, good, *see* good teaching
temporality, 17–20
Trigwell, K., 4, 19, 21, 22, 112, 126,
150, 153, 154, 155, 158

understanding
forms of, 123
integrated and separationist, 35
prior, 26–7, 30–7, 42–3, 46, 51,
53–4, 56–8, 66, 72–4, 79, 84,
118, 122–3, 162
see also knowledge objects
unit of analysis
academic department, 158
subject/course, 70, 71

variation
in approach to teaching, 21–4,
152–7, 162
classroom research on, 42–50, 56,
80–1, 131–4
see also research
in experience of teaching, 142–52
in models of learning, 16–21
in same field of study, 37, 43–9,
108–9, 111–14, 121
in students' approaches to learning,
41–2, 84, 86–90, 92, 94–5,
98–100, 106–7, 110
in students' learning outcomes, 24,
96, 107, 110, 111–18, 120–5,
126–8, 130–6
in students' orientation to study, 41

in students' perceptions of their
  learning situation, 59–65, 80–1,
  106–8
  see also perceptions of learning,
  students' perceptions of
in students' prior experience, 26–37

von Glasersfeld, E., 13
Vygotskian perspective, 13

Walberg, H.J., 92
Watkins, D., 93, 127, 170
West, L.H.T., 32

The Society for Research into Higher Education

The Society for Research into Higher Education exists to stimulate and coordinate research into all aspects of higher education. It aims to improve the quality of higher education through the encouragement of debate and publication on issues of policy, on the organization and management of higher education institutions, and on the curriculum and teaching methods.

The Society's income is derived from subscriptions, sales of its books and journals, conference fees and grants. It receives no subsidies, and is wholly independent. Its individual members include teachers, researchers, managers and students. Its corporate members are institutions of higher education, research institutes, professional, industrial and governmental bodies. Members are not only from the UK, but from elsewhere in Europe, from America, Canada and Australasia, and it regards its international work as among its most important activities.

Under the imprint *SRHE & Open University Press*, the Society is a specialist publisher of research, having over 70 titles in print. The Editorial Board of the Society's Imprint seeks authoritative research or study in the above fields. It offers competitive royalties, a highly recognizable format in both hardback and paperback and the worldwide reputation of the Open University Press.

The Society also publishes *Studies in Higher Education* (three times a year), which is mainly concerned with academic issues, *Higher Education Quarterly* (formerly *Universities Quarterly*), mainly concerned with policy issues, *Research into Higher Education Abstracts* (three times a year), and *SRHE News* (four times a year).

The Society holds a major annual conference in December, jointly with an institution of higher education. In 1995 the topic was 'The Changing University' at Heriot-Watt University in Edinburgh. In 1996 it was 'Working in Higher Education' at University of Wales, Cardiff and in 1997, 'Beyond the First Degree' at the University of Warwick. The 1998 conference was on the topic of globalization at the University of Lancaster.

The Society's committees, study groups and networks are run by the members. The networks at present include:

Access	Mentoring
Curriculum Development	Vocational Qualifications
Disability	Postgraduate Issues
Eastern European	Quality
Funding	Quantitative Studies
Legal Education	Student Development

Benefits to members

Individual

Individual members receive

- *SRHE News*, the Society's publications list, conference details and other material included in mailings.
- Greatly reduced rates for *Studies in Higher Education* and *Higher Education Quarterly*.
- A 35 per cent discount on all SRHE & Open University Press publications.
- Free copies of the Precedings – commissioned papers on the theme of the Annual Conference.
- Free copies of *Research into Higher Education Abstracts*.
- Reduced rates for the annual conference.
- Extensive contacts and scope for facilitating initiatives.
- Free copies of the *Register of Members' Research Interests*.
- Membership of the Society's networks.

Corporate

Corporate members receive:

- Benefits of individual members, plus.
- Free copies of *Studies in Higher Education*.
- Unlimited copies of the Society's publications at reduced rates.
- Reduced rates for the annual conference.
- The right to submit applications for the Society's research grants.
- The right to use the Society's facility for supplying statistical HESA data for purposes of research.

Membership details: SRHE, 3 Devonshire Street, London W1N 2BA, UK. Tel: 0171 637 2766. Fax: 0171 637 2781. email:srhe@mailbox.ulcc.ac.uk
World Wide Web:http://www.srhe.ac.uk./srhe/
Catalogue: SRHE & Open University Press, Celtic Court, 22 Ballmoor, Buckingham MK18 1XW. Tel: 01280 823388. Fax: 01280 823233. email:enquiries@openup.co.uk

FACILITATING REFLECTIVE LEARNING IN HIGHER EDUCATION
Anne Brockbank and Ian McGill

A book that puts new forms of relationship and dialogue at the core of teaching and learning. It is likely to give courage to those who are daring to reflect differently on their teaching and learning practice, and to those who recognise the limitations of technology as some 'panacea solution' to challenges of mass higher education.

Professor Susan Weil

This book offers hope and the practical means for university and college teachers seeking a new experience of learning for their students and themselves. The book deals with learning which is real, genuine, relevant to learners now and for the future, and which is significant for their lives. Such learning embraces their relationships, work and careers, community, society and their world.

Anne Brockbank and Ian McGill provide direct support for teachers who wish to move from teaching toward facilitating learning, thereby transforming the relationship between teacher and learner and between learners. Information technology, whilst useful, is not a substitute for the learning advocated here; facilitation enables learners to use technology productively and complementarily as a part of the learning process.

This book enables teachers to acquire an understanding of facilitation and to enhance their ability to facilitate rather than teach in the traditional way. The authors emphasize the centrality of engaging in reflective dialogue with both colleagues and students. They explore the significance of emotion and action as well as cognition in learning. In addition they examine how teachers can best create the conditions for reflective learning.

This is a practical book for university and college teachers which will help them facilitate their students' reflective learning.

Contents
Part 1: Learning and reflection – Introduction to our themes – Learning: philosophies and models – What is learning?-a review of learning theories – The requirements for reflection – Reflection and reflective practice – Part 2: Facilitating learning and reflective practice – Academic practice and learning – Developing reflective practice: the teacher using reflective dialogue with colleagues – Developing reflective practice: the student using reflective dialogue – Becoming a facilitator: facilitation as enabling reflective learning – Facilitation in practice: basic skills – Facilitation in practice: further skills – Part 3: Exemplars – Action learning – Academic supervision – Mentoring – Conclusion – Bibliography – Index.

304pp   0 335 19685 3 (Paperback)   0 335 19686 1 (Hardback)

DEVELOPING LEARNING IN PROFESSIONAL EDUCATION
PARTNERSHIPS FOR PRACTICE

Imogen Taylor

This is a timely addition to the literature which provides a challenge to professional education: both through its portrayal of a highly innovative problem-based course (and the rich detail of students' experience) which shows how a learner-centred approach can impact on participants; and through its location in much wider contexts of teaching and learning in professional education and in debates about the relationship between university education and professional practice.

Professor David Boud

At a time when attention is being directed increasingly towards lifelong learning, this book offers an extremely timely guide to the development of the learning skills needed to make this a reality. Readable, relevant and full of practical illustrations, it will be widely read by educators in a variety of professional contexts.

Professor Patricia Broadfoot

This book is about professional education and developing the required knowledge and skills to equip students for the pressing needs of professional practice. Student professionals from health care, teaching, business, law and social work must learn how to practise both independently (to respond to a constantly changing environment) and collaboratively (to respond to the complexity of today's society); also they must learn how to work in partnership with the consumers of professional services. Imogen Taylor explores how professional education can develop approaches to teaching and learning which both help learners to be reflexive, self-monitoring practitioners and meet the requirements of professional accrediting bodies. She draws upon her own research into students experiencing professional education based on small group, problem-based learning; on an extensive range of relevant international theory and research; and on her own long experience in professional education, training and practice.

This is an important resource for all those educators and trainers in professional education seeking to improve their own practice.

Contents

Part 1: Setting the scene – Introduction – Uneasy partnerships? – Part 2: Beginning learning – Transitions: traditional expectations and non-traditional courses – The personal is professional: using pre-course experience for learning – Part 3: The learning infrastructure – Learning for teamwork – Facilitating independent and interdependent learning – Restraint, resourcefulness and problem-based learning – Assessment: the crux of the matter – Part 4: Promising outcomes – Non-traditional learners: valuing diversity – Perspectives on education as preparation for practice – Partnerships with users of professional services – Appendix: enquiry and action learning (the structure) – References – Index.

224pp   0 335 19497 4 (Paperback)   0 335 19498 2 (Hardback)